A Life Different

ELIZABETH ANTONOVA

ISBN: 979-8-88640-472-2 (sc)
ISBN: 979-8-88640-473-9 (hc)
ISBN: 979-8-88640-474-6 (e)

Because of the dynamic nature of the Internet, any web addresses or links contained in this book may have changed since publication and may no longer be valid. The views expressed in this work are solely those of the author and do not necessarily reflect the views of the publisher, and the publisher hereby disclaims any responsibility for them.

THE EWINGS
PUBLISHING

One Galleria Blvd., Suite 1900, Metairie, LA 70001
1-888-421-2397

CONTENTS

ACKNOWLEDGEMENTS

I would like to thank the people who helped to make the publishing of my Mother's memoir possible. I am grateful to Michel Sily of Barry University, Assistant Vice-President for Web Marketing, for converting the 1940 printed manuscript to a computer program making it possible to be edited, and for being helpful and supportive.

I thank Sister Linda Bevilacqua OP, PhD President of Barry University, for taking the time to edit the manuscript. I also thank Alfred Allan Lewis, author and playwright, for fine tuning the final draft.

I thank my sister, Natasha Kimmel, for her help in selecting photographs and poems to be included. And my thanks to Henry Adams, who was also helpful in many ways.

But my very special thanks go to Virginia Adams, who took the initiative of convincing me to put this book together. I mean this sincerely. I always wanted to do this for my Mother and with Gini's help and continuous encouragement it was accomplished. Without her this book would not have been published.

A LIFE DIFFERENT

This book, written by my Mother, is a factual account of what happened to her aristocratic family when the Bolsheviks seized power in the October Revolution of 1917. Every situation at the time was recorded in my mother's diary. The reader will soon understand how vital her survival depended on what was said – to and by – her, and the words quoted as direct discourse are as nearly as possible a faithful account of her experience during that horrific, outrageous period in Russian history.

Elizabeth Antonova and her family were all too obvious a target for the paranoid, xenophobic and culture hating Revolutionaries. Her lonely, deprived months in prison were punctuated by relentless interrogations by devious, brutal inquisitors. Under great psychological and physical duress she withstood her persecutors by adamantly insisting on her innocence, and finally – at long last – she triumphed.

Although Elizabeth Antonova's life contains much suffering and sadness, the book is an exhilarating read, affording the privilege of intimacy with a wonderful writer and courageous woman who embodies the nobility of the human spirit.

I am so very proud of her.

Olga Melin

MY EARLY YEARS

When I was born my grandparents, expecting an heir, were disappointed in a second girl, but my mother believed that a tiny star rejoicing in my coming twinkled merrily in the Crimean sky. Mother's tale was that the star's gaiety passed into my smile. In a tender yet persuasive way she used to repeat the fancy; subconsciously intending to instill hope and confidence deep within me. "Quickly wipe your tears," she would say when I ran to her with a bruise or cut seeking consolation. "How can the little star shine through if you cry?" During the school year, the belief that my star would never fail seemed to help in my difficult relationship with mathematics; and later in my youth when we were living through the drastic changes in Russia with its destruction and misery. This legend often kindled in me a hope of better days.

My father, Dr. Anton Kraevsky, was the descendant of a distinguished Russian family whose old estate was near the historic city of Pskoff in the north of Russia. An idealist throughout his life, he chose to give his inheritance to a disabled friend of his school years and worked his way through the University of St. Vladimir in Kieff (Kiev) tutoring children. Soon after Father received his medical degree he married a beautiful girl named Olga with deep blue eyes, black hair, and an unusually flawless complexion – my mother. She was born in the south of Russia to wealthy parents. Having lost her own mother early she was brought up by her maternal aunt in Yassy, Romania and learned to speak perfect Romanian. Soon after she returned home she met Father on one of the estates near Kishineff. The tall young doctor and the lovely girl with humanitarian ideas and flair of European elegance made a handsome pair.

My parents had three children, my older sister Vala, a son who died at birth, and me. By that time, Father was a successful doctor in a Crimean district near Yalta. He and his wife were equally popular with the poor people of the Village and the wealthy aristocracy whose magnificent estates, contrasting with the poverty of the village, were located at a considerable distance. As there was no school in the village Mother would accompany Father on his visits to the ailing poor, and while he was helping them she was teaching reading and writing to their little ones.

Luxurious carriages sent by our wealthier neighbors would stop at the gate of our garden to take my parents to dinners and parties. Father often refused the invitations, knowing he was needed elsewhere, and spent long hours with the sick in the hospital.

One of my earliest memories is of an evening when I watched my mother dress for a ball before her candlelit dressing table. This picture is now as vivid as the feeling, the emotion which sprang from it: Mother is leaving…Mother is going to the Great Ball. I see her through the half-open door…how beautiful she is …I do not want her to go away … I feel like sobbing but I shall not upset her …She must go to the Great Ball and her little daughter who loves her, who loves her very much, must not cry. In the mirror I see her face reflected – marble-white with sparkling violet/blue eyes. She is my mother, but others must see her… Once more, Mama, kiss me goodnight… I only wish it but she feels my thoughts. She comes to me. I am enveloped in perfume. I reach out my arms to her and smile… She cannot see the two little tears run quickly down her daughter's cheeks. It is quiet in the nursery… the moon is

3

shining… I am tucked in my blanket and in my grief. She will never know that in my heart I am crying… appearing happy for her peace-of-mind. In her lovely velvet gown with the little puffed sleeves and long white gloves she will dance at the Great Ball. When you love, you do not cry… you do not hurt those you love. I knew this, although I was five.

Another vivid memory is of our large green living room, where the Christmas tree always stood. The Christmas tree seemed to fall right from heaven, as we children never saw it being decorated. Only on Christmas Eve, when the living room door closed for some time was suddenly wide open, it appeared in all its resplendence, with red and white candles glowing and contrasting beautifully with the green of the heavy fir tree. The lofty little silver angels, though fixed to the branches, created the illusion of flying around it. The colorful bulbs were intermingled with glossy tangerines. Glass icicles streamed down the tree; the nuts in gold and silver paper were skillfully hung, and above was the star of Bethlehem, to which our attention was especially attracted as to the one that guides us to our little Lord, and through Him to all good.

After Christmas, it seemed to us children that we lived a long, long time until another great holiday came – Easter. Easter was celebrated in the red living room. How strange. Right now I could draw the plan of our house, the first I lived in, and yet I know we left it when I was six years old. The widely stretched table was decorated in the traditional Russian way. It was laden with holy breads blessed in church and decorated with little sugar lambs and roses; the tallest bread in the middle, and on both sides smaller and smaller ones in the shape of towers, gradually reaching the ends of the table and forming a triangle. The place of honor in the very center was for a special Easter cheese delicacy full of almonds and glazed fruits. There were sweets, a variety of wines, cold roasts of turkey and ham, a suckling pig. I remember how I cried when I found out that the little pig with the red apple in its mouth was dead. I did not touch a piece of it then, nor at any other time in my life. Tarts, cookies, cakes, fruit, nuts and candies were in abundance. The servants, who had been busy for many weeks before Easter, were given a three day holiday. Nothing was cooked during these days, everything being served cold. Only on Easter morning would Father come into our nursery. He would hang a pretty Easter egg at the heads of our beds and kiss us three times. He seldom kissed us, careful not to pass germs on to us as he was always in contact with the sick, but Easter was different. How we waited for that kiss! I remember Mlle. Cecile, our French governess, blushed when Father gave her the Russian Easter kiss together with the presents she received on that morning. Being French, she did not know it was a typically Russian custom for the master of the house to greet his entire household on Easter morning. For the next three days everyone who said, "Christ is risen" is answered, "Indeed He is risen", and kissed three times on the cheek even though they might be total strangers who met on the street.

Because our parents were occupied with their social work, my sister and I were left mostly in the care of Mlle.Cecile with the result that every day language and prayers were in French, and our Russian stumbled a little in the background. Mademoiselle seemed a heroine to us except for days when there were thunderstorms. Then, full of fear, she would reverently light a candle before the icon of Christ that hung in a corner of our nursery, grab us in spite of our resistance, and make us kneel with her for what seemed to be a very long time rattling off one prayer after another until the storm subsided. Although we were quite lively Mademoiselle never seemed to be tired of us, and when a German governess was engaged to take charge of us every other day, Mademoiselle, who was a little jealous, reluctantly accepted her free days; not until a few months later did the two become friends.

I remember how proud our Fraulein Mina was of me when one morning, running barefoot after our old dog, Barbos, I cut my foot on a long piece of glass and did not make any special case of it. She carried me into Father's working room, boasting about my courage. I nearly lost it though when Father dug the glass out, deep from under my bleeding sole. Oh, how painful it was. I felt like yelling in revolt, but by some strange contrast or because the seed of fortitude was beginning to germinate in me, eyes full of tears I burst into laughter instead. As a recompense for my stoic behavior I was allowed to rock in Papa's chair – an unexpected privilege, a dream suddenly come true as we hardly ever entered Father's work room. Then we went to the sun parlor and listened to records, parchment rolls that played lovely tunes out of a large square box. It usually was our chief diversion on rainy days, but that morning was bright and the sun parlor in the form of a glass lantern was golden with sun. All the plants in pots were shiny green, each leaf having been individually washed. A Chinese red rose, which looked somewhat like a Florida hibiscus, had just opened up. The canary, having received her half fig for the day, was picking on it with accompanying music in the same atmosphere that made me soon forget the pain on my foot. Fraulein Mina was wise.

This sun parlor was our pleasure room. We, who had regular study hours since we were three years old, never worked there but sang, were read to, or listened to music. The air of this room was always cooler than elsewhere. From a special kitchen built in the back of the garden where only bread was baked, the smell of fresh boolochki (sweet egg rolls) would often reach us. I loved that smell and never forgot it. I was most sensitive to smells in general. I loved my mother's perfume, light as a breeze in spring that brings the scent of all the flowers. I enjoyed the smell of the earth after rain, the fragrance of cut grass, the mixed scent of tangerines, and pine needles at Christmastime; but some heavy smells made me very unhappy and sick – not for hours, but days. Mother told me of an incident. No one ever knew why I disliked and always ran away from a lady friend of hers. The lady was quite upset about it and once made up her mind to catch me. Laughing and joking, saying that she was going to get me this time, she ran after me into the garden, back to the house and finally when I crawled under the bed, she pulled me out by my fat little three year old legs and hugged me and kissed me. How horrible it was for me! I was so afraid of her. I became very sick to my stomach, ran a high temperature and threw up for hours. It took a week for me to be on my feet again. Father and Mother wondered at the reason for my sickness as I was a perfectly healthy child. When some time later the lady came again, Mother watched me closely, saw me hold my nose and run away faster than before. She realized that her baby couldn't take the heavy Oriental perfume that her friend wore in abundance. Of course, I did not know why I disliked the lady, but to me she and her perfume were just sickening and I ran away, instinctively protecting myself.

The memory and the names of first playmates probably stay with one forever. Tala, Verochka, and their brother Liova Ovsianiko Koulikovsky were our nearest neighbors. We often walked to each other's house, passing the picturesque little church by their estate where we were all baptized. I remember the old oak tree with its cool shadows, not far away from the lily pond. The tree was encircled by a broad, octagonal bench – our permanent "home run". Any other garden I visited later in life brought back the picture of that beloved giant tree which was a part of all our games. The other children, the boys Tolia and Boria and the girls Sonia and Nadia Falz-Fein, whose estate was quite a few miles away, had a modern playground with giant steps, trapeze rings, slides and ladders. Our governesses would chat while we were playing. Their mother was very fond of our mother and loved to spoil her with gifts. I still have a green leather jewelry box with my mother's monogram which the charming Sofia Stepanova brought her from Carlesbad, and two beaded collars from Paris. Mother never wore them, thinking they were too glamorous, and left them for us.

We had much joy and ease in our childhood, but from Mother we knew that there were other less happy children, about whom she often spoke after her visits to the village. Several times a year she would urge us to give some of our toys to the little ones who had none, teaching us to share even the things we loved best. She never failed to be with us at bedtime. Together we repeated the simple little Russian prayer which somehow brought God close to us. **Tzar of heaven, Counselor, Soul of Truth, abiding everywhere, fulfilling of heaven, everywhere, fulfilling everything, come and abide in me. Cleanse me from all evil and save, oh Gracious One, my soul.**

With a feeling of her sweetness and the soothing music of her voice blessing us, we fell asleep. Father, entirely engrossed in his profession was distant and mostly inaccessible. We thought and spoke of him with reverence and awe.

SCHOOL DAYS

My first day in school was rather unusual. Two months after school had begun I was brought by Mother late in the afternoon. It was the day of a national holiday, one of the many anniversaries of the Imperial family. The schools, The Institute of Tzar Nikolas I for Girls of the Nobility in Odessa and the Corps des Cadets for boys, were having a concert that night to celebrate the event. All I remember of that first evening was that just before the concert for some reason I was brought into the presence of the French teacher who spoke to me with much kindness and whom I loved at once. After a friendly chat the tall man picked me up and carried me from one classroom to another showing me off. "Here is a little girl, the youngest in all our school," he would say. "She speaks French like a little French girl. You should take lessons from her, not me. This child could put all of you to shame, even though you are the graduating class." This was said to the beautiful tall girls who stood around us. He would ask me some amusing questions to which I laughingly replied, entertaining the pretty girls who listened attentively. It certainly was not what I had imagined my first day in school would be. During the concert M. Louis Goriss still did not let me go. I sat on his lap in the first row next to Mme. la Directrice and during the intermission he introduced me in the same boastful and witty manner to all the staff of the school. He kept chatting with me quietly, showing me photographs of beautiful ladies on the cover of his gold watch.

9

The next day all I heard was, "Here, here she is, the Novenkaya, (the new girl) who speaks French so well." One of my classmates came to me and in a rather commanding tone said, "I want you to be my friend." Not waiting for my answer she announced to the class, "Listen here, girls. I inform you that Lisa and I are going to be official friends." I was not accustomed to being with so many girls and stood there bewildered, not uttering a word. Throughout my school years I remained an example and an authority in French, and many times I wished I were not. Only several years later did I learn what preceded my entrance into this school and why all the fuss.

After many years of devoted service Mademoiselle was called back to France to take care of the children of a relative who had died. It was the year when my sister Vala was taking her entrance exams for the second year in school. Mother took me along and asked the inspector to let me go through the examination also. I passed with a brilliant score in French and German which were an important part of the curriculum at that time, but my age was the obstacle. I was not yet nine years old and girls were accepted in the first grade only at ten. Mother was very anxious to have both of us in school since Mademoiselle was no longer at home to help. Mme. la Directrice, V.P. Kandiba born Baroness von Fredericks, formerly a lady-in-waiting of the Dowager Empress suggested sending a telegram to Tzar Nikolas II with the official request that he grant permission for a girl who excelled in languages to be accepted in spite of her age. This was done in May and only towards the end of October came the favorable answer from the Tzar allowing me to enter school. That is why I came two months late.

The girl who forced me to be her friend was very poor at French and wishing to improve kept me constantly at her side. Instead of studying arithmetic in which I was quite weak, I had to help her almost all the time given us to study. Another not too helpful incident occurred. Once when the girls were up to something I had the misfortune to mention that I was brought up to respect my elders and to obey their orders. This slip of the tongue was a catastrophe for me. All the girls in my class, being older, took advantage of it. "Lisa," one would say, "I forgot my book in the hall. Will you bring it please?" or "Hurry up, girly. Take this pen to Katia," and so on. It took me a little time to catch on. At first almost mechanically I would run to do this or that, not thinking much about it; but when it began to cause me trouble I would refuse to run their errands and they would come back at me saying, "That's not fair. You, yourself, said that one has to obey the orders of those who are older." Quite a few times because of them I was late to class or dinner, and at the end of the semester I had a twelve (twelve being our highest grade) and a minus for behavior. A rather contradictory remark explained this minus. "Too kind a little girl" was written on the bulletin which my father overlooked. When my report card reached him a return letter informed me that if I continued to receive minuses for behavior, he would take me out of school and send me as a goose girl to watch the geese. On the whole the girls were very friendly to me and the joke of running their errands was soon dropped forever. I was getting accustomed to the new life and felt fortunate to have my sister in the same school. Yet, often when alone in the piano room where I was supposed to practice, I gazed out the window watching the red sun setting behind the bare branches of the trees – and cried and cried for Mother.

The following year early in September Mother, my sister and I were slowly walking toward the immense now familiar official building – our boarding school. We had arrived by boat from the little city on the Black Sea, Port Skadovsk, to which Father, after seven years practice as a district doctor, was transferred in the capacity of a military doctor. According to Mother's plans the three days before school in the large city of Odessa (which we did not know at all) turned out to be a wonderful holiday. In a coach running smoothly over the pebbled roads, we were taken around the city, saw the main temple in the center of town, the famous Uspensky Cathedral with its five impressive domes, and passed along the Boulevard Nikolas whose trees were glowing with the multiple colors of a rich autumn. We stopped by the monument of the Duc de Richelieu – a French duke who came to live in Russia after the French revolution and became Governor General of the city. We walked down something like two hundred steps to a little Church of St. Nikolas which Mother had insisted on seeing. Climbing back up was not easy but afterwards we enjoyed our dinner in the cool and sumptuous Hotel de Londres, the best in town. The next morning we saw the museum, the railroad station and all the monuments. After that the same coachman, his horse taking a swifter trot, took us to the outskirts of town where the summer villas seemed to compete one with the other in beauty. All were situated on a hill running straight along the coast of the Black Sea. The last day was the shopping day. In the Passage, a large arcade with a glass roof where every commodity could be found, Mother bought for herself a chic green hat. Sister and I concentrated mostly on little souvenirs which during the long year in school would remind us of the three happy days spent with Mother.

Walking toward the immense cold looking building, none of us feeling too happy, I started confiding in Mother about Anna Z – " I never really wanted to be her friend, she forced herself on me and it doesn't make me happy. There is something wrong, very wrong. She makes me do things – takes my time to help her with her French – and doing those things for her, I am not pleased. I feel that she is not a real friend for whom I surely would like to do most everything."

"There are children like that, and also grown-up people, who force themselves on others and under no circumstances should you continue such a friendship. The sooner you break it, the better," Mother said.

"I tried to a few times but she told me that I will scandalize myself forever, as according to the rule of our school nobody is supposed to break a friendship once started."

"Nonsense! There is no such rule, my dear. Be firm and do not worry. It will work itself out for the best and you will smile again."

The old doorman, Dimian, in his red and blue dress livery opened the school door, greeting Mother with a low bow. In the downstairs reception hall we were able to visit with Mother another half hour, listening to her parting advice. Then she blessed us and reminded us to write to her at least twice a week. I looked and looked and looked at her, as though trying to hold her image in my eyes forever. How pretty she was in her blue silk suit and new little green hat. How hard it was to realize that in a few minutes she would go away and I would not see her until spring. She was the whole world to me. To me she was the most beautiful, the sweetest, the kindest mother. To part with her was very, very trying, and for many days after I woke up with swollen eyes.

Days went on and my friend Anna did not feel like granting me my freedom. Somehow she managed to laugh off my plea; then she would become exaggeratedly sweet, making me feel ashamed to drop her. Around Christmas I caught a cold and was taken to the lazaret (the school infirmary). When I felt better I was more determined than ever to take action and sent her a note breaking all ties. Like a bomb she fell into my sickroom, exploding heavily, threatening me again with a school scandal. That night my temperature ran up again. When allowed out of the infirmary I finally performed my coup de theatre. Managing to enter our classroom just a few minutes before the teacher, I climbed on his pulpit and waving my hands high, shouted: "Girls, girls! Listen, quickly! I am breaking my friendship with Anna, and I want you all to know it!" "Bravo! Bravo!" came back the unexpected approval together with loud applause for which, much to my regret, we were punished by the teacher whom we were supposed to wait for in silent reverence. This victory was a triumph, a true liberation, and the memory of it was, and is, most helpful even now when similar characters cross my way.

In school we had French and German days, the same as for many years at home. How different from our young Fraulein Mina was the severe old Fraulein Grutzmacher. On her days, we had better watch out. Just a look! What a look! She used to bend her head low, chin to chest, so as to fix her sharp little eyes on us from above the frame of her glasses. One glance was enough. We were afraid of her; that is why we did not like her. She did not know how or maybe did not care to be our friend for the teachers to be close to their pupils was not quite fashionable those days.

Mlle. Bernand, who wrote on my first grade bulletin "Too kind a little girl," was as sweet as my own Mlle. Cecile. She was only with us for two grades, and then left to be married. Always I shall be grateful that she was there when I entered school. The first morning following the concert, awakened by the rising bell I saw a smiling angelic face looking at me. "Good morning, little Lisa. Have you had a nice sleep? I am your French Dame de Classe and I have come to help you with our routine." This was Mlle. Bernand. "Let's start," she went on. "Do you want to? Well, first things first. I have chosen an easy number for you – number six." I looked confused. "It means that all parts of your uniform and underwear will have No.6 printed or embroidered on them. This makes it easy for you and for the laundry. Every girl has her own number. Do you understand?" I nodded. "Now get up, open your bed to be aired and join me later." It felt good to be guided by her even in the immense wash room where, as was customary every morning, I had to wash half of my little torso in cold water. I felt warm with Mlle. Bernand around.

At 7:30 in the morning all the girls lined up. We were going down from our dormitories on the third floor to the main hall, where all the students (about three hundred) had their morning prayer. This was the large hall where Sunday receptions for the parents and relatives and the pupils took place – also concerts and balls, and of course, graduations with sometimes sixteen pianos standing in a half circle on which thirty-two hands played some heroic, mostly Wagnerian, piece to start the graduates bravely on their own. From this hall we went down a marble staircase into the dining room below. After breakfast a half-hour walk in the garden, sun or rain. In the winter season boards were put on some of the paths to protect our feet from the wet ground, enough for us to make a circle or two on them in fifteen minutes. I think it was wise on the part of the school authorities to make us take this short, brisk walk just before studies began. With rosy cheeks, mind and body refreshed by the clear air, we would quickly hang up our coats and run to the classroom. Our studies were held on the second floor in classrooms on both sides of a very long corridor where we would limber up after every forty-five minutes of study.

In each classroom, the teacher's assistant (who was there to watch behavior and order) had her little table, and the teacher, his lectern. The rooms were very large with plenty of light from immense windows facing the garden. Our desks were comfortable and roomy, with two girls in each. There was a different teacher for every subject. I was sorry to find that my "publicity agent" Monsieur Gorisse was teaching only the four upper classes, and that we had a very original almost African looking little old lady, Mme. Gannibal, for our French. From nine until noon three usually serious subjects were given, then lunch and another walk for a much longer time – about an hour. During this second walk, weather permitting, we would run all over the garden and to the playground, which was not as perfect as the one of my early friends the Falz-Fein, but was still well equipped with a very tall sliding hill (gorka) which we especially enjoyed. After that, three more study hours of which two were devoted to singing, music, painting and gym.

In spring, we younger ones were very busy, each being allowed to make her individual garden, clearing the space under a lilac bush as I remember mine was, or under some tree. Each was like a little rock garden and we competed with each other in originality and neatness. The best one received a new plant from the gardener as a reward. This usually happened at Easter.

Dinner was at six and we were not allowed to talk while eating. It was extremely boring for me as I seldom enjoyed the food in school and only made believe that I ate. I was getting thinner and thinner but no one seemed to notice it. I think it was in the fourth grade that we read about

Grecian stoicism which originated a new mode, a certain fad, to try to exercise will power. Once on Sunday when my favorite dessert was served I decided, under the influence of Grecian stoicism, to abstain and sent mine to Sonia B, a plump girl who loved nothing more than food. While the waitress was carrying my plate across to Sonia's table the Inspectrice Maria Ivanovna questioned her about it. By that time, everybody knew that I was not a good eater, but to think that I had refused a delicious macaroon seemed to the lady too much of a fuss. At once she ordered me to leave my seat and stand in the middle of the dining room for punishment. In her indignation she called me, who was as thin as a reed, "You stout monkey" and let me stand there long enough to think of some other less embarrassing method of proving my stoicism.

For about half an hour after dinner we were free to do as we pleased, run around the corridor, read in the classrooms, or play games in the large empty reception hall. The study hours were from seven to nine, then the evening prayer in each individual classroom; after that we went up to the dormitories, washrooms, and to bed. Lights went off at nine o'clock for the "little ones" and at ten for the "big ones," the three upper grades -the school having seven grades in all. In these Imperial schools, the lowest grade was the seventh, next came the sixth, and so on, the highest being the first, the graduating class, when the girls completed their education and received the "attestats," their diplomas. As I mentioned before, twelve was the highest mark for studies and behavior and seven the lowest passing grade. All the rest were unsatisfactory marks which could come down as low as one (ediniza), which probably would mean expulsion.

The daily routine was as I have described previously, except for the mornings when we took our steam bath. The steam rooms were in the basement. Every ten days the rising bell would ring earlier than usual and with special coats over our long-sleeved flannel nighties we went by the back stairs (a rather gruesome procession) four flights down to the steam room. There the maids were waiting to wash our hair and bodies.

We sat with hair loose on long hard benches all in a row like Loreleis on a rock. Sometimes the steam was so thick we felt like ships lost in the fog unable to see a hand stretched before us. It took me a few years before I began to like this kind of bathing. Now when I come to a new city I often look for what is generally called a Turkish or Russian bath and if there is one I never miss it.

As a result of systematic undernourishment my resistance was very low and I was often taken to the infirmary. Every time before getting seriously ill, probably running a temperature, I had the same nightmare. From the opposite corner of the dormitory a woman in a dark violet dress with large yellow spots was approaching me growing taller as she drew nearer. Terrified, I would recognize her as the same person who frightened me in my early childhood running after me and finally dragging me from under my bed. The nightmare reached its peak when I tried desperately to run away from her but found myself unable to move. Invariably the next day I was taken sick. I had all the regular children's diseases, and in the third grade contracted measles followed by a very severe case of scarlet fever from which I almost died. Those with contagious diseases were immediately transferred to a building completely outside the school – the quarantine. I was in great danger. Once when my worried sister came to inquire about my condition she heard the school nurse issuing the order to prepare the complete gala outfit of No.6, Lisa Kraevsky, who was not expected to live through the night. Turning her head the nurse saw the frightened face of my sister. She gave a sigh but said nothing. After a consultation four city doctors had given up on me. Father was called and took over the responsibility of my care. He believed that lukewarm bathing would relieve my pain and take the poison out of my system. That critical night after two baths into which I was plunged and held in a sheet as in a hammock, my delirium stopped for the first time in a week and I slept a quiet, natural sleep.

I remember the feeling, a split second of half-consciousness, when you cannot make out who you are, from whence you came, or where you are going. Just then my eyes opened, and in the farthest corner of the room I saw the figure of a lady in a long white dress standing in a praying attitude under the lampadka (a small oil lamp) which threw a soft light on the icon of Christ. All of a sudden I felt she was praying for me – the lady was praying for me. It was not my mother. It was our Maman as all the girls called her, our Directrice Madame Kandiba, the solemn Baroness von Fredericks, usually looking so inaccessible and regal, who stood there humbly asking the Lord to spare the life of her little pupil – the Maman who remained in our memories forever as a model of authority combined with kindness and grace. To see her standing there in my sickroom thinking of me and praying for me gave me a wonderful feeling of warmth. I could feel her love all around me.

From that distant corner of the room my eyes returned to my bedside and there I saw Father, all in white, watching, watching me with his eyes and with his soul. "Lisa," I heard. "Papa." Later when Father told me all the history of my sickness and recovery, he said that even one word, coming almost in a whisper, was too much for me. My eyes closed heavily but a smile brightened my face all the while I slept. When I felt better the quarantine nurse took pleasure in telling and re-telling me how during the worst days of my sickness, the whole school prayed for me in classes and in church. Mlle. Dreving A.A., my French Dame de Classe right after Mlle. Bernand, was the most fervent in these prayers. How pleasant it was to think of her. She was beautiful with a saintly cameo-like face. When she knelt in church she somehow leaned forward in what seemed to us to be the most tiresome attitude. Yet for hours she knelt motionless, during Lent especially, in uttermost concentration. In our minds she was a saint. What else could she be with so much praying? I have often wondered if it was not under her influence that, a year after my sickness, I began to check upon my own concentration on prayer. Sometimes late at night in the long, long dormitory with only a little light before the holy image, I was the only one still praying, kneeling on my bed, often for hours, trying to say my prayers from the beginning to the end without other thoughts creeping into my mind. Maman, who frequently at night walked through the dormitories where all her girls were fast asleep, would notice me praying and patting my head would say, "God has heard you, child. Now go to bed – you need your sleep."

Since the early days of understanding, partly through Mother's simple teaching, partly by itself, my relationship with God as my Eternal Father had been pretty well established; but hearing that others were praying for me made me understand the importance of prayer and also made me feel grateful to my Creator for having answered them. I dreamt of being in our school chapel again and lighting a large candle there, one that would burn for many hours carrying my thanksgiving to God. We all loved our school chapel. It was spacious and beautiful. The walls were decorated in white and blue and trimmed with gold. The holy icons, real masterpieces, were painted in cheerful colors by outstanding modern artists. There reigned an atmosphere of quiet beauty, making the long hours spent in church much shorter. Our chapel days were every Saturday evening and Sunday, all the national holidays and every day during the Lenten period. Our own girls sang in the choir. I loved the evening service especially, with all its sad melodies. I felt its peace and though I longed for home more than at other times, in church I did not feel lonely. During the longer liturgical service in the morning I often let my imagination wander to far away places and did not listen too attentively; but at a certain moment when, arms extended, the priest chanted "Gore Imeem Serdza -We lift our hearts to the heights"– all my being stirred, my heart beat stronger, tears would come to my eyes and I felt that I, too, could reach those celestial heights.

Our beloved very, very tall Reverend Father Ioanne Strelbitzky, who also taught us religion and catechism, officiated mostly alone but sometimes with the help of a deacon. When the three hundred girls stood in the chapel, or knelt as one, our blue dresses and white pelerines formed a colorful streamlined design which was lovely to look at. Our uniform was very pretty indeed. The base of it was a very heavy, stiff material of turquoise blue with a tight hooked bodice and full skirt. The bodice had little sleeves and an open neck. Over it we wore a wide white apron and attached to the short blue sleeves were long washable white ones. Over the décolletage we had a pelerine, a little circular cape coming down almost to the waist which was held at the neck by a bow tie which we took special pride in fixing properly, although some of the girls never succeeded in doing so. We always walked with hands clasped in front. The things we carried were in the large pockets sewn in our underskirts, not in our dresses. There we had our hankie, comb, candies, pencil, eraser, and many other things. On gala days the white parts of our uniforms, made out of cotton, were replaced by ones made of fine French batiste, and the little bow ties looked like butterflies perched at our necks. These extra gala dresses worn only by the two upper classes at the Year Ball and the Graduation Ball eliminated the cape and the sleeves. A little lace ruche was gathered around the décolletage, and on the left shoulder was a rich red satin bow, the ends gracefully falling down the arm. Long white kid gloves extended above the elbow and a fan completed this beautiful outfit. The three colors in it represented the Russian national flag – red, white and blue.

Flashes of this passed through my mind as I was sitting outside in the little garden of the quarantine house, where so recently I had been at the brink of death. From where I sat I could see the immense edifice of our school and thought of my sister and the girls. No one was allowed to cross the gate of the quarantine so I only heard the voices in the garden from behind the wall. I would have liked to have run around with them but I was too weak. In the spring they brought me outside where I would sit in a chair. The lilacs were in blossom and I loved their fragrance. The nurse gave me a branch which I held carefully. There were many lilacs in the garden of my early childhood... and now I was a big girl of eleven.

I thought of Mother. Poor Mother! What had she lived through knowing I was in danger! Here at my side on a little table were all her letters. Each had a little surprise inside; each had words of encouragement, words of faith, of trust in my recovery and well being. How I longed for her. What wouldn't I have given to have her by my side? I always longed for her. No wonder. Anyone who met her once wanted to be with her again and again. Why? I think because of the constant radiation of her goodness which together with her exquisite beauty made almost everyone she met a friend or an admirer. A wonderful thing happened to me sitting alone in the garden dreaming of my mother. My mother came and sat by me for many afternoons. The spring air and Mother's tender love hastened my recovery. How thankful I was for her presence. How thankful I am even now that my parents knew what that security meant to a sick child. Without it there could be no true relaxation, and without complete relaxation no quick recovery.

Ten days later, Mother took me home. The doctor together with the school directors decided that after such a severe illness it would not be advisable for me to return to classes as there was only a short time left before the end of the school year. At home I had to stay in bed every morning later than usual. When Mother came to bid me "good morning" she always thanked God for my recovery, and left alone I kept thanking and thanking Him for it, and for Mother and for something I could not quite understand that filled my heart to the brim, something invisible but great which had become very important to me – my faith.

Another summer under the warmth of Mother's love, another winter in school, another summer and another winter, and now it is spring again, and the end of the third class (fifth grade). Thus two years passed without any special events. I was still doing very well in languages and had 10 as a mark for all the other branches. I was popular with the girls and the teachers – they called me the joy of the class. It seems that I had a contagious laugh and often in class sitting in the first row trying to control it, my shoulders would shake and the girls sitting behind me would giggle first and then all at once burst into such a torrent of laughter that even the teacher and the Dame de Classe were pulled into its irresistible current. M. Gorisse finally had been with our class for a full year and spoiled me with privileges. There were even some signs of jealousy or competition between him and our German teacher as to which of the two languages I spoke better.

I had no other serious sickness, still I was not strong. Additional food was provided for me to protect me from anemia but I had no desire for it and it did not seem to do me any good. Mlle. Vosnesensky, who came to us on transfer from some northern institute, had replaced the prayerful Mlle. Dreving. She always looked very slick, as though she had just come out of a cool pond and this, together with her very wobbly gait, made us call her "Ootka" (the Duck). Her best friend, another Dame de Classe who was very thin and tall and somehow curled around Ootka, looking just as slick, was nicknamed "The Eel." Nicknames were very fashionable in our school. The new Inspectrice for instance, was called "The Raven." I still have a clever caricature of those ladies made by one of my classmates.

Once during rest period Mlle. Vosnesensky called me to her desk and held a long conversation with me. At first, for quite a while, she knitted silently. I sat down on our shiny parquet floor as we usually did when talking to her informally, both my hands on the arm of her chair, head high, looking at her. "Listen here, my dear," she began, "I have done quite some thinking about you lately, and have come to the conclusion that for your own good you should stay at home a whole year and rest instead of starting next autumn with the very strenuous and difficult studies of the second class, the last before your graduation year."

"You mean, Mademoiselle, that I should part with my class and upon my return continue with girls I was never with before? Oh, no!"

"Friends you will make with any girls, in any class," she went on. "But remember that after all the ailments you had in earlier classes, you really have never rested as you should. Your appetite is still poor and you are very thin. Of course, according to your age you should be the smallest in the class and so you are, but if you do not take proper care of yourself in time and overwork your brain you may remain just as little as you are now, for life, and then the boys on the street will run after you and shout, "Dwarf! Dwarf!"

"Oh no, Mademoiselle, that couldn't happen! Am I really that small?" I asked, getting to my feet and looking down the short length of my body to my feet. After this conversation for the rest of the day I could not speak to anyone; I did not prepare my lessons, I think I did not even sleep, but thought and thought and thought.

The next morning at breakfast I consumed everything that was given to me, my extra egg and cocoa, everything to the last crumb. Then instead of going for our regular morning walk I ran to the orthopedic teacher. "Please, Dr. Gorin, let me exercise with your class."

"But my dear girl there is nothing wrong with you, no curvature in your back as I remember, and you really do not need any orthopedic correction."

"Oh, please let me exercise on the parallel bars. I will not disturb anyone." He couldn't say no to me. From then on for a half hour daily I climbed and hung from the parallel bars trying to stretch myself, and when the girls passed by me I asked them to pull me by the feet. At first my whole body ached but nothing could stop me. My mental command, stirred by the dread of remaining a dwarf, was so powerful that even my appetite increased to an almost abnormal degree. I ate the meals I could never touch before, and ate them with relish and joy. Leaving for home, I told Mademoiselle that I had no intention of parting with my class, nor did I expect to be a dwarf. After a whole summer of physical culture and excellent care, I returned to my class. I was a pretty tall girl of almost fourteen, tall enough to walk in the sixth pair instead of the first as I had done for the previous five years of school.

Mlle. Vosnesensky was right. The scholastic work in the second class was incomparably more serious than in the previous years. Besides such branches of mathematics, physics, history, geography and pedagogy we had the reading of the classics of Russian, French and German literature such as Pushkin, Lermontoff, Turgenev, Racine, Corneille and Moliere, the German Goethe, Lessing and Schiller. It took almost all the time during the day and often part of the night. We sneaked into the not too elegant quarters – the lavatory, the only place that had a little lamp. We took the risk not only of being punished, but also of ruining our eyesight, and read pages and pages of prose and often memorized long passages of poetry. With so much studying our horizons certainly widened and though, as I said we hardly had any leisure, there was time left for dreaming – and we were dreaming. Next year we would be out of school; next year we would be free. Each of us would go in her own direction, try her own strength, try her first steps in the school of life. Some dreamed of traveling, some of taking a higher education, some of becoming actresses. The majority of the girls were dreaming of boys they thought they were in love with. Others were dreaming of falling in love. When a young girl dreams of something into which she puts her heart she is always sad. The old Fraulein Grutzmacher, familiar with the vague expression on a young girl's face, herself apparently void of any feelings, would brusquely move her knitting needles right in front of her victim's face and say, "Stop dreaming! Go back to work!" Indeed, our freedom was too far away yet, and all we had to do this year was work.

Here before me is a precious possession – a notebook of impressions, observations and descriptions of events that happened during the last year in school. Sincere and unrestrained, my adolescent pen ran across the pages of this notebook which became at that time, and later remained, a permanent friend with whom I shared my thoughts whenever urged and able to do so.

NOTEBOOK

I do not think I shall keep a diary, yet I feel that this week's events should be described lest memory fail to retain some of the minute details. Besides, it is my last year in school. Later on it probably will be pleasant to read and remember some of these days with the extra privileges given us by our dear Maman as well as some other, maybe less exciting moments of the quiet sheltered life behind the walls of this Imperial school. The excitement of this week was our meeting the Tzar, Emperor Nikolas II, while he was passing through the city of Odessa to a destination, of course, publicly unknown. His Majesty was to arrive at our port in his yacht, the motor ship Standart. We were to be lined up to greet him on his way from the harbor to the train. For two days almost all the regular routine was off. Instead, in the large reception hall we rehearsed the meeting of the Tzar. We were taught how to walk, how to hold the row, how to stand, how to curtsey, and what to say while greeting His Majesty. That memorable day at 8:30 in the morning, in our new turquoise frocks and gala aprons and capes, the whole school started out in sixty-seven elegant carriages, four to five people in each. The teachers who were to meet the Tzar with us were in the carriages with the little ones. At first we were lined up in front of the Imperial train. It was not a favorable spot and we were disappointed in the city mayor, who had promised our Maman the best place. There we stood for half an hour examining His Majesty's luggage and that of his suite.

Soon we heard the salvos of the cannon. In a small boat the Emperor was approaching the shore. A welcome hurrah did not cease as he walked through the rows of representatives and organizations that had come to meet him. I could not see him. I was in terrible despair as I had dreamed of seeing him well. Several times Monsieur Gorisse tried to help me stretch, but with no success. Then suddenly, just as the Emperor was passing through the last row, an officer of his suite offered to move us towards the pavilion through which the Tzar had to pass. Maman issued the order to proceed, Monsieur Gorisse pulled me by the hand, and in the wink of an eye we were in front of the pavilion. I was in the first row beaming and trembling. I thought, I'll just lose my mind when I see him so close. Now he was moving toward us. I shall never forget this moment! He stopped for a second and embraced us with his kind glance. Like a wave of the ocean all white and blue, the three hundred girls of our school curtsied before the Tzar, with a clear: "We are happy to greet Your Imperial Highness." To which he answered, "Thank you for your joyous welcome." Now he was approaching Maman under the shower of flowers we threw around him. I watched Maman making her graceful court bow. She looked so majestic. The Emperor stood by her and I heard him mention that he enjoyed looking at our happy faces and would report to the Mother Empress that the pupils of the Institute of Odessa looked healthy and happy. He shook hands with Maman and proceeded, passing close, very close to me. It was no longer a dream. I saw him! I saw him! Once more, this time in solemn silence, the white and blue wave went down and rose to its crest. On the step of his train the Tzar turned and waved to us; then he disappeared. I thank God for having had the happiness of seeing him, even hearing his voice right next to me. This I shall never forget. And never shall I forget his dear features, his sad blue eyes.

Our Directrice was not in a hurry to leave and my eyes followed the disappearing train until I no longer could see it. Only then I noticed that above the park there was an inscription in immense letters: "GOD SAVE THE TZAR." We let almost all the crowd go by before we started out. The weather was fine. The day before we were worrying about the rain and Maman jokingly advised us to write on little pieces of paper the names of forty bald men, and then throw the names out the window. After that she assured us the weather would have to be fine. We had never heard of this trick before and did not fail to try it. I do not know whether the bald men are supposed to dislike rain more than others and specialize in praying for fine weather, but the result was remarkable. We returned through town in the same carriages with only one difference – now the inhabitants of Odessa gave us an ovation. The entire Deribassovskaya Street was full of people waving and cheering us. Only some groups of shabby looking students made unfavorable remarks on our account.

Back at school we had dinner. Maman came with the teachers, made a short speech with good wishes for the well being of the Emperor and we sang the Russian hymn, followed by three hurrahs. Our first class had the privilege of drinking a toast with the teachers which we had never done before. After dinner we had a "Te Deum" in our school chapel with a special prayer for the Emperor. Maman came to our class and we thanked her for the great treat she had given us. She informed us of another surprise – tomorrow our class was to spend a whole day in the school "Villa Ochepovsky" by the sea. That night I thought about the Tzar and prayed, remembering what I had heard about the tragic accident during his coronation (which some took as a bad omen), and hoped that the rest of his reign would be happy.

I have no time to describe our nice party at the Villa, but this I must. There is no end to the goodness of our Maman. At 2: 30 PM we went out to the Imperial yacht Standart, still moored in the waters of Odessa Harbor awaiting the return of the Tzar. This privilege was only for graduating class. Maman, the two dames de classe, the inspector, N. Krafchenko, and a few teachers went with us. Group by group, in small tugboats, we approached the Standart. The chic naval officers greeted us courteously and took charge of showing us around. The one with our group, Captain Constantinoff, was very handsome but not at all talkative. Tzar Nikolas's room was very simple, full of family portraits with inscriptions made by his own hand. Above the portrait of the Empress was written, "Alissa." The Tzar's working room was without any pretense. On his desk was a pair of binoculars. I picked them up and looked through them. I wanted to take a piece of stationery with the inscription Standart but had no courage. I sat in the chair in front of the table, and once more walked through his room before catching up with the group. Oh Lord, did I ever think it would be given to me to be in a place where the Tzar lived, to sit in the chair he sat in, and walk through his rooms? How thankful I must be to our school. Had I been at home, I would never have had the chance to be on the Standart.

Too bad Sister Vala had graduated last year, and could not see any of it! All my dear ones now live far away in the District of Voliny near the Austrian border, where Father was transferred a year ago. I know my next letter home will be a long one.

Now, where was I? Oh, yes – The Empress Mother, Maria Feodorovna, had inscribed "Maria" on the glass door of her cabinet, followed by the names of the ports she had visited while on this yacht.

The room of Alexandra Feodorovna, the Tzarina, was ornate with religious pictures, among which were many Madonnas. There was also a wonderful portrait of Tzarevich Alexis. The handsome boy stood with a toy shovel in his hand and beside him his irreplaceable bodyguard, Sailor Derevenko.

I forgot to mention that next to the quarters of Nikolas II was a little room containing all the gifts presented to him in Odessa, among which I noticed a magnificent icon of the Holy Virgin; also an album, a present to the Tzarevich, on the cover of which his face was carved on wood, and inside pictures of the technical school that had presented the album to him. In the children's quarters the interior was very simple – three rooms in all, connected by a staircase with the suite of their parents. Olga and Tatiana had one room, Maria and Anastasia the second, and the third for the Tzarevich Alexis. From there we went to the Tzar's dining room, passing the one used by his retinue. We were shown where he usually sits and who sits next to him. (The little Tzarevich eats at a separate table.) The dining room was large, with many plants. On the walls we saw some printed notices. There was the exact weight of the Tzar, his family, and his officers, taken religiously every week. The weight of the Emperor was 4 poods, 10 funts and three-quarters; Alexis, 1 pood, 14 funts. I don't remember any more, except the extraordinary weight of Prince Orloff – nine poods! (One pood is approximately 40 pounds; one funt is one pound.)

Soon we were called down to the officers' dining room where refreshments were waiting. Nina and I sat together and the officers served us hot chocolate with cake and candy. The officer at our table seemed very dull. "Yes, yes" and "No, no" were his only answers. The Chief Engineer of the yacht held a little dog from Malta, which he called by that name, and there was another little dog at his feet named Valetta which he had acquired in the city of that name. After the refreshments we were to leave. Nina and I ran again to the deck, almost knocked down the Admiral, curtsied deeply to him and ran away. We had found out that we were allowed to take souvenirs from the Standart and I wanted one at any cost. I succeeded in tearing a flower and a leaf off a plant in the room of the Tzarevich, but many girls took stationery with the Tzar's crest. Tamara Morar took an eraser used by the Tzar, Alla Alexeeff took thread from the sewing box of Alexandra Feodorovna and matches from the Tzar's table, Nastia received a ribbon with the name of the yacht. Postal cards with a picture of the Standart were given to all. I was very happy to receive one. Much to my sorrow, the little flower I held so carefully withered at once.

We returned to shore in groups as before. I was in the last party and sat next to Maman. She thanked the Captain for the cordial reception and I heard him say that he would like to see us again, when or if, we returned to Odessa. For a long time the officers waved to us with their hats and handkerchiefs and we reciprocated. It was wonderful! Once back to the street, I was shocked by the contrast between the comfortable though not luxurious yacht where the Emperor often lived, and the dirty streets with ragged people.

As soon as we reached the school we had to grab our geometry books and study, study, study. The straight lines of Pythagoris' plans and the neat square rooms of the Imperial yacht seemed to jump simultaneously before our eyes. Olga Kostieva and I worked together and got off the subject very often. Mostly we thought of the Emperor whose presence we felt on the Standart despite his absence. Could it be that never, never again we would see him? Next day, unexpectedly I received a good mark, 11, for geometry. I think the end of our pleasures has come and we might as well begin to work very hard. What a happy month of October!

Last night, a week after our visit to the Standart, the Tzar was supposed to arrive back in Odessa. In the dormitory, when almost everybody was asleep and Nina and I were still praying, we heard nine cannon shots – the arrival of the Tzar – then three whistles from the yacht which meant his departure. An inexplicable sadness filled me. Where did it come from? Why do I feel like this every time I think of him? After all, he is a tzar, a monarch, he has everything. All Russias are his and yet I am so sorry for him.

Autumn is in its full power. It is humid and cold, dark and unpleasant. My birthday and right after it my name day have passed. I received a parcel from home with the things I love – Mother's cookies, halval, quince, jam and chocolate. My school mates gave me all sorts of little trinkets. I love the grayish-green jade bottle best and have it constantly in my pocket. Sister wrote that most probably my next birthday would be celebrated in Switzerland – Lausanne or Geneve, maybe. Could this be true? Will Papa really send us abroad? He is so intelligent. He always knows what is best for us. But I wish he were a little less severe. I can never come really close to him and speak to him simply, without previously preparing what I am going to say. How I wish I could be less formal with him and sit on his lap and joke with him as other girls do with their fathers. Who knows, maybe it is all for our good. I feel a little bit ashamed, but I must write to him now and ask for more money. We shall have our yearly ball and all the accessories must be bought with our own money – red ribbon, fine laces, and silk gloves this year. Except for the ball there will be hardly any other holidays before Christmas.

Going back to my name day, I wish to tell my book something that seems so wonderful to me. Every year on that day, St. Elizabeth's Day, the miraculous icon of God's Mother of Kazan is brought from the Cathedral to our school, and with holy chants is carried at the head of a procession through the entire building as a blessing. The day of my saint and the day of the celebration of the icon of the Blessed Virgin of Kazan correspond. In my heart I think this is a special blessing for me and I rejoice over it. I am thankful for this joy streaming deep inside of me, which somehow I do not share with others – a joy that is a secret between God and me.

Lots of news. We are editing a magazine, "The Days of Our Life." Sonia, Nina's sister, and Mila are the editors. I have already made a contribution of a short story and a poem.

There was a wedding in our church – the daughter of our Inspector, Assia Krafchenko, married a certain Mr. Tuneeyeff. She looked pretty, exactly as I expected a bride to look. I never was at a wedding before. The ceremony impressed me, although it was rather a private family affair, not a pompous one.

We were told that the ball will definitely take place, if no one of the Tzar's family passes away. I am glad Father sent me the money.

Our class relationship is destroyed by the grouchy Fraulein Grutzmacher. She is too unjust for words and I resent injustice more than anything else. We avoid speaking to her for days and she tells us as often as she can that we are the worst class she ever had.

Ootka, the Duck, (our other class supervisor) is not too good either. Yesterday she made changes in our dormitory and took Nina away from me. We are heartbroken but she doesn't care. She punished Nina for being too noisy at a wrong time in class, which has nothing to do with the dormitory. She was simply nasty, because she knows how happy we were to have our beds next to each other. We seldom talked but prayed at the same time, reminding each other not to be noisy in class lest one should forget. Sometimes after the lights were out, we were still taking notes on the subjects of stories we would write for the magazine, having pencil and paper at hand, especially for poetry. Ootka is breaking this coziness of ours. I feel like crying. We shall miss each other so much.

Our official ball took place, and did not leave any impression. I was terribly rushed sewing the lace around the sleeves and neckline, but in time all was ready and at eight o'clock sharp we entered the big formal hall. The cadets were already lined up and we stood opposite them and at the first sound of the music we began to waltz. Some of the cadets were very awkward. I liked only one, a blond with fine features, and would have enjoyed not only dancing with him but also talking a little. But then came Mr. K. M., our singing (voice) teacher. He told me quite a few flattering things I did not expect to hear, but instead of rejoicing over them I was bored. In the crowd I could not find my cadet again. Though I danced a lot, I did not feel enthusiastic about it. I think the whole affair was overrated.

Maman is leaving for a short vacation since she never celebrates her name's day, St. Barbara's Day, the 4th of December, here at school. In the evening our class went down to her private quarters with our gifts – two large hand-carved wooden vases made by Zoya in an ancient Russian style. We put fresh tea roses in one vase, and yellow and pink carnations in the other. Maman came out with her precious St. Bernard dog and was exceedingly appreciative. Reading our letter of good wishes, she asked teasingly, "Do you really mean it all?" She kissed each and every one, and with a "Christ be with you" she left us. Maman is so just, so kind. She is the only one in the whole Institute who is always the same. Mademoiselle and Fraulein are often obstinate and illogical. If it grieves me now to see Maman go away for a short while, how shall I feel when the hour comes for me to leave school forever?

For the first time in years I am going to spend my Christmas vacation at home and I look forward to it. Mother is coming and in five and a half days from now I shall be home.

Christmas at home was full of snow, sleigh rides, parties and compliments; many people mentioned that I was pretty. I was really surprised that at the parties quite a few young men sought my attention. I had often heard that I had a nice smile and almost everybody mentions my dimples, but I did not think I was pretty! Our friends' son, K. B., who attended the cavalry school apparently lost his head over me. Sister and I were very successful at a "bal masque." She wore an exquisite Tatar costume with long fluffy trousers, pointed slippers of dark blue satin embroidered with shiny stones, a jacket also richly embroidered, and the flat little Tatar hat covered with a veil. On the hat, intermingled with the pearls and multi-colored stones, shone tiny electric lamps which Sister could light at will since the battery was concealed next to the buttonhole of her jacket. It was a novelty and the lamps had a great effect. Vala won the first prize and I was so happy for her. I was a Pierrette and wore that classical pattern with great comfort, the ivory colored light wool being very agreeable to the touch. Immense old-rose silk pompons, four on the outfit and three on the hat, were its only decoration. We danced without stopping and next day I had to rest with my feet higher than my head.

During the two weeks of vacation I saw much snow. In Volinia winter has more snow than in Odessa. Sleigh rides were an enchantment. We went shopping, visiting, to parties – always in sleighs, plus special sleigh-ride parties when five or six of them raced. Every morning from my window I admired the old linden trees looking young in their robes of glistening white. I had a wonderful feeling realizing that I was home, that Mother was in the next room. I must not just sit and dream of her as I do in school, but run in my nightgown and kiss her good morning.

We had guests or went out almost every evening. Only once we were all by ourselves, and Father spoke of our future trip to Switzerland, telling us that the more education we acquired the better for us. He was in a good mood and teased us about our admirers, then turned the conversation to the subject of the importance of standing on your own feet – of being independent, and not hurrying to get married just because you cannot rely upon yourself, but must be "sewn to a pair of pants." He explained that marriage should be based on mutual respect. He also stressed that we should read more, that we should get acquainted with the characters depicted by great writers, and take less example from the society of the day. Father was so nice and approachable that night. I was happy. I thought much of what he said. Mother took me back to school. Alone with her on the train, I felt relaxed and sheltered, contented and sad at the idea of another separation, but this time only for five more months. Then she will take me out of this formal and secluded school forever.

I am back in my classroom again. My great consolation is my friend, Nina. What a fine girl, what a wonderful friend she is. I hope she and Sonia will go to Switzerland also. Since Christmas, my study habits have become even worse than before. I find myself dreaming, remembering the parties, or thinking of the future summer – long walks and horseback riding. Pencil in hand, I scribble my initials, E. A. K in different ways, and then automatically come the numbers 1-9-3-0 all over my blotter. Why do I do it? The year 1930 is so far away, and yet these figures have some fascination for me. 1930, 1930. I keep on writing it everywhere. Maybe something unusual will happen to me that year, something wonderful. I love these numbers. I do not know why.

Catechism, algebra, geometry, cosmography and physics simply refuse to enter my mind. Reading is still the best. I have just finished Turgenev's "Nest of the Nobility." Reading always leaves me with a desire to be better. It lights the flame of ambition, mostly for inner improvement. For instance, I think of the heroine of the "Nest of the Nobility," her character and her actions. I wish to be like her, as kind and as truthful. I wish to protect my own opinion and to love as beautifully as she did. I read with enthusiasm. Father is right, the characters brought to life by great writers cannot help but make an impression on one's mind and the theatre too. Last Sunday the city Mayor's box was offered to us. A little group went with Mademoiselle Vosnesensky to see the "Sunken Bell" by Hauptman. The actor Bogroff whom we had seen in a few plays before Christmas was playing Heinrech and Schuchmina played Reitendelein. How charming she is. Every motion of hers is full of grace. I sat breathless. Mademoiselle was all attention also. During the intermission we offered her some chocolates and she frowned. With an expression of quiet disappointment she said, "After seeing such an ideal performance how could you think of your stomachs!" Out of respect for her feelings, we did not touch a candy in the theatre, but as soon as we were out – oh my, how they vanished! I hope the Mayor's box will be offered to us again. I must try to have a 12 for behavior.

Nina loves the theatre even more than I do. She is a good little actress herself, having participated in some plays in Batoum where her father is the Governor General. She knows more about the theatre than I do and has her own opinion about acting. I have no opinion – I just enjoy theatre. At our numerous concerts Nina's recitation was almost professional. I was told that I was not too bad, although I have never studied elocution or dramatic art. I love to memorize passages in French from the tragedies of Racine, from Le Sid or Andromaque and recite them. I love to write. I am so glad that all I have written was accepted by our school magazine, even poems which were mostly humorous.

Sometimes life becomes unbearable here. At our free period we went to the large hall to play. Then Mademoiselle appeared, suspecting that we were up to something. Of course with her around we lost our enthusiasm for playing. We cannot take one step without these blue dresses of the Dames de Classe sneaking after us. Mademoiselle is spying, Fraulein Grutzka is shouting. Seven years of this is far too much. I am disgusted with these grey walls, with these angry faces, scoldings, bad marks, punishment and persecution. I am glad I shall be out of school at fifteen. To think that the majority of the girls finish at seventeen, practically spending their best years here! The geography teacher was unjust in marking my work. I must speak to him, but how shall I do it with so many spies around?

Today we were voting on the celebration of the hundred days before the end of school – "stodnevka." Some voted to have a secret celebration with wine upstairs in the dormitory or in the reception hall. Some, the group Nina and I sided with, wanted to ask Maman's permission. The majority agreed with us. Nina and I were chosen as delegates and went downstairs to Maman for consultation. Maman not only allowed the celebration, but also offered for our convenience a few things such as tables, a samovar, etc. It was an intimate gathering. Until 8:30 we chatted and danced all by ourselves, then everyone came for tea and a small concert program was given. Alla and Zoya recited, Maria played the piano and the general mood was utter harmony. At 11 o'clock we went upstairs. I fell asleep with a heavy heart, thinking that in one hundred days I shall part with all my school friends.

I have left my notebook alone for quite a while as there is no time to write. I enjoy my book very much, mostly because I come to it light-heartedly, as to a friend to chat on the spur of the moment, not regularly, day after day, as other girls do with their diaries, whether they have anything to say or not. I like my way better and probably shall continue writing like this in the future.

Russian literature was our very last class in school. Shortly written exams will begin and never again shall we sit at our desks as pupils before their teacher. I happened to be the last called to recite one of the short poems of Pushkin. It seems strange that in sixty days or so we shall bid farewell to the Institute where we have spent seven years. They passed with extraordinary rapidity. Soon each of us will walk on an individual road, a hard one maybe, because the "Road of Life" cannot be strewn with rose petals only. There will be obstacles to surmount. These will be the lessons of life, so different from the lessons in school.

The written exams have passed. French was the first, during which Monsieur Gorisse was most cooperative, being in one of his superlative moods. The subject was on the theme I have recently thought so much about – Fortitude in Life, based on the French tragedies, "Le Sid" and "Horace." Maman's assistant, our Inspectrice, "the Raven," pierced us with her sharp eyes at every move and at every whisper, but it did not help her much as Monsieur Gorisse already had established an atmosphere of naturalness and ease. In Russian we had a choice of subjects: (1) Gogol's humor per his comedy "Revisor -The Superintendent," or (2) "Hunter's Notes" by Turgenev. I wrote on the Humor of Gogol. I love humor! Our German teacher the sentimental Heinrich Johansen gave us "Happiness Is Not Lasting" with examples from "Die Leiden des Youngen Verters" by Goethe. This was easy. But oh, the last written exam was mathematics! I struggled for two and a half hours with the two algebra problems and did not solve either one! Somehow at the end I managed to copy one from Nina's paper; the other was never done and never presented to the teacher. What a flop! Never! I hope I never will have anything more to do with this great science. It is not for me. I was glad to see the last of it.

Immediately after the written exams we moved our desks from the regular rows to any part of the room we wanted. Mine is now by the window. The spring wind plays with my hair. While writing I often lift my eyes from the book and look at the familiar faces of the girls around me. How dear they are. I love them. God bless their lives no matter where they go.

Spring is here. No more heavy winter coats. I should say never more shall we wear those school coats which were extra heavy and clumsy. They are replaced by the short spring jackets, much to our delight. Our garden is green again. Here and there hyacinths are trying to push through and Easter is not too far away. This afternoon I saw a little girl, a beginner, busy making her garden by the same lilac bush where I used to work the first spring I spent here. Time goes on. Not long ago I was the smallest in the whole Institute.

I was glad to find out that on three out of four written exams I received the highest mark –12 – with the notation "Excellent work." I felt I deserved a reward. Any little thing would do, even a bowl of ice cream or some unexpected candy; but there was no fuss whatsoever about my excellent marks. How silly of me, anyhow. It just shows how immature I am. The marks by themselves are a splendid compensation.

I also wanted to loaf a little, to roam through the garden aimlessly, thoughtlessly, inhaling the lilacs, but no, the oral exams followed at once. By now we have passed catechism, physics and cosmography. On all three I pulled a ticket I knew best and had prayed for. (Each subject was divided into parts called "tickets," some subjects had 40 tickets, some 25, and some as low as 12. Before each exam these tickets were spread face down on the green felt cover of the long table at which all the teachers and officials sat. As in a lottery the pupil would pull one and looking at the outline recite accordingly.) My good mark in geometry balanced my failure in the written algebra problems, giving me a decent average.

It is so hot already that we can no longer work on our subjects in the garden. Maman allowed us to change our low hair-do to braids on top of our heads. It is much cooler this way and we look different – so much more grown up.

It is Easter Day. During Holy week we kept a strict fast and received the Sacraments. On Easter Eve after the church service and holy procession, we broke the fast at the traditional midnight supper with Maman, which took place in the large reception hall instead of in the dining room.

Last night before going to bed, we discussed our aims in life. Mine is to study; then to be useful to people in one way or another. If I ever get married it will be to relax in my own nest, living peacefully, with mutual love and respect. As to the family, to be sincere, I cannot picture myself bringing up children. Anyhow, that is pushing the horses too far. My aim this summer is to come closer to my own father. Until now my sister Vala and I have never really had a chance to talk with him. Maybe it was our fault. He is so kind. He wishes us to continue our education, unlike Mila's father who does not allow her even to think of anything but marrying some rich man. How awful!

The oral exams are coming to an end. I feel dizzy. At times I cannot keep my eyes open. I miss Mother terribly. Studying, studying, studying, for one whole month and a half, often reading at night in the petit cabinet until dawn! Mother would not allow me to work so hard. The German was good. I picked ticket No.18, Schiller's "'Wanderyahren," and recited with enthusiasm. I heard the officials whisper to each other, commenting on my typical German pronunciation. I am quite at ease with German and French. I wish I also knew English. I could have taken it privately in our school but Father thought I was overworked as it was, without another language. Before the Russian exam our studies were disturbed by the taking of group photographs. I stood in the last row next to Monsieur Gorisse. Each group photo will cost us four rubles, plus the expense of the ones we have to present to each teacher. I also have to take one with Nina and one all alone. I was playing a little lazy and did not read all the Russian, picked the ticket on the "Biography and Elegies of Joukowsky," and received a 10.

Next came geography. It seemed incredibly hard – 26 tickets from the book of Belochoff and 26 from the book of Matchenko. I gave up. I did not read it through. I hoped and prayed for Ticket No. 14 and could hardly believe my eyes when I pulled it. I answered satisfactorily and received a 10. Our teacher, Chuykoff, was pleased with us.

Sixteen days are left before the end of school. I expect Mamochka and Sister on the 16th or 17th of May. We shall have substantial expenses before graduation. So much is needed: a new dress, a new suit (my first), hats, gloves, and pocketbooks. I shall have to pay visits to many people right after graduation. I guess I am no longer a child. Mother wrote that she had bought the material, beautiful Swiss-embroidered batiste, for my graduation dress. What will the pattern be?

In the little reception hall, the French exams are in full swing. I was fortunate to be the first to answer in the first group, early this morning. Now I am free. In a little while the second group will go downstairs. All the girls are terribly frightened; so much depends upon Monsieur Gorisse's changeable mood. I told them that today he seems to be rather even-tempered. They all wanted me to bless them before they went and I certainly did not fail to do so. They also made me promise that I would pray for them.

Next to my desk stands a little cupboard on which many candles are now burning before some of our personal icons brought down to us from the dormitory. I have prayed for all of them, asking Our Lord to take their fear away and return their self-confidence. He, who sees everything, who knows everything, can do it.

It is so peaceful that I feel like writing. I observe that my diligence in studying decreases considerably. I think I am tired. I had to reread for the French exam, "Le Sid", "Horace", "Andromaque", "Avare" and "Misantrope." How could I do it with all the interruptions in connection with our graduation?

Nevertheless, this morning I approached the long green table with a buoyant step, curtsying deeply, most probably smiled. French could not fail me, I thought, I love it too well. Monsieur Gorisse, disregarding the solemnity of the event and the strictness of the officials, (whose number increased by many guests who had come to hear us), greeted me with his familiar, "Bonjour, bebechik," and then elaborated on my school history. He made it very easy for me, asking questions he was sure I could answer, disregarding the ticket I pulled, making it more of a visit than an exam. Rules certainly do not exist for Monsieur Gorisse. My fatigue suddenly disappeared and my voice was sure as I answered every one of his questions, completely relaxed and unafraid, despite the fact that everyone sitting at the table was listening and looking at me with what seemed to be one big attentive eye. Before I knew it I curtsied again, and it was all over. I know I was not too studious, and yet I cannot reproach myself. God knows I was really overworked and tired.

The wind nearly blew our candles out. A thunderstorm was approaching and the thin lightning just slid over my pages and dress. It makes me think of Mlle. Cecile. She was so afraid of thunderstorms. We had to pray with her in French, repeating: "Notre Pere qui etes aux cieux." I was such a baby then! The thunder increases. The air is heavy and in a moment a quick spring rain will refresh all. I think of our Volinia. There the thunderstorms are very frequent. The little city itself is of no interest, but the outskirts are lovely with picturesque old castles on hills, especially the one that belonged years ago to the Polish Count Radzivill. There are birch groves and pine forests and the air is tinged with the fragrance of the fir trees. Mother and Vala are en route. Maybe, maybe I shall see them tonight.

Mother and Vala arrived a little too late to visit me last night. Today, Sunday, I was so happy to see them, to kiss them, but that was all. It was absolutely impossible to talk things over as there were too many school companions of Vala, and other acquaintances in the Sunday reception hall. To spoil this precious hour entirely Monsieur Grutzmacher talked to Mother until the last minute. I think Mother and Vala both look well.

We prepared all week for history. And then the last exam – pedagogy. Seeing Mother every day gave me new energy and I worked better and quicker in spite of the fact that the seamstress was coming often to fit my dress and suit, which were adorable. I loved these visits with Mother in the cozy and more private downstairs reception hall. We are so happy. It is especially pleasant as I know that she no longer will go away alone but will take me along, out of here forever.

My graduation dress is simple: open neck, full sleeves, full skirt, rather short (Mother did not want it too long.) with a blue satin sash which ties in a bow in the back. The Swiss embroidery and the blue bow are lovely. My white kid shoes go well with it. The suit is a beige tailleur with beige shoes and a straw hat with field flowers to go with it. This is all that is to be made to order for me. Most girls think it important to have many dresses, but I am satisfied. A couple of extra dresses would not change me, could not make me better and the vanity of appearing every time in a new outfit is stupid. Mother bought me a beautiful leather album with my initials in silver, E. K. A few of the teachers and some of the girls have already written their wishes for me. Right now is a quiet hour when the girls are finishing writing in each other's albums.

Two days are left before the end of school. We already have had three rehearsals for the graduation. We are going to play Richard Wagner's "March of Tannhauser" in thirty-two hands. These two days will pass like a moment. Am I happy or sad? It is impossible to determine right now as the dinner bell is ringing.

At the graduation Mother looked lovely in her white chiffon dress over crisp salad-green silk taffeta. "It is a great day for you and for us," she whispered to me as I passed by her that morning, and I felt the importance of it to the core of my being. Everything was ceremonious and impressive. Even the "March of Tannhauser," which I was sick and tired of practicing for weeks sounded brand new to my ears as we played it with an enthusiasm we had never before displayed. The school personnel and the parents listened with obvious admiration. The graduation class recited, sang and delivered speeches.

Maman's speech came from the heart. It left no doubt as to her sincere affection for our class. The last we saw of her was in her private quarters when, dressed in our civilian clothes and ready to leave, one by one we received from her a little volume of the New Testament inscribed by her own hand. Then she kissed and blessed us like a true mother.

We will spend three more days in Odessa; time to pay visits to some friends and teachers and to see the famous actor, Kachaloff, in a few plays – this Mother promised – then home to green Volinia and two months later to Switzerland.

HIGHER EDUCATION IN EUROPE

We are staying in the house of our old friends, the Falz-Fein, who live at Gogol Street, No.7. They would not allow us to stay in a hotel. Their city mansion is even more luxurious than their country home, which I remember so well. It is now after midnight. Mother kissed me goodnight and asked me not to stay up too long. How delicate of her not to order me to bed. She understands that I have had more than enough discipline. She spoke to me as though I was quite a grown-up person and yet, more than ever, I felt like being her baby daughter.

This afternoon when the old doorman Dimian in his gala livery, respectfully opened and closed the school door after me, I was ushered into a new life, ending the cycle of childhood and adolescence forever. Yet, in relationship to Mother, I shall always be a little girl, and I know that right now her treating me so seriously is rather forced.

LATER: The two months after school ended we were afforded the first real vacation we ever had. No governess this time. Picnics, horseback riding through the thick forests of Volinia, stopping for milk and black bread at some peasant's house – how I loved it! Sometimes I talked with them for hours, amazed at their natural wisdom and their appreciation of my sincere approach to them. Friendliness glows on their open faces when they are not afraid of you. The children, with flaxen hair and blue eyes, their chubby bodies covered with something very brief, stood around studying me. I became close to one family and visited them often, bringing gifts and clothes to the little ones.

I remember our visit with Mother to the ancient castle of the Polish Count Radzivill, now the residence of our friends, General and Mrs. Svignin. It stood high on the hill and its red brick roof was seen from far away as we approached it one glorious summer afternoon. It was a delightful and memorable vacation for me. A change of surroundings is usually beneficial in one way or another. The hottest part of the day I spent in the library reading and sometimes just touching the rare volumes I had never seen. In the afternoon I took an invigorating swim in the lake which from the window of my room looked like a frozen skating rink. At twilight I strolled through the winding path of the old park which was scented with pine and white tobacco flowers. We usually spent the evenings with the hostess and her guests in one of the living rooms before an ever blazing fireplace. Concerts were often given there, even by famous artists. During our stay a young Polish violinist played more than once. I was fascinated – I dreamed of him, neglecting the pleasant companions of our riding cavalcades.

Our departure to Switzerland was a big event for the little city of Radziviloff. So many came to see us off; but my attention centered on Father. I thought it was not fair to take Mother away from him but he thought we were too young to go alone and his word always counted. He was animated and cheerful. I heard him speak to a man of the benefits of the Swiss climate and the good example that would be set for us by the diligent Swiss people. He seemed to take our departure very well and I comforted myself with the thought that he would join us next spring. Mother, Vala and I were now on the train to Switzerland and Russia would be left behind for at least two years before Father plans for us to return home. We dashed through picturesque Vienna, Austria and many other cities and finally stopped and settled in Lausanne, Switzerland where we found a lovely apartment situated on a green hill overlooking the lake of Geneva. Lausanne! Lausanne! Kind, honest people. Plenty of milk, plenty to eat! Day and night the view from our balcony brought enchantment to me. The chain of the snowy Savoie mountains bordered its transparent blueness. The gliding white and pink sails were reflected there and sometimes a sudden madness occurred when the bise (violent wind) was blowing and the angry lake roared like an ocean.

Father was right. The even beat of the Swiss heart was very beneficial. The city that he chose for us to continue our education had, and probably always will have, a remarkable spirit of cultural achievement – and that was transmitted to me. Thousands of students from all parts of the world came there to study in private schools or in the old university; everyone seeking further instruction, more knowledge. With our perfect knowledge of French, it was easy for us to adjust. Soon Vala and I became students at the "Ecole Superieure des Jeunes Filles Etrangeres" (Special School for Foreign Girls) and progressed regularly until the end of the school year. The strenuous work seemed easy at the thought that on Sundays we would go to Oushy and hire a boat and row and sing on the lake until late. Often we took the tram to Montreux, passing Lutry and Vivey. We spent hours in the Chateau Chillon where Lord Byron was inspired to write his immortal "Prisoners of Chillon." On the columns were inscribed many famous names such as Byron, Victor Hugo, Dumas, and others. I dared to add my own to the last column. We went to concerts, plays, and listened to many lectures at the University of Lausanne. In the spring we took a pilgrimage to the "Field of Narcissus." There were always enough of these tender fragrant flowers, no matter how many thousands of people came and took arms full home. At dusk, we would return to the cheerful house in which we occupied the whole second floor. Our loving Mother would be waiting for us with a smile in the tiled Swiss kitchen where we would devour a delicious hot meal of soup, a roast with plenty of potatoes and other vegetables, bread, cheese and milk. We were hungry and ate heartily. This was the first year we began to face life in general, not only in schools. A completely new life began for us here and we met it with joy and dignity.

In April, expecting the arrival of Father and an elderly friend, Lydia Kasparovna, we moved to a larger more elaborate apartment in the central part of town – Longeraie Numero 1 – very close to our school. From here the lake view was simply breathtaking and below in the garden the lilacs were already in bloom. Some students lived in the same house and it did not take long for them to start serenading us under our window. (Why were examinations scheduled in the Spring when the weather was so beautiful and I would much rather be spending my time outside with friends instead of inside studying?)

When Father came to Lausanne we were busy studying but, with Mother's guidance, he became acquainted with the city and began to plan our future trip through Switzerland. The old Lydia Kasparovna followed Mama and Papa when she could, but when left at home she assigned herself to the duty of supervising our study and general activities, of which there was no need whatsoever. She told Mother to give us only milk chocolat – never the bitter kind – the latter being too stimulating for young girls. She did not approve of our students' serenades and gave us a million instructions as to how to behave on the train when our school organized an excursion to Neufchatel and Chaumond where we had a picnic. I remember that miles and miles before we reached Neufchatel we smelled the delicious Swiss chocolate – not without a certain physical torture. I can smell it even now. The best chocolate factories are built all around Neufchatel.

Around the end of June, the examinations were over. Vala and I passed the advanced course in French literature, French history, and historical grammar with distinction. In my book I wrote:

This morning in the solemn quietness of the Church of St. Francis the "Certificads d'Etudes" was given to us. This is the second important document I have received certifying to my scholastic achievements.

My, did I work hard these last ten months! These were really serious studies and I gave them much more concentration than I ever did in school at home. I deserved this diploma and I am proud to have obtained it in Switzerland, in the French Swiss Canton de Vaude, city of Lausanne, which I love. Our parents, knowing that we had done our best, embraced and enthusiastically congratulated us.

For this occasion a very becoming white linen suit with pink French cuffs was bought for me as well as new shoes and a lovely hat. I had no luck with my hats this time. Twice Father did not approve of my choice, finding them too eccentric, but at last I found one that suited both his taste and mine.

In the afternoon our family and Lydia Kasperovna took a large boat across the lake to the French resort at the foot of the French Savoies, Evian les Bains, known for its curative waters and kid gloves. Evian les Bains is practically opposite Lausanne and on a clear night each one sees the flickering lights of the other. We drank the famous water, bought some gloves, and returned to our boat. The lake was stormy but it looked beautiful. I should go to bed now as tomorrow we are departing for Geneva. Soon we shall leave Lausanne also.

Papa thinks we should study for one year in France and speak more 'French' French and not the Swiss French which has a little different pronunciation. We shall probably go to Grenoble. On our way to France, Father's plans and his itinerary worked out with precision. We went through about two-thirds of Switzerland with unending admiration for this picturesque country. We spent the most time in Berne then went back to Lausanne. All my life I think I shall feel that Lausanne is partly mine. I wanted to stay longer there but according to Papa's schedule there was no more time for it, so we packed and left.

Now we are in Grenoble and Switzerland is in the past. We understood that during the winter we were to attend a certain course at the University of Grenoble, but Father came out with another surprise. His worry was that our brains might become stale if not exercised and as a result we are now enrolled at the University in the second semester of the summer course for foreigners. How much can a girl's brain take? What fun this summer course turned out to be! There were so many young people from Germany, Italy and England and for the first time we found ourselves in a mixed school. Entering late, we soon noticed that we had become the topic of conversation of the other students. They called us the "Russian linguists." Right now the students are putting on two plays and Professor Rosset has given me the main role in both—"Because of your impeccable French," he said. I had never acted before but I accepted the challenge and was terribly excited.

We are settled with Father and Mother at a rather modest place by comparison to Lausanne and board is included so Mother can relax. All is well – not much studying now – mostly rehearsals for the play which keeps me very busy. Vala did not want to participate. The first play was "Les Finesses de Jasmine" in which I had the role of a girl cashier romancing with an interpreter who, by the way, was being played by a charming Englishman, one Mr. Dixon.

Because of these plays I became acquainted with many people – even a Hindu. In spite of the fact that for a whole year I was only in the company of girls, I felt very much at ease with the young boys and spoke to them as if they were girls, without any extra fuss. Some boys were obviously interested in me and because of them I wanted to act especially well. Finally on the 16th of August the plays were performed. That day we had four rehearsals – two in the morning and two in the afternoon. The first thing I did that night was to look through the peephole in the curtain at my admirers in the first row. That made me feel even better.

Both plays were a success. Judging by the animated faces and the laughter in the audience, everyone was really amused. Mother and Vala told me that I acted very well. Many people took me for a French girl and the next day at the University my popularity visibly increased.

Pictures were taken of all the cast and I was anxious to see them developed.

To know that our greatly admired Professor Veil enjoyed our performance gave me great satisfaction. How wonderful his lectures were! I left the auditorium a few times in tears, emotionally living through the lives of the great Romantics such as Lemartine, Hugo, Musset and Vigny. Their lives were so vividly presented to us by his oratorical skill and because of this I memorized pages of French lyrics.

For a few days we had been living in the pension of Mme. Riondet where we had two lovely rooms with balconies. Mother insisted that each of us have our own room. Dear Mother – she knew how I preferred to be alone sometimes.

We have just said goodbye to Father and Mother – goodbye for a whole year. My beloved Mother! How happily we lived with her in Lausanne, and now she will be so far away from us. Father also took it a little hard. The next day I felt the same emptiness that I used to feel when left alone behind the walls of the Imperial School without Mother's care and tenderness. I thought of Father's tears; to know that he was not only a stoic but also a man who could be overcome by emotion, made him closer and dearer to me. In my mind I followed them from one city to another, and only when I heard that they were safe at home did I begin to think of the reason and the purpose of our stay in France.

We were left here, I thought, to acquire more knowledge and become more self-reliant. From now on, I alone would have to give account of my actions and reactions in life. The power of mind over body is surprising – head high, sure that I had grown somewhat taller, I accepted the challenge. A new desire for achievement took hold of me – a zest for progress, for conquest in every field. The summer course was finished with high grades and there was a recess, a surprise vacation, before the beginning of the winter session. One by one our summer school companions were leaving for home, and the tradition was to celebrate the departure of each of them. We were invited to every farewell party and some fuss was made about us – flowers, corsages, dedicated poems, special songs, souvenirs, etc. We did not think of it as exceptional until someone in our pension mentioned the fact of our extreme popularity at the University. I must say that our schoolmates treated us with great respect.

The Italian group was the closest to us. In their company I soon began to speak a little Italian, sang their songs and even learned to recite some passages from the "Divine Comedy" of Dante taught by Luigi Grafinia, the poet of the group. We took small excursions around Grenoble and had picnics and long walks in the dreamy parks of the Ile Verte and Ile d'Amour. The interest these boys had in us was more general than individual and the compliments they paid us came almost in chorus, as did the serenades we often heard at our windows.

Longer excursions were organized by the University to acquaint us with the beauty of the Province de Dauphinee, the last one being an excursion to Grande Chartreuse. With youthful exuberance we delighted in the picturesque roads with the Savoyan Alps for background, the small mountain lakes, hundreds of noisy brooks from which we drank stretched out on our stomachs, and the symphony of the autumnal foliage. The walled Monastery with its Florentine fountains seemed to sleep in a deep valley. The monks were no longer there but we, the visitors, were still given a sample – a miniature bottle of that amazing light green liqueur, the secret of which they alone knew. "Partir c'est mourir un peu," (To part is to die a little) said the poet Graffinia, waving to us from the train that took the last Italian students from Grenoble to Milano. Yes, to part is to die a little, but only a little. Memory will carry forever the fraicheur (freshness) of the dawn of life.

By mere force of habit, lazily at first, we returned to the familiar routine of studying for the winter terms. On the 10th of October, the anniversary of the death of Count Leon Tolstoi, I was the only student to speak from the platform to professors of different faculties. My heart was throbbing, yet on the outside I was told that I appeared utterly composed. Beautiful pink roses and a basket of flowers were presented to me at the end of my speech but I never found out who sent them. The next day between lectures many shook hands with me, telling me how much they enjoyed my speech and asking hundreds of questions about my previous studies.

Hans Arndt, a student from Berlin and a genius of languages (so we heard), was apparently to study with us, and for a long time. Because of his solitary ways we were interested in him. We found out that he had finished college and was taking some extra courses while awaiting his nomination as Professor for the Chair of Patois in the south of France at Montpellier. He was tall and fair with a chiseled face which even in complete repose conveyed the potential for action and efficiency. One day he introduced himself in a business like manner and said that he would be interested in preparing the next assignment of French literature with me. Taken by surprise, I started to tell him that I usually worked alone, but then I quickly added that to study with a professor might be very enlightening. Hans knew how to study. The intensity of his concentration was great and I learned the advantage of such power. Each assignment was done in half the time I would have used had I studied alone and much time was left to talk, to read, and walk. Hans acted like an older brother. I even wrote to Nina that her place was temporarily taken by a young professor friend, adding that it was pure nonsense to believe that there was no pure friendship between boys and girls. Once in a while, rather objectively, he would pass a casual remark about my appearance. "The lines of your nose are simply perfect," he would say; or "Do you know that you have the most adorable little ears?" When alone I would look into the mirror longer than usual, wondering if my eyes, the dimples of my cheeks and the rest of my face didn't amount to anything. I admired Hans' knowledge, perseverance and will power and, sometimes, as one does before a teacher, I tried to display my better versatility by treating subjects in which I thought he would not be so competent; but invariably he was. His farewell kiss made me drop all illusions of the possibility of a friendship between opposite sexes and, deeply perturbed, I did not close my eyes all night, lost in reflection. After he left I drowned myself in my studies. Even the time used for dinner in the cozy dining room of Madame Riondet seemed wasted. It must have been at that particular period that I acquired a large amount of knowledge which later gave me confidence and satisfaction. Busy with my scholastic achievements, I did not realize what was happening around me until a little Swiss girl who sat next to me at dinner told me that a Danish doctor, one of our pensionaires, was greatly interested in me. One afternoon a few days after my birthday in November, coming home from the University I found roses in a beautiful Royal Copenhagen vase on my desk. The card read, "Happy Birthday. Better late….H.M." Soon the Danish doctor who used to come to Mme.

Riondet's only for meals moved into our pension and sought every opportunity to see me and speak to me. I thought it wise to pretend I did not notice. I simply greeted him with a polite smile, never giving him the slightest encouragement by word or glance. Yet, that very indifference changed his desire into an obsession, and when around Christmas we began to plan our visit to Sonia and Nina in Lausanne, we discovered that the Danish doctor was also going to Lausanne.

Our trip and the three days stay with our schoolmates passed like a dream. We went from one Christmas party to another, visited our Swiss friends and former teachers, strolled through familiar streets and entered pastry shops where we were handed our favorite cakes. In spite of the raging winds and great frost we could not resist the temptation of going down to Oushy to stand by the lake for a few minutes. Afterwards, a few cups of hot chocolate restored our bodies to normal temperature. Hans Mose the Danish doctor was often in our group. He was quite entertaining and congenial throughout our stay in Switzerland and I began to enjoy his company. On the way back to Grenoble he told me that he loved me, and for the rest of the year this was a disturbing factor.

I was too young to understand his devotion and far from being pleased, mistook it for weakness of character.

Before we knew it Easter came and with it the opportunity to visit Italy with a group of girls organized and chaperoned by Mme. Delord, Directrice of another pension. As soon as we mentioned this to our parents we received a favorable answer and we were overjoyed. Avignon, Marseilles, Italy – what an impression Italy and its past produced on our young minds.

How thankful I am for the wisdom of our parents who did not hesitate to give us a chance to broaden our horizons and stimulate an interest in the historic past of Italy. Soon after our return the final exams began and plans for our return home followed. At this time a certain uneasiness began in the general atmosphere of Europe. In one of his letters Hans spoke of the possibility of war and advised us to rush home.

Hans Mose went with us as far as Dijon. The farewell was hard for him but I was not too sympathetic. The fact that we were to spend a few days in Paris made me dizzy with happiness and there was no room for anything else. Paris in the spring, the Champs Elyses, Bois de Boulogne, Jardin de Luxembourg, all these were unforgettable. To leave brought a melancholy and the desire to return, a powerful nostalgia evoked only by cities that have a soul.

We passed Lieges and Cologne. Approaching Berlin I was the happiest girl in the world because Mother would be there to meet us – our charming loving mother. What a compensation for the sadness in parting! Next to her at the railway station stood a young man; a stranger I thought, and only after having kissed Mother did I notice that the stranger smiled at me. "Goodness gracious, Hans Arndt! You and Mother are together?" Waiting on the platform they had engaged in conversation and found out they were waiting for the same passengers from Paris. Though not definitely informed, Hans had not mistaken the date of our arrival. During the three days in Berlin Hans served as our guide. The Mausoleum of the Kaisers where violet light bathed the marble of the sarcophagus impressed me. I also loved Potsdam, the part of Berlin where the Chateau Sans Souci stands. We went through the palace and lingered quite awhile in the library where Voltaire, guest of Frederick the Great, spent many years of his life. We roamed around the palace admiring the gardens. Hans was sad. "War is in the air," he said, "and I may not see you again." At parting he kissed me reverently and, pressing me for a moment in his arms, whispered, "Forgive my farewell kiss in Grenoble." I remembered the passionate kiss that made me lose faith in the pure friendship between men and women; but time, the faithful aide, had already stored this impression in the treasure box of experience, and I smiled at this talented man whom I admired but did not love, without any trace of resentment.

BACK HOME – THE REVOLUTION

We returned to Russia, and to our new home in the city of Odessa. Father, at first glance, approved of the tailleur suits and Parisian toques (hairdos) of his "French girls;" yet serious as usual, added "I expect your intelligence to have improved parallel with your elegance." Coming from Father, that was a compliment. We were happy that he liked our appearance and felt sure we would be able to display a certain mental maturity and a greater capacity for discussions, if and when involved in a long conversation with him. Switzerland and France were no longer real – just memories; but friends we had made there kept in touch with us by mail and seemed as close as before. Arndt wrote often and his letters were beautiful though always a bit pessimistic, sure of the approach of world disaster – war. Hans Mose's letters were heartbreaking at times. He missed me unbearably he said, and once wrote to Father asking for my hand. I told Father to answer him that I had no plans for marriage at the time, but not discouraged by this answer, he kept writing.

The war broke out. Mobilization – Father's departure to the front hospital – our anxiety and prayers for him, for our soldiers, our country. We began to work in the Red Cross and visited the sick and wounded who were shipped from the battle front to our city. Concerts and benefit balls were organized. Gatherings were held in private homes to help support soldiers and their families, many of them already orphaned. We kept very busy, and only at the twilight hour or at night would our memories take possession of us. Vala and I would sit and chat about our life abroad, remembering everything, even the most minute details – a place, a word, a song.

The work in the hospital was very absorbing. At home in the afternoons unknown to Father I took ballet lessons, which for many years saved me from despair over the conditions of my country and the whole world. To dance was to forget myself, to forget about the war for awhile at least. The rest of the time I took it too much to heart. The instructor said that he found me most capable and he was especially proud of the precision of my steps and the elasticity of the high leap. It was too late though to specialize in classical ballet, so I was trained for character dances. Often he told me that I could become a professional in this field – an idea which had never entered my mind.

Dark clouds were gathering on our horizon. Father, after two and one half years of work as a surgeon in the field hospital, became ill. It seemed that some meat preserves supplied to the battle front had pieces of lead in them. Father's intestines were injured by a chip of the metal and, suffering a dangerous hemorrhage he was taken to the hospital in Moscow. The healing took time, and a few months later when Father came home to Odessa he spoke very seriously about the general situation, advising us to brace ourselves to meet the hard years ahead. I could not exactly grasp the danger of war and its consequences, yet I understood that there were signs of the coming revolution.

"Keep your morale high, children," Father would say. "Watch your appearance and take the best bit of advice I can give you – NEVER FORGET TO BRUSH YOUR TEETH! The first time you neglect this your morale will go down quickly."

"It will not be hard at all," I said. "We could not neglect doing that even if we wanted to."

"Hard or easy, write it on your forehead, and it will help you through the coming hardships." Now I wonder at Father's wisdom. How could he have foreseen that a little habit could be so significant at a time when all values were totally depreciated? How could he have known that just this little advice would gain fortitude, when volumes of advice would not have sufficed to protect young people from bending and falling? How right he was! His seemingly ridiculous formula was not easy to follow. Many times the temptation to avoid what we thought was a permanent habit presented itself most powerfully. Hungry and frozen, I often did not feel like going twenty blocks down the hill and twenty blocks back up to bring home two pails of water, but Father's advice was written on my forehead. I went, knowing that the next morning we would need this precious water to "brush our teeth." How often in the sleet, halfway home, I would fall and have to return to fill my pails. For a long time, when reaching my destination my two pails were the equivalent of only one until a young man I met at the faucet where hundreds of people stood in line, generously presented me with two wooden circles which kept the water from splashing.

My little oil lamp smokes badly. I see there is hardly any oil left. I must have written for many hours. It was pleasant to write about Switzerland and France, but I noticed that my pen stumbled more than once when I began to write about trying times. I do not wish to write about it, besides, it is our sad reality. I am tired and sleepy and my hands are frozen. The shooting has subsided and dawn appears. Oh, how cold it is! I am tempted to go to sleep as I am, attired in my dress and coat. Shall I really have the courage to undress? Yes, I will. In fact, I feel much better now after having relived in my memory the happy days of Switzerland and France.

LIFE DURING THE BOLSHEVIK REVOLUTION

What has happened to my country? Since the abdication of Tzar Nikolas, her sons, calling themselves "Whites" and "Reds," murder each other for power. Blood is shed – brother kills brother, communication is destroyed, food and fuel supplies are cut off and even the water reservoir is damaged. Spotted typhus rages and people die in the streets from fever and hunger. Write, write, urges the inner voice. It will be hard, but I must try. Just now it is the only thing I can do. How can I otherwise forget myself, sitting here in a cold room in the city of Odessa – a starved stricken city in a country at civil war, and listen to the whistle of bullets intermingled with the plaint of my empty stomach? It is a matter of self-protection that I occupy my mind now. To concentrate on the past, happy or not, may help to detach myself from this puzzling present. To be totally absorbed in writing may even subdue the pangs of hunger in my healthy body, unprepared for starvation and therefore impatient with it. Mind over matter! I hope it will work.

Mother thinks our turn is coming. Delicately, she tries to make us understand that we cannot escape the common lot but we are young and do not want to believe it. For two days already we have been shut up in our apartment because of fighting in the streets below our window. Thank God our family is reunited, though it is hard for me to know that Father, Mother and Vala are hungry. Mother always says that she could not wait for us and has already eaten, and makes us take the crust of bread that is hers. All that we had today was a rather small piece of mildewed bread and cold water as there was nothing to heat the water with; we had only one glass each as we do not know how long the fighting will last. I cannot sleep. I hear the bombs explode. Blood is shed – blood is shed! I just got up and went to kiss Father, Mother and Vala to make sure that we are still together. Losing the integrity of one's country, one clings more closely to the family.

Our poor Mother Russia! The rage of your sons distorts your beautiful face. Where are your rich fields of wheat, bending under the caress of the wind? All of your fertile land is an arena of murder. How very far away are my school days. Go ahead – write. Write!

March 4, 1917: What a coup d'etat. Oh Lord! How strange – how incredible! There have been troubles in Petrograd – the establishment of the provisional government, the liberation of all political prisoners and finally today the Tzar renouncing power for himself and his son. I cannot grasp it all yet. I read and re-read the Manifesto of the Tzar – his last one – where he says that he and his son renounce the throne for the good of his country. It touches my heart with the same compassion, the same deeply felt note of sorrow that I experienced for him even in the best days of his reign. I know he had no willpower, that he was easily swayed even in important decisions, and that he was implicitly under the influence of his wife, and yet the pity for him never leaves my heart. No more dynasty of Romanoff! What is happening? And what is going to happen next?

March 7, 1917: This morning the soldiers marched through our streets with red ribbons attached to the points of their bayonets, singing the Marseilles. The people greeted the army.

March 14, 1917: Our hearts are heavy. From time to time we hear stories of crimes that make us shiver. Six admirals killed, many officers shot, and these assassins think they are right in doing it! The Grand

Duke Nicolai Nicolaivitch is no longer Commander-in-Chief of the armies. The war is still facing us. I am afraid that the drastic events in the interior of the land will bring serious discord in the army. I greet the new government as if it is going to be good for all the people and help Russia. I wish, oh how I wish, to have confidence in it. This is a decisive moment when Russia, fighting for her own freedom, must reach her salvation. If not, only You 0 Lord, can save her.

May 21, 1917: Spring again. Acacias are in bloom; their suave fragrance makes me dizzy. This year I am less taken by it all. Times have changed. I find myself engrossed in the enfoldment of events as well as in the study of the past, so as to better understand the present — but spring has her power. She demands admiration and for centuries obedient humanity has given it. I, too, must give mine. I forget my books and admire the snow white of the acacias in bloom, superb under the blue rays of the moon. I expose my face to the scented breeze and inhale the spring — yet, the ecstasy is not the same. The beauty of this May night fills me for awhile with a profound sense of peace, and more than ever I feel the desire for inner perfection. For another moment I bend over my balcony rail admiring the moonlit flowers and then, back to my books.

August 24, 1917: What is to become of my unfortunate country? Is the agony just beginning? Prime Minister Kerensky? I lost faith in him long ago. General Korniloff? Is he to become the new dictator? Can anyone stop this ferocious onslaught of the masses or will we be doomed to go through the horrors of civil war? I read tonight that the mansion on the estate of the Princess Viasenmsky is destroyed and the young Prince cruelly killed by a group of soldiers — the first demonstration of the hatred of the lower classes of the nobility who for centuries were the privileged ones.

September 10, 1917: Last night, thinking of the cruelties we hear about, I dwelt upon the irrevocable law of sowing and reaping. I came to think that if the Russian nobility suffers now, and if they suffer much in the future, it is because of Time's sublime revenge of the people unjustly oppressed for centuries by our forefathers; and we, though not guilty ourselves, but children of these guilty ancestors, will have to bear without complaint all that is being prepared for us by the posterity of those oppressed classes. We will have to forgive the madness that comes to them with the joy of being free. In their revenge our suffering will be great; but that of their forefathers was not less.

Sept. 18, 1917: I look for strength and energy in myself to face this chaos, in which people lose all that is human in themselves and descend to primitive ferocity. Tonight my mood is less lenient, less capable of pardon. My reflections of Sunday, September 10th, seem vain and I am ashamed of the Russian people who, having their freedom, are making such bad use of it.

November 2, 1917: We have never had such a thunderstorm at this late date – a torrential "spring" rain with thunder and lightning. On the political horizon, however, the storm is much more terrible. In the north, in Petrograd, civil war is already beginning in all its horror. This uprising of the Bolsheviks, enemies of Russia, will bring us inevitable peril.

December 1, 1917: The Civil War spreading all over Russia is reaching us here in the south. All supplies are cut off – no food. All day long we hear the cannon roar on the outskirts, but we do not even know between whom the battle is raging. Orders are given not to leave our houses.

December 20, 1917: Christmas is coming – the first Christmas in the free and already miserable Russia. Civil war continues and everything is condemned to complete destruction. The Germans wait for us to destroy ourselves with our own hands. They may not have long to wait. Every day brings worse news than the day before and my disillusionment in my people grows. In spite of the sadness of these days, Vala and I could not resist getting a little Christmas tree and we succeeded in finding a very pretty one. Christmas without a tree would be an even sadder Christmas.

January 1, 1918: The year 1917 disappeared into the black night, as if taken away by a tempest, escorted by the lugubrious howl of the wind which reproached it for having been such an evil year. The New Year tries to smile at us through this bright and luminous morning. Lord, if only it will bring us some consolation!

January 16, 1918: The Bolsheviks are trying to get the power in their hands. War rages. The air is constantly shaken by the burst of bombs and the rattle of machine guns. From the sea, the city is menaced also. God knows what can happen to us in five minutes! Same day – 6 P.M. Now a battery of large cannons from the boats are entering into action and seem to be aimed directly at our part of the city. We cannot rejoice anymore over the fact that we live on the third floor of a very tall house. It is a good target. If only we can all die together! A great sadness grips my heart; every shot from the guns, every roar of the cannon, every exploding bomb means death. Death is flying in the air and chooses its victims.

January 17, 1918: At 3 A.M. the bombardment from the vessels started anew. We got up and went to Mother and Father's room to be together. What a night! Every moment we expected the house to crash. Early in the morning some soldiers pushed themselves into our house. What an abominable scene: a band of tough, half drunk, armed men suddenly all over our apartment demanding the immediate delivery of any weapons we might have. There was only Father's revolver for which he had a permit. They took it and with it our field binoculars (Zeiss). By what right? Sent by whom?

January 18, 1918: We did not sleep again. At dawn all calmed down and in the morning the town became alive. The Bolsheviks have won and it is to their power that we shall now have to submit.

January 20, 1918: Vala and I walked through the streets today. The whole aspect of the town has changed. Soldiers and sailors roam about aimlessly with guns on their shoulders. Once in a while they aim their weapons at a passerby who shrinks or runs away, much to their amusement.

January 30, 1918: No one understands exactly what is happening. Politically, we are moving again in the dark. The rumor is spread that the Rumanians contemplate occupying Odessa. We were even expecting to welcome the English fleet in our waters, but today I am inclined to think that they will not be the first to visit us. We must think of saving some flour for who knows what may happen to us.

February 3, 1918: Days go by, monotonous and sad, yet there is in me much strength and courage to live on. I cling more than ever to my dancing lessons. During these hours at least, I experience a carefree happiness – a primitive joy, I presume, for it is purely physical. Apart from that, I read and study a lot, and tired physically and mentally, sleep soundly and well. I just finished reading "Victoria" by Knut Gamsun. The story is moving, so beautiful and sad that I could not help crying. It becomes harder to correspond with friends. The letters are often lost, but I do not give up. Our friends find some extraordinary way to reach us, which is even more precious. I like the company of a few young men whose conversation is stimulating, but find it is a waste of time to be with others who bore me to death.

February 18, 1918 – Old Russian Calendar

March 3, 1918 – New European Calendar, ordered by the Bolsheviks.

We are on the eve of events. The Germans, we hear, plan to occupy Odessa. The rumor is spread that they are already in Kieff.

February 28, 1918 to March 13: The Germans are in the suburbs of our city. The last two weeks of Bolshevik power have been most trying. The terror continues and many are killed. We all live apprehensively, deprived of any legitimate news; perking our ears to rumors each worse than the other, general massacre, bombardment of the city, etc. There are no more sailors or soldiers walking proudly around. Actually, no authority as such is left here except for thieves and gangsters armed to the teeth and, therefore, most dangerous. They have demanded (not for the first time) a sum of 20 million rubles from the people under the threat of total destruction of the city but have not succeeded in getting it. It is now too late. This morning the German planes were flying over our roofs displaying the white flag, symbol of peace. Maybe there will be peace for awhile, but at what price? Some people will never find it after the irreparable losses caused by the brutality of the short but furious occupation of the Bolsheviks. Only one year ago for a short time, it is true, we rejoiced that our Russian people oppressed for so long were finally free; but the Russian Proletariat became drunk with power and acted accordingly. Leaders, finding the time propitious, started their experiments, putting forth all their socialistic and international ideas. Those leaders, void of love for Russia, did not fail to demobilize the army. They did not think of the honor of Russia, and thus these bands, inflamed by the socialistic ideas which they could barely understand, tried to execute their ideals of liberty, fraternity and equality by starting a civil war – Russian against Russian, brother against brother, killing each other and terrorizing the population. In their drunkenness they would have finally destroyed their own country as well as themselves had not their former enemy, the Germans, introduced themselves. Such is the outcome of this terrible war – four years of war. Maybe we need the orderly Germans to stop this anarchy, yet in many Russian hearts it leaves a deep wound. To think of the brave millions who died for their country! What a shame! What dishonor! I cannot understand it all. My head is ready to burst. God Almighty, is it true that Russia is dead?

March 2 – March 15, 1918: Germans are everywhere, their faces triumphant and smiling! If through chaos and disorganization in our country they act like conquerors, they must remember that on the other side, the war is not yet over.

March 4 – March 17, 1918: We are being given the possibility to breathe, but the air is too heavy. I went to church. There I saw so many eyes in tears, faces expressing grief, so much mourning; but on the Cathedral Place an Austrian orchestra played inspiring tunes.

Germans – more of them arriving every day. I do not go out much; I prefer to stay home. Lately I have written many Russian and French poems. I believe that most of all I like to dance and write poetry. It sounds futile but it helps nowadays. Upon the request of Olga V.K. (the daughter of my school directrice), I teach French literature to the higher classes of her school. It is a responsible job and O.V.K. thinks I do it well but schools are not too regular these days.

March 14 – 27, 1918: I received a letter from Hans Mose. What a contrast their life and ours: joy and well-being there, misery, suffering and shame here. His affection does not diminish. He still hopes to meet me again someday. His letters took two months to reach me.

April 16 – 29, 1918: The Germans take hold of everything. No "Rada," no Ukrainian government anymore. The south of Russia becomes the province of our enemy. All inhabitants are being disarmed by the Germans. What else shall we see? No spring for me this year. I do not notice the fresh green or the lilacs; I hardly look at the sea. It hurts me to think it is no longer ours. I often find peace in the churches and while there feel among my people.

April 22 – May 1, 1918: I wish we were more light hearted, but we are not. How we used to rejoice at Easter!

May 31, 1918: We were both sick – first I, then Vala. The epidemic of the so-called Spanish Flu is severe. I feel better today but cannot go out yet. I finished reading the "Matelot" of Loti, and it made me think of Mother. How we must love and cherish her and thank her for all she has done for us. Mother's love has no limit. My eyes fill with tears of gratitude, tenderness and fear before the inevitable.

July 20, 1918: Last night in the Cathedral thousands and thousands of people mourned the death of the Emperor Nicolas the Second. At the funereal sound of the Cathedral bell people knelt right on the street where they walked, expressing their grief and reverence for the late Monarch. Our Tzar shot! Whose hand was lifted against him? Why, why, 0 Lord, did they kill him? Rest in peace, dear unfortunate Tzar.

My heart bleeds at the thought of your suffering. So many Russians who loved you did not, or could not, save you. What a crime! What sin! No country, no Tzar! No details of the assassination were known to us then. Much later we learned that, upon the approach of General Koltchak with his army from the side of Siberia toward the city of Ekaterinodar, where the Tzar's family lived under guard, the Bolshevik government of the north had issued the order for the assassination of the Tzar and his entire family. The Bolsheviks had undoubtedly feared the possible consequences of the General's approach.

It seemed that the precise, practical, orderly Germans had succeeded in returning the city to its normal state, more or less. People began to meet socially. Parties were given here and there and many people who had left, returned.

Friday, August 24, 1918: Trip from Odessa to Kherson. Since yesterday I am on board the luxury yacht "Vanity". Mrs. Falz-Fein, Tolia's wife, the former Maria Petrovna Regier, invited me to take this trip with them and to spend some time at their estate "Tchernomorie." I was undecided but Father, knowing how much pleasure the trip would give me, helped me to make up my mind. We took off Thursday morning – Maria, Boria, Tolia, myself and the crew. A fresh and favorable wind blew for five or six hours, the time needed to approach and pass by Otchakoff and enter the sweet waters of the Dniepr River. Red wine and sandwiches were served on board all the time. At 7 P.M. we anchored for the night opposite the village of Kasperovka. After a fabulous hot dinner and the best of wines we all went to sleep in our berths. This morning we proceeded with a speed opposite the one with which we started yesterday. There is no wind; we hardly move. I have no complaint though, for I admire the Dniepr and the beauty of its shores.

Saturday, August 25, 1918: At the "Estate Tchernomorie." A carriage with four brown horses brought us here to Tchernomorie. On our way we passed the house where I spent the first years of my life. My eyes devoured it and all the familiar places. Joyfully, I inhaled the air that gave me life. Place of my birth! With the years its charm grows as does its melancholy. All here seems to have kept something of my soul.

August 30, 1919 – 10:30 PM: The last evening in Tchernomorie. Unexpectedly, I have spent eight beautiful days here – remembering, dreaming, roaming through the park in which we played as children, entering the church where I was baptized, spending mornings by the sea where the beach, beautifully kept, surpasses any beach we have in Odessa. Joy and melancholy intermingle. Boria sang tonight. I am happy I heard him before leaving.

September 1, 1918: The S/S Roumianzeff brought me home. On board, an Austrian officer introduced himself – Baron von Reichlin-Meldogg, the first man of the occupying forces to whom I have spoken. He is not young but he is refined.

Thursday, September 6, 1918: Pepa R., one of our lovely boyfriends, died from this inexorable flu. Pepa was life itself. How can I believe that he is dead?

Wednesday, October 3, 1918: We hear that peace negotiations begin. The Germans ask for mercy. To our own misfortune, we separated ourselves from our allies and now we are deprived of the joy of celebrating the victory with them. But no one can take away from us the desire to rejoice in their triumph.

October 19, 1918 – Night time: At times my soul is overwhelmed with sorrow for people – the unfortunate who are hungry but too proud to ask for a piece of bread and walk erect until they fall, unable to overcome their pride. I pity the discouraged, the weak; I pity even the happy ones for their happiness is not lasting. I pity all with their shortcomings, their errors, and those who get lost on the tempting road of evil. I cry and pray for them.

October 22, 1918 – Old Calendar; November 4, 1918 – New Calendar: It is St. Elizabeth's Day – my name day. My room is flooded with golden rays. It seems to me that everything here awaits this important moment, this last caress of the sun. Not one small object in my room is neglected. This moment is too short. The shadows tremble.

October 25, 1918: News again! The Franco-English fleet is expected in our harbor. Events present themselves with unbelievable quickness. No more Kaiser Wilhelm in Germany. Republic replaces Monarchy — changes, changes, and we go through the most drastic ones. Here in the south of Russia more than anywhere, we witness this. The French and English will be on our ground, and we shall give them all that is left of our resources, as we gave to the Germans and Austrians. Not much courtesy is to be expected; they will help themselves. Yet, instinctively, I rejoice in the arrival of the people who were not our enemies, people whose losses we deplored and in whose victories we rejoiced. What amazes me though, is that now since fortune stopped smiling on the Germans, I do not find myself with the same animosity as I felt before. I see them as instruments in the hands of the ambitious Kaiser Wilhelm. On the whole, Dear Lord, all this enmity of people is so abnormal, so unnatural. Some day it will disappear and divided nations will merge in brotherhood.

November 2, 1918: The volunteers, mostly officers and cadets (calling themselves "Whites"), gather together to stop the terror of the masses of Bolsheviks (called "Reds").

November 9, 1918: Impatiently we wait for the French and English fleets. Oh, but they seem to take so long. Winter has come and no food, no fuel, and no shelter for many.

December 5, 1918: Only yesterday the French army arrived. For more than two weeks there were various troubles in the city and its vicinity. The English boats which arrived first had no fighting forces and the volunteers were not numerous enough to stop the Ukrainian troops led by Petlura who had devised: "Independent Republique of Ukraine." Panie Getman Skoropazki abdicated and Petlura and his followers are all over the Ukraine fighting the volunteers who are retreating. Finally, four days ago, Petlura entered our city. "Head of

Petlura, Tail of Bolshevik," said our newspapers. Once more, war was fought on our streets. When the French issued this order for our city of Odessa to be ruled by the Volunteers, Petlura indignantly protested and fought – fought until he was forced to retreat. Again, so many lives lost.

January 4, 1919: Recently we met two elderly English officers at Madame Popovsky's and later were invited for tea on board their steamer – the first pleasant experience in 1919. Though there were many other ships on our harbor, my greatest wish was to visit the English boat and meet the British officers. Young as I was, the possibility of falling in love with an officer of the British fleet seemed the height of romance. Now within half an hour I was supposed to be there and, of course, was all excited about it. Only a small group had been invited. I pictured well-bred tall young men, mostly blue eyed and fair haired, who would greet us. I knew that strong tea, almost black (which I greatly disliked) would be served; but after all, it was not the tea that mattered. "French will be spoken" I assured myself, since much to my regret I did not know a word of English.

ENGLISH – MY NEWEST LANGUAGE

At the last moment I ran to study myself in the mirror again. The blue coat with the grey chinchilla collar was very becoming and the small hat of the same fur perched on the side of my head looked coquettish. After going through a blizzard on the way to the harbor, it was a pleasure to find ourselves in an atmosphere of warmth and elegance. The Captain and his officers were most courteous but I felt a little nervous because I heard only English spoken. The tea was very black indeed, but the officer sitting next to me was very handsome – not blond, but dark, with deep set mystic green eyes. I wondered if he spoke French. He did. He spoke it beautifully and told me that he was the only one on board who spoke the language. "I am very lucky to sit next to you," I said, "because I don't know any English yet, and only plan to learn it." He encouraged me, saying that with my knowledge of French and German I would master it in no time – "Especially if you allow me to give you your first lesson." He smiled warmly. I liked his smile, his voice. I liked him, and felt some emotion toward him that I could not understand. Our conversation was swift and animated, and he certainly did not hide his interest in me. Suddenly, a shadow darkened his face and he told me that in a few minutes he would have to go on duty. I did not try to hide my disappointment and he also looked sad as he asked me to write down my address so that he could send me my first lesson in English. "You will memorize it, won't you?" he asked. "I will," I said, watching him go; wondering how he had become so important to me in such a short time. Who was he?

The party was going on, but I did not feel like looking at anyone else. I was even glad now that I did not know English. Next morning in the cold winter air, I paced the street in front of our house looking for our postman. I could not have awaited the fulfillment of my destiny more eagerly than I awaited this letter, probably containing no more than a few lines in a language I did not even know. I took the letter from the postman and tore it open. Much to my surprise, I understood its meaning. "Two shall be born, the whole wide world apart, and speak in different tongues, and have no thought each of the other's being, and no heed; and these, o'er unknown seas to unknown lands shall cross, escaping wreck, defying death; and all unconsciously shape every act and bend each wandering step to this one end – that one day out of darkness they shall meet and read life's meaning in each other's eyes." (From the poem "Fate" by Susan Marr Spalding) "You must know English, you must know English" resounded in my ear as I rushed back into the house to study my first lesson. "You must know English"! I wondered if it was my own inner voice or the voice of the prophetic-looking Englishman that I heard.

English became my new, all-absorbing occupation. I looked for English books – a dictionary, a grammar – inquired about teachers, and reprimanded Father for not having included English in our early education. Father, who could not understand me at all, tried to dissuade me, saying that it might spoil my good French. "Besides," he said, "whom do you expect to speak to? The Grafton has been ordered to Novorossysk and probably will not return. So when will you use it?" But my urge to know this language was too strong to allow anything, even Father's arguments, to interfere. I walked around repeating, "Two shall be born... etc., etc." while looking for someone to give me the second lesson. At the University I found the name and address of a professor of languages, and went there without delay.

71

That night the order was given for everyone to remain indoors. We did not know who was fighting whom now, since so many different bands besides the Reds and Whites were trying to grab control of the city it had stopped being a novelty. However, in spite of the warning I walked out of my house around seven o'clock hoping to find the professor at home. The streets were completely empty. Stealthily I proceeded close to the houses, hearing the whistle of bullets now and then. I was careful not to cross the open Cathedral Place and half stooping crept alongside the buildings framing the square. In the middle of Deribassovskaya Street, now called Lassal Street, I heard a fusillage of shots. I was frightened, but fortunately had very little distance left to run to Professor E.'s house, immediately to the left of Lassal Street.

"By all the gods of Olympus, where does this vision come from?" cried the Professor, with Shakespearean pathos, opening the door to me. "What service can I render you, fair lady?" His greeting, elaborate yet friendly, was most welcome.

"I wish to take English lessons from you, Professor E.," I said, smiling and shaking his hand.

"Well, well, you must want it badly, child, to come tonight."

"It is true. I could not wait. Your address was given to me and without notifying you, I came. Forgive me, please."

"Nothing to forgive. I am delighted. The only trouble is that I have no English text books of any kind here with me." We entered his study – a professor's nook – books everywhere but all accessible, all in their places, the entire room most orderly. He pushed the ladder from one side of the room to the other, climbed it and took down a volume from the upper shelf. "Percy Shelley is the only book I can think of for the start. No doubt you know other languages." We sat at his desk and he read and explained from four to six stanzas at a time, making me read and translate. I took notes of the meaning and pronunciation of the words I could not guess. I surprisingly understood much, since many roots were similar to French and German. "You're doing well," encouraged the professor, "Your pronunciation is good." He smiled, visibly pleased with his pupil, and went on without interruption – one page, two pages, three …

Observing the old man, I did not doubt that he had been disciplined with himself and others. He was pleasantly enthusiastic and gracious. "I think that will do now," he said.

I smiled, "All right, if you think so."

"I know you could read the whole poem through, and I like your eagerness, but for the first lesson this will suffice."

"May I confess," I said guiltily, "that this is not my first, but my second lesson? My first was, "Two shall be born…. and I went on and on with the poem I knew so well. We parted, quite pleased with each other. I held the book of Percy Shelley tight in my hand as I hurried back home through the temporarily quiet streets of Odessa.

From my friends I learned more about my professor's achievements and my respect for him grew. He had compiled grammars in sixteen languages, which he knew to perfection, for Russian schools.

Three days later I returned for my lesson and Professor E. met me in the friendliest way. "Now let me hear you read the three pages first, and you will translate later." He reclined in his armchair and closed his eyes.

"O, sweet is the …. Sweeter than all is your tone of affection….."

"Perfect, perfect," he said when I finished. "You read extraordinarily well, and I can hear by your intonation that you understand it all. Excellent!" He opened his kind eyes. "Let's go ahead now. But where is the book?"

"Oh, sorry. One moment, Professor, I left it on the couch with my purse."

He stared at me. "You mean you recited these three pages by heart? Incredible!" I flushed with pleasure and went on with our lesson. When I was ready to leave he mentioned that my diligence was a new experience in his teaching career, again complimented me and said, "You will speak English in no time." I did not suspect then that the uneven tempo of our trying lives would make this my last formal English lesson, and the progress I made later would be the result of steady self-teaching.

DEATH, DESTRUCTION
AND GREY HAIR

Later, one thinks of all these people and at the same time makes reflections upon one's self. It appeared that I was very well liked, but I told myself from then on I was going to avoid all that was not good and cling more and more to beauty, truth and harmony. I wish to be able to respect myself at every moment, under any condition in life, and to pass evil without being soiled by it.

March 21, 1919: The French gave up our town to the Bolsheviks. It seems that Clemenceau sent a telegraphic order to give up the city without firing a shot. I feel bitter against the French, who from the start did not show any character. Fearing the Germans, the French left and the Bolsheviks just took over. Before Bolshevism became permanently established as the only government, we witnessed their most cruel revenge on the long fighting volunteers. Father, as a distinguished surgeon from the war was offered an opportunity to leave the country. He refused, saying that his torn bleeding land needed doctors more than Europe did. He advised us to go, but of course we stayed with him.

Calamity followed destruction, and sickness spread. Father was needed now as people were dying on the streets from sickness and hunger. From morning until night he helped the stricken in the poorest quarters, never taking a fee, and he often asked us to give something from the little we had to some lonely man or woman. Very delicately Mother tried to make us understand that we could not escape the common lot. Still I was often deeply disturbed. If we escaped starvation and typhus we would still live under a strange new regime which considered it a crime to be of noble birth. One night I was awakened by a strange noise in the street and, despite the orders issued to keep our windows closed, I rushed to the window. A rumor had passed that 800 cadets, children of nobility, were to be executed. I saw the back of an overloaded truck break open, and hundreds of bodies rolled out in a pile onto the street. Horrified, I turned away. Such slaughter! Pale, naked bodies of young men – almost children, spotted with blood – not yet stiffened – still graceful. Paralyzed, I sat in a chair unaware of the cold until Mother came to wake me. "What happened? What happened to you?" she cried, rushing to me and putting her hand first on one temple and then the other. I could not speak. "What happened to you, dear child? Your hair is grey. Grey!" Tears were running down her face.

"It doesn't matter, Mother," I whispered.

By then food was more scarce than ever, and we like thousands of others were getting only bare necessities, trading our things with the peasants, who for awhile were much better off than the city people. Once in the market place I saw yards of priceless French lace sacrificed for a pound of butter and pieces of sterling for a quart of milk. Much of our expensive bed and table linen went for fruit and vegetables. I remember how, on an autumn day, a peasant brought in two big bags of flour and carried out our entire dining room suite. From the balcony of our apartment I saw him load onto his cart our table, the carved, marble-topped buffet, the little samovar table and the dozen chairs. I watched these pieces of furniture, familiar since childhood, sadly shaking in the drizzling rain on their way to a strange, new home. At the time I found it hard to believe that Father and Mother could do such a thing in their right minds. I told Mother of my utter amazement at the transaction. She sighed. "The furniture will not feed us, darling, but the two bags of flour will remove the fear of hunger from our house."

Many people found their way into high ranking jobs by displaying devotion to the Bolshevik regime, but many preferred to die. Workmen's unions were inaugurated and everyone with a trade or profession was expected to register. Although many of our friends had done so and were in possession of Workmen's Union identification cards, without which one could not obtain bread, Vala and I were reluctant. One day when we were gathered for dinner, Father said, "Well, you cannot go against the tide of history. As a doctor I was given a card automatically, but you, Vala and Lisa, must make at least a little effort yourselves and try to become members of one or another union according to your capabilities." It was a quiet suggestion, but we knew that Father meant business and that we must take the first step toward becoming part of the working element, in contrast to the non-workers who were, so to speak, outcasts deprived of all privileges: fuel, clothing, and so on.

ENFORCED EMPLOYMENT

The next day Vala and I went for the registration but the queue was so long that our turn never came. The time was not wasted. Because whereas it had been my original intention to register only as a teacher of French, I had learned while listening to various conversations and opinions that the union for theatrical performers such as opera, drama, comedy and ballet, offered far greater advantages. The following day we succeeded in registering as teachers of foreign languages, but the conviction that the theatrical union had more practical advantages did not leave me. Putting in my pocket the teacher's permit card, I went to try my luck at the desk where theatrical workers registered. After registration I was told to come back in two weeks for an audition and a theatrical job.

I had to go through two commissions – a kind of examination which all the artists had to pass under this new regime before they were nominated for a job. I was well received and I must have danced well, since none of the judges doubted that I was an accomplished ballerina. And then, hooray! I became a member of that most envied organization, the Union of Theatrical Performers. In such strange times this union was the least attacked, the least suspected of all, and that fact gave me the courage to tell Father that I had studied ballet as well as gymnastics, and that I had done well enough to gain some recognition in the field.

I told him proudly, "Father, I am now registered under a stage name, Cyane, as a ballerina of Oriental operas in the opera house in Odessa."

Father gasped. "You! Our little bear?"

"Yes, Father." He shook his head in genuine wonder. "And you didn't break anything? I can't believe it!"

Oh, the expression in Mother's eyes when she asked if everything had turned out all right. Only a mother's eyes could have looked like that. That evening was even more cheerful than usual, and the next morning when I came down to breakfast I asked Father how he had slept. "Slept!" he cried. "I didn't even think of sleeping. How could I? I was practicing ballet all night long." He rose from the table, executed an odd pirouette, and said drolly, "Who knows? Maybe I can make the Opera, too."

MORE NOTES FROM MY DIARY

December 24, 1921: I have just returned from church. It always lifts my spirits and makes me feel much better. The choir was excellent. How they sang, those half hungry men! We need such singing – our souls do.

Sunday, January 16, 1922: After a fortnight of severe dry cold came the snow. I like the immaculate whiteness of these lightly falling little stars, but I am very sad today. A letter came from Berlin and I rejoiced, certain it was from Hans Arndt from whom I hadn't heard in years. But it was from his mother informing me of his death. She, whom I had never met, wrote to me with love, saying that her son instilled it in her, adding that my photograph which Hans kept on his desk will always remain there among the things precious to her.

I had decided to drop ballet and began teaching French, but the job at the Workmen's Faculty where I taught brought hardly any income. By the time I paid my expenses I hadn't much left for our general use. The desire to find work that would enable me to help the family a little more was constantly in my mind. Father for the most part treated his patients gratis. Therefore, the moment I heard of the opening in town of an American office known as the A.R.A. (American Relief Administration) I went to apply for a position. This was a new experience altogether. How should I go about it? What should I say? In what capacity should I apply? My knowledge of English certainly ought to be profitable, I thought. I didn't consult Father or Mother, or even take Vala into my confidence, but kept my plans to myself.

I started out bravely, but the closer I came to the given address the more nervous I felt. Does everyone get this nervous when applying for a job I wondered? From the biting frost I entered a warm well decorated office and came face to face with two good looking blond Americans. I began at once to worry about my English, and when taking their pipes out of their mouths the Americans greeted me, I am sorry to confess that I could not even repeat after them the "How do you do?" that I heard. My total ignorance of English seemed obvious and a Russian employee emerged to dismiss or hire me. I was stumbling over my own name and the busy Russian clerk taking me for an illiterate, assigned me without further consideration to the warehouse. "You will start at 8 A.M. tomorrow. Instructions will be given there." That was quick, I thought, walking out quite reassured. "Goodbye, Miss," said the two Americans. They had not moved an inch from where they stood and must have been amused by my dashing in and out. "Goodbye," I called back. Smiling broadly and not even thinking of reproaching myself for my previous timidity in English, I skipped gaily home.

On my job at 8 o'clock the next morning, I was given an apron and told to carry packages of rice, sugar and cocoa from the cart outside the warehouse into the storage room to be sorted. I was told that besides the weekly wages, I would receive two standard food packages a month. I was in heaven, and with an enthusiasm never experienced before, began to work as a laborer. At home no one knew what I was doing. I made up my mind to break the news only when I placed the first food package on our table. My muscles ached from the unusual exercise, but I was so happy that it did not matter.

Monsieur Gorisse, who was still interested in me, obliged immensely by taking over all my classes at the Faculty which made my resignation easy. I also gave up the few lessons at the school with Maman's daughter, Olga. Only the impossibility of practicing with Bekeffy made me sad, but there was no choice since my family had been undernourished for three years.

Our foremen were Russians and at first the Americans seldom entered the warehouse, but on the fourth day an elderly American gentleman came to supervise our work. In my sincere zeal to do well, I carried four bags of sugar to the other girl's two, and more than doubled their rice and cocoa. The old man stood and watched us for an hour and then he made a sign to me. Balancing the bag in my arms, I rushed up to him. First, he tried to make himself understood with expansive gestures then asked in plain English, "Why do you carry twice as much as the others?"

I put my cargo on the floor, straightened up and answered, "Because I am very strong, sir."

"Why, you understand English! In fact, you speak it," he cried. "My dear girl, your place is not here in the warehouse. I'll arrange for your transfer right away."

"I thank you very much," I said.

He winked at me and left muttering, "What a mistake!"

That afternoon I was transferred to the general office in the information department, sort of A.R.A. post office, where we helped people to find their relatives in America, wrote letters for them in English and addressed the envelopes. It was heartbreaking to see the sick, hungry, almost dying people covered with vermin who came to this office with no knowledge of addresses, crying, and begging us to find a brother in New York, or a sister in Chicago whose married name they did not know. We tried to comfort them and in the most desperate cases, where there were large families, we helped at once with food packages.

IN MY DIARY AT THIS TIME:

February 12, 1922 – Odessa: No more teaching. Since the 8th of this month I am an employee of the A.R.A.; working in the information bureau of the organization. Before passing to this office I had three days of work in the warehouse, of which the muscles of my arms and back are still aware. After such physical labor any other work seems easy. I am happy to work in the A.R.A.; in this way I can help my family considerably because in great part my wages will be paid in provisions.

Our supervisor is Mr. John Hynes, a real thunderstorm when something displeases him, but otherwise a very charming person. His assistant is Mr. Harry Harris, who looks like a very young man. I saw them both the first time when I crossed the threshhold of this office. Since then I have met them socially at the home of our friends, the Popowsky's, with several other Americans. When Mr. Hynes and Mr. Harris were introduced to me my English suddenly seemed to flow, and it was a source of amusing conversation when they remembered why I was assigned to the warehouse because everyone was sure I could not understand a word of English. I danced quite a bit and the next morning Mr. Harris told his American colleagues how well the Russians danced. Old Mr. McSweeney was also there, boasting to everyone of discovering me in the warehouse. He is a real tonic for the nerves. I am sorry to be obliged to abandon my regular lessons with Maestro Bekeffy, yet this sacrifice is well worthwhile and he allows me to practice every Sunday from 11 to 1 o'clock.

At last my English, to which I applied myself so diligently in spite of Father's discouragement, brings results and gives me some privileges. Whereas before I had no practice at all except for the two lessons with Professor K., now I have almost too much. I pray that all will go well on this new job. Never before have I had employment of this sort and I am glad that everyone is very kind. Tomorrow is Sunday and tonight I feel the fatigue of the whole week.

February 26, 1922: I am very sad. All this past week I have felt depressed and annoyed with this or that – some misunderstanding with Father which made Mother unhappy, certain unpleasant experiences on my job where we work with all kinds of Americans, many of them greatly different from Mr. Hynes and Mr. Harris. Some are obviously not well brought up since they do not find it necessary even to greet us in the morning; or perhaps they take us for very ordinary girls beneath their notice. At first this disturbed me greatly but I have made up my mind to see nothing but my work which enables me to bring provisions home. I do my best to get accustomed to my position because, after all, we are the "proletariat" today, and there is no reason to remember that we were "de gens du monde".

I am tired again. I have so much to do with the public, and whereas I am often beside myself with the arrogance of others, I am deeply affected by the grief of the meek ones. At the end of each day I am hoarse from having talked so much. If only the coming week may be less exhausting, dear God! The only joy of these last days was the good news from George E., who has been liberated from the Lubianka prison in Moscow.

March 3, 1922: I get a variety of impressions at my work between the well-fed complacent Americans and the shaking, hungry, frightened people who come for help; but little by little I begin to be accustomed to it. Our first package of food has been received. Flour, rice, sugar, tea, cocoa, lard and evaporated milk practically cover our dining room table. Mother, Vala and I cried for joy, and we all blessed America and the Americans; but Father seemed a little hurt that I had done it all in secret without his advice.

I am happy that Mamochka (Mother) will eat better. She likes rice and from now on she will always have some good tea with milk in the mornings. This last winter she deprived herself too much and it shows on her. She is so very thin. Everything seems to improve now. We are a little less pressed materially and one feels better in general since the worst of the winter cold is gone. The winter was very severe.

Here is another letter from Hans Mose in which he speaks again of his wish to have us all in Denmark. Diplomatically, he adds that his wife also wishes us to come. "Venez, donc, Venez," he writes, et cela sera pour moi la plus grande fete se ma vie." Farther on he says, "Life is strange, Lisa. God knows that I loved you with all my heart, all the strength of my youth – a pure and beautiful love. It was also my first love. Maybe that's why I suffered so. It's also true that two or three years later I found myself and returned to normal. Sentimental as we people of Germanic origin are (and I am sure you are going to laugh at this), I spent many, many hours under your window in Grenoble just to see your silhouette behind the curtain. I still love you. Your place in my heart is the same. No one could ever take it." Such a letter, after so many years! I replied thanking him for his kindness and sincerity of his words.

March 7, 1922: Another letter from Hans Mose. He writes that he knows someone who recently left Russia quite safely. He thinks that now there is an opportunity to leave which may never present itself again. Poor, dear Hans. He calls us again, but I shall never go.

March 16, 1922: Since last Friday I am forced to stay in bed with a cold. Were it not for the cough and pain in all my body I wouldn't mind resting for a few days. Sickness tires me more than work and now when I realize what a few days of fever did to me, I can honestly say that I would prefer to do double work in the office. Work would never make me as weak as this. I drink a cup of tea and feel exhausted. It is an effort even to lift my arm. How little we are worth after all. But my sickness will soon pass and I am sure I will regain my usual strength. Thank God, it is not one of those typhus diseases so frequent in town.

Many people have come to inquire about my health: some of the girls at the A.R.A., my new co-workers, and many old friends. Monsieur Gorisse blew in like a hurricane, worrying about me for fear that I had typhus. Dr. C. H., the ever faithful, brought me a bouquet of violets. Two more letters came from Hans Mose, informing us that he had sent parcels – one through A.R.A., the other by the Nansen Red Cross. Dr.

Leonid K. knew nothing about my sickness when he dropped in last night. At the request of Father, with whom I discussed my condition, he returned this morning for a consultation. This was rather embarrassing for me but this was Father's order. Before leaving Leonid wanted to ask me something, but I do not know what premonition made me skillfully stop him. I was too weak to listen to anything, good or bad.

Saturday, March 26, 1922: People die from starvation – hundreds of them on the streets and in their homes, like the unfortunate M. P., Professor of Mathematics, who died leaving a sick wife and two small children. Members of a family die, one by one, sitting close together in a tragic huddle on the street. However, the dead are dead. Those living cadavers, those phantoms roaming around, are far worse off. I come home so distressed that often the bread I put in my mouth sticks in my throat. I feel guilty eating when millions are still hungry.

April 3, 1922: Someone next door plays the violin very well. I love it. It always sets me in a particular mood. All one lives through is embraced by the sound of music. I wish I could have heard the violin longer but the player stopped.

We went to midnight Easter services with Father, as usual. Then we sat around the table, not as luxurious as the ones of our childhood, nevertheless far richer than those of the last years thanks to the A.R.A. Our meal was harmonious, with Father in the best of moods, for which we were all so grateful.

This morning I visited the mother of Leonid K. They are in heavy mourning since the recent death of Professor K. While visiting with them Vala urgently called me home. She was in great distress, unable to speak English to the two Americans, Mr. William Pratt and Mr. Clement, who were paying us a friendly Easter visit. I personally found them most attractive and we were pleased with their attention. It made our Easter day even brighter.

April 5, 1922: Yesterday we attended a party at the mansion of American friends. We all amused ourselves – the same Russian crowd, about five families well known to each other, and the Americans, whose numbers increase: Hynes, Harris, Clement and Parker among the younger ones, an old captain around forty-five whose name I did not know, Dr. McElroy, Mr. McSweeney and Mr. Spratt (very distinguished). We were all happy and we danced. I tried to be equally nice to everyone, and I think my impartiality displeased Mr. Parker a bit. This morning in his office he seemed a little sulky. Just why, I can't understand.

Today when I arrived home from the office I was immediately aware that something unpleasant had happened. The son of our former maid, Angelina, whom we now shelter with her children Stepa and Shoura, had fallen from the staircase and hurt his head. Stepa looked bad. Oh, how I suffered for him and with him the rest of the day. Each time he calmed down and I could sit at my desk for a minute the sad impressions of today mixed with the happy ones of yesterday. Chaos in my mind – glances, words, the melodies of fox trots, and the horrible pallor of the youngster and the anxiety of fear for his life.

It is midnight. I am tired after the party of yesterday and the worry of today. Stepa is breathing rhythmically in his sleep now. I think of William Parker. Why is he angry with me? Is he jealous? Oh no, this would annoy me too much. One thing that I can say about him is that he is a really fine young man. As to that bold, ardent Mr. Clement, the terribly handsome one, I have told him that I will never dance with him again. Mr. Spratt, whom I met for the first time, is a true gentleman and Mr. McElroy is also, though with a glint in his eyes. Mr. McSweeney, Bon Papa, is charming and sweet. I see them all before my eyes and can hardly believe I had the opportunity to enjoy myself so much in their friendly company after seven years of such a life as ours. It is high time to go to bed now. Stepa is quiet and I hope he will sleep through the night.

April 14, 1922: More parties – One at Xana's with three naval officers from the American destroyer "Charles 241," Mr. Autree, Mr.

Fleming, and Mr. Desenberry. The officers wished to reciprocate but were not allowed to invite us on board the destroyer, and so arranged a dinner party at Pushkinskaya Street, Number 32. George Merrick Dusenberry came for us considerably ahead of time and we sat in our living room chatting. George is certainly well bred – he must have come from a good family; but then, all the officers have excellent manners. George's interest in me seems to grow from minute to minute. Around seven we went to the party which took place in a large hall draped with naval flags. The dinner and everything that preceded and followed it was very chic. This party was mostly for the younger crowd, but the captain of the destroyer "Childs" and some older Americans came later. We came home by car. What luxury!

The night before last Mr. Autry and Mr. Dusenberry spent their last evening in our house. Dusenberry was charming and nonchalant, but at the end of the evening he grew serious and spoke open heartedly to me revealing sincerity and a warm feeling. In general I find the Americans less complex and more spontaneous than the Russians. Their directness sometimes shocks me. Even though they allow themselves little familiarities, one never feels hurt, since there is a certain naiveté about it all. Mr. Dusenberry was sorry to leave and hopes to return soon.

Last night William Parker dropped in and I could understand that the visits of the officers did not please him too much. William likes me I think, but tries not to show it. When the A.R.A. auto came for him around 10 o'clock in the evening he kissed me on the forehead and left. This is Thursday. On Saturday we are invited to Mme. R.'s and "America" will be there too.

Sunday, April 17, 1922: The A.R.A. is doing much good. They have begun to feed the poor children, starting with those in the suburbs. Soon they will start with those in the city. I succeeded in placing our Angelina in one of these outfits and she never stops blessing the Americans for their generosity. Usually dinner is served at two in the afternoon, but many of them gather at the doors at six in the morning.

For dinner they receive cereals with milk and sugar and hot chocolate. Since I have been on the job I have been able to obtain parcels of food for many of our neighbors whose misery and helplessness is obvious, such as the family of Z. in which the mother recently died and the son is tubercular. We do all we can to help this poor condemned boy's morale. Happily, he is not aware of his sad condition. Unfortunate country, unfortunate people! When, finally, will the graph of our destiny move upward? All one hears now is sickness, death and hunger.

The work of the A.R.A. was stupendous. As I think of it now, it seems to me that never enough credit was given officially for the help they brought to Russia, when hunger all over the immense country had reached its climax and the nation was threatened with total starvation. The Russian people considered Herbert Hoover as their savior, and even now I do not feel it is too late to tell Mr. Hoover that his photograph, obtainable in any A.R.A. relief station, had its place of honor in millions of Russian homes. His name was on the lips of everyone who survived. On behalf at those who never had the chance to express their gratitude to you, as one of the survivors I humbly wish to express our deep appreciation for the wonderful help brought to my starving country in its most critical hour.

Contact with the filthy, insect ridden people soon brought typhus to our office. This disease, usually transmitted by lice, scourged many regions of Europe during World War I and lingered in Russia long after because of lack of soap and elemental sanitary conditions. I was the second stricken. For the first two days I saw Father's kindly face bent over me. I also remember how heartbroken he was, when advised by Dr. P., Mother permitted my hair to be closely cropped. "To cut that beautiful hair!" he exclaimed. "Didn't you know, Olichka (Olga), that this measure is only necessary in hospitals to avoid spreading the disease? Lisa will be taken care of at home."

Father's words of concern were good to my ears before I lapsed into unconsciousness, though hair or no hair didn't matter to me as my sickness was taking a quick course, and the little argument about my hair was the last I heard for many, many days. Mother told me later that even at the height of my fever I demanded my toothbrush and automatically brushed my teeth morning and evening. It was amazing how Father's advice, given at the beginning of our hardships, had become so deeply rooted in my subconscious.

After seventeen days between life and death I came back; but something in the atmosphere of the house depressed me. Mother and Vala came and went as in a dream and their smiles didn't seem as natural as usual. My diary contains the record of these days of convalescence, written with pencil in a very weak, uncertain hand.

May 18, 1922: Since April 28th the typhus has kept me in bed and only in the last three days have I begun to recuperate. Excessively weak, I nevertheless feel that little by little life is returning to me – an incomparable, unique condition.

May 19, 1922: Only yesterday I found out that a few days after me, Father also fell ill with typhus. Oh, Lord, how I sensed it! I questioned everyone about my father, wondering why I did not see him.

May 31, 1922: Lord, help me to pray. Help me to feel You near me so that my prayers may enable me to live with my grief. We have lost Father. Is it true? Are they true, these words I dare not write? We have lost Father.

Yes, it is true. He died ten days ago on Saturday night, the eve of the Trinity.

June 4, 1922: The bells have rung just as they did when Father died. The bells were ringing and his breathing grew weaker and weaker until it stopped. Mother and Sister were beside him. They dared not cry, dared not say a word, so solemn was the moment, so beautiful and calm was Father's face. And I, still sick in bed, knew nothing. I remember how ardently I prayed that the Lord would save Papa, and how with a trembling hand I wrote a letter to a priest with a request to pray for him, but at that very time he had already left us forever. It was 7 o'clock and

Vala came in and said that Father was resting very calmly, that he slept and that Mother had gone to rest for awhile. Now she was free to go to church, she said. "Go," I told her.

Alone in my room I felt prey to an inexplicable anxiety. I thoroughly believed that Father was resting, and yet a worry and an unnatural fear covered me with sweat. This hour – the hour that Vala spent in church – was the first hour after Father's death.

There was no light in my room. The shadows cast by the moon reached my bed and frightened me. I was afraid to make the slightest move and listened to the terrifying silence of the house, impatiently waiting for Vala. She returned and I told her about that horrible hour. She tried to comfort and calm me but I slept very little that night. What surprised me was that every time I moved Vala would run to me and kiss me. "Go and sleep," I told her. "What is the matter that you run to me every minute?" All night and the next day I did not hear Father's sighs. "Father seems very quiet," I would say.

"Yes, he is," they would answer quite naturally.

I almost knew the sad truth already. My heart told me but I did not want to believe it. At five in the afternoon I could bear it no longer. "Vala," I said, "tell me if Father is gone."

"Yes," she said, "last night at seven – I cannot hide it from you any longer." Gathering all my physical and moral strength, I said that I wanted to bid farewell to my father. They understood that nothing would dissuade me, and a little later I was carried in an armchair to Father's room. In his workroom on his bed, covered with light gauze, I saw him. On the windowsill near which his bed had been moved, there were flowers and a picture of Christ that Father loved, "Jesus in the Desert," before which a small lamp was burning. Dr. Chmelnitsky and another friend held me up. I knew that I had to control myself for Mother's and Vala's sake. I looked at my father, his handsome face so calm and full of peace. I kissed him on his forehead, on his cheek, and on the corner of his mouth. I kissed his beautiful hands and the little icon on his chest. Crossing myself and blessing Father, I asked him to bless us from on high. I couldn't go away from this bed where Father seemed to sleep. I clung to him again and again; but at last they took me back to my room, trembling all over, and for a long, long time I felt an open wound in the place of my heart.

Later, I heard the chant of a choir on our staircase. They were taking Father away from us forever. There was nothing in me but grief. Can I ever express what I felt in those sad moments, left alone in my room? I now heard the singing from the street and I listened to it, sobbing, as it reached me from farther and farther away. They took Father to the Cathedral where he lay in state until the afternoon of the next day. I was told that an immense crowd followed him – all the people that he had treated with so much compassion. Poor Father, how he exerted himself, how he gave himself to the sick. Hundreds of people whom we never knew loved him and lamented his departure as that of a good doctor and a kind man.

Father is no longer with us. His room is empty. Now that I can walk I go in and touch his bed, his pillow. I kiss the gravure of "Jesus in the Desert" which he loved and about which he once spoke to me. Dear Father, I know that this is only your physical death, your passing from this earth. Your soul lives in the vast universe. You still live but we suffer so much not having you.

Tuesday, June 14, 1922: Lustdorf – a resort close to Odessa. Is it true that it is I who sit on a terrace surrounded by an abandoned garden so beautiful that I call it "The Enchanted Garden"? Is it truly I who listens with astonishment to the silence in this charming place, who finally sleeps all night through, after nights and nights of terrible insomnia, and wakes in the morning to the song of the birds? Yes, I am in Lustdorf, and this morning we spent a long time at the seashore. I could not recuperate in the city so Dr. Chmelnitsky helped us to get settled here. The auto of the A.R.A. brought Vala and me to Lustdorf last Sunday. Unfortunately, I'll be able to profit by this sojourn for only a week and a half, and then I will have to resume my work.

Wednesday, June 15, 1922: I read the "Life of Jesus," by Ernest Renan, the book Father was reading before he got sick and which I think he had no time to finish. This winter and the preceding one he read aloud to me many fragments from the volumes he loved, which were mostly philosophical and religious books of Tolstoy. Last winter he read Vladimir Solovieff, and read and re-read I don't know how many times, the Gospel of Tolstoy and his personal letters. Last month he read hardly anything, returning too late and too tired after visiting from twenty to thirty patients a day; but in the previous winters, by the light of a little oil lamp in our dining room we all gathered together, he with his stack of books and I with mine. He wanted me to listen right away to his reading, but my ultimatum was, "No philosophy until I have had my page of English." Sometimes he read only short passages which struck him by their originality, and I listened, wondering why these ideas were most familiar and not at all of interest to me. Father often expressed regret at not having read philosophical books in his youth, and in order not to regret it as he did, I am going to try and read some of them. I'm sure to like these books, which perhaps can explain some of my own thoughts, and certain states of mind and heart, some of my moods and desires. I feel as though I had taken this book which he did not finish right from Father's hand, and it is with the "Life of Jesus" that I am going to begin my new reading, though it is purely historical and has nothing in common with religious philosophy. As yet, I have no idea what Ernest Renan will say of Jesus. No matter. Nothing could possible change my own ideas on Jesus Christ and my faith in him.

Sunday, June 19, 1922: Last night Mamochka arrived. I had wished it with all my heart, and I am so glad for she needed the country air. She needed a change – she who has seen nothing but the street we have lived on for so many years. We went to the sea last night and also this morning and Mother went into the water. I find her looking a little better, but she is still very pale and thin. I feel sad because tomorrow we shall have to leave here. Mother had some formalities to attend to and Vala thinks my presence in the A.R.A. is necessary, since if I linger I may lose my good job. Thus, one leaves the old garden, and no longer will I read on the terrace nor go down to the sea. I feel like a new person. However, something tells me that five or six more days here would help me not to feel my sickness at all, for though I walk quite well my feet still feel heavy and running is almost impossible. I also cannot lift myself on tiptoes. We are leaving tomorrow at six o'clock, and Tuesday I shall go to work. I ask God for strength and courage. It is as though I were starting a new life.

June 20, 1922 – Odessa: Mother and I are in the city again. Vala took the little Shourotshka, Angelina's child, and went back to Lustdorf. I see that I am not quite myself yet, but I know that it is high time to become normal in every way especially as tomorrow I begin to work at the A.R.A, and this is the work that is going to sustain us. Between Father's sickness and mine, Mother incurred many debts. But courage – courage – we shall pull through. Tomorrow morning I shall see Mr. Hynes, who will tell me where to work now. I have returned – changed. During Father's and my sickness the Americans showed concern and supplied us with medications we could not find in our pharmacies. Tomorrow I'll be able to thank them personally.

Now it is up to me to take the reins in my hand and try to replace Father in our family. The A.R.A. in Odessa was most kind but they paid only average wages, not enough for a family of three. Besides, I was ambitious and wanted to show Mother that I was capable of earning our living. Subconsciously perhaps, I had a wish to live in a larger city than Odessa. At any rate, when I was informed that a person knowing foreign languages (receptionist, interpreter) was needed in the English agency of the White Star Line at Moscow, I applied for the position and received a favorable answer.

Preparations began. Mother, though grieved to see me go, cooperated beautifully. Her greatest concern was my winter clothes. In Moscow the frost is heavy and creeps up on you without the warning of the wind we have in Odessa. Your ears turn white and then there is trouble. She even ordered a pair of warm boots for me, to be made out of Father's winter coat. It was August, 1922. The date was set. Tickets for Moscow, hard to obtain because of the great influx of population to the capital, were ordered by the A.R.A. because one of their representatives, E. D., whom I had once met at a party, was being transferred to Moscow and we were leaving together. I was excited about going but disturbed at the thought of leaving Mother and Vala alone. Something had to be done though.

The Odessa A.R.A. showered me with favors. They gave me a farewell party, paid for my ticket under the pretext that I was still their employee and everyone came to see me off. Dr. Smith presented me with a lovely kit – a regular little drugstore with aspirin and other medications almost impossible to obtain, and best of all I was given a beautiful warm blanket of light gray wool.

By some coincidence, our friend Professor Kovaleff, was leaving on the same train. It was a nostalgic farewell. Even Mother kept smiling, seeing all the attention given to me. It made me feel good and I tried to show my appreciation to everyone; but just before the train left, as though at the touch of some magic wand, the whole crowd seemed to have disappeared and I only saw Mother. Her eyes – Mother's eyes – in them was all the love a person can express. During the entire trip I was spoiled by the attentions of both E. D. and Professor Kovaloff. As we approached our destination we spoke more and more of the difficult living conditions in Moscow. E.D. offered to drive me around to facilitate my first steps in an unknown city and Professor Kovaloff promised to inquire among his friends about a room for me.

This problem was far from the center of my mind – the job was most important. The wages were three times higher than in Odessa where there was no requirement for many languages. My new job was all that I was thinking about. In spite of all the frightful stories about the impossibility of finding a room in Moscow, the lodging question seemed unimportant to me. My new job, my new job – I was anxious only about that.

The chauffeur of E. D. was waiting for him when we arrived in Moscow and we drove from the station to the house of my friends where I was invited to stay for three days during the absence of their son. E. D. promised to take me in his car to the office of the White Star Line the next morning. A sudden order for reduction of personnel, instead of the increase previously planned, had been received and put into effect at a meeting the night before. An official letter stating these facts and expressing regret for the unforeseen change of policy was handed to me without further explanation. It was a shock, and its effect must have shown on my face because E. D. sensed the situation before I opened my mouth. I shall forever be thankful for his firm hand on my arm at that moment.

My first thought was to return home. This seemed to be the most sensible solution, but my baggage and E. D.'s was reported lost, and the railway officials suggested that I wait until it could be found in order to identify it in person. Thus, my martyrdom in Moscow began. Frankly, it was softened greatly by the incomparable kindness of E. D. Upon his suggestion I took a position in the Moscow A.R.A., similar to the one I had in Odessa.

The search for a dwelling – a task close to the impossible – was not such a lugubrious one in his company. The moment that I sat comfortably in his Cadillac, my troubles seemed almost nil. Though the three days stay with my friends had almost ended, the hope of finding some place to live kept surging through me after every vain attempt. After work each day we drove through Moscow with its numerous encircling walls, and I began to recognize the general plan of this intricate old city. Summer was over and the chill of autumn was in the air. Gliding through the endless boulevards we saw its imprint in the various shades of leaves hanging over the ponds, so much loved by the Moscovites! In the evening we visited the centuries old churches, the amiable yet most reserved E. D. always there for my inner and outer comfort. I began to love Moscow. In the afternoon of the fourth day, when my friend's son arrived and took possession of his room, we found a place – something that could hardly be called living quarters – just a sofa in the living room of an apartment house situated in a rather uninviting section of Moscow called Krasnaya-Fresnia. The rent was fifteen rubles a week.

It took a few days to realize the extent of the inconvenience of my new abode. The first morning I was awakened by a two-toned childish shriek. It came from beneath the cloth covered table next to my sofa. I jumped, horrified, thinking the children were injured. I lifted the edge of the tablecloth and saw there two little blond angels crying, their faces completely covered with something like a yellow paste. The two little rascals, thinking they had stolen sugar from their mother's market basket, had treated themselves with dry mustard, and were letting the whole world know about it. The blond angels, Tolia and Mika, my landlord's sons, four and five years old, turned out to be real little devils with no lack of imagination for mischief. The next day, for instance, they sprinkled coffee on one of the roomer's laundry which was just rinsed and ready to be hung.

My landlord, a fireman on duty in the opera house every night, liked to have his tea hour upon his return home after midnight. It was apparently his best meal. He and his wife, and often a few friends, would sit and sip their tea, sometimes for hours, at the same round table next to my sofa. A request for a screen which would give me a little privacy and allow me to be in bed during this nightly festivity, was not granted. They needed the only screen they had for something more important than that. Consequently, every time I heard the fireman return home, I would get out of bed and spend their tea hour sitting on the edge of the bathtub, reading a book or writing letters.

After a while my American friends simplified my domestic problem by daily inviting me to their box at the opera, and after the performance for a snack in their American quarters. I always made sure to return home about the time when the tea party was over. On the whole, however, the lack of primitive comfort and the late hours were not good for my health. I was beginning to tire easily, and though I enjoyed the ballet and the music of Tchaikovsky's "Swan Lake," which I heard about twenty times, during the last few performances I did not even hear the music, but slept comfortably in the red plush chair in the box.

The luggage question worried me a lot. All that I had was in that trunk: winter coat, shoes, boots, all of my warm clothes. It was October; the approach of winter chilled the air and I felt none too comfortable in my light, spring coat. We inquired daily, but no luggage – neither E. D.'s nor mine. Actually, I could not return without it and I wouldn't dare tell Mother of its loss. Therefore, hopefully, I waited.

Mother's letters were frequent and cheerful. The fact that the government obliged her to rent Father's office to a Swiss Red Cross representative made her much more comfortable financially and I lived very thriftily and sent some of my wages home. Though I read between the lines that Mother longed for me, she wrote that I shouldn't worry about her and Vala, but remain in Moscow as long as I liked it so well. For my birthday, the 2nd of November and my Name Day, the 4th, I received presents from home: Mother's cookies and quince jam. To be alone these days was new to me and I felt very homesick, but somehow Mother's immense love warmed me even at a distance. E. D. brought her package sent to the A.R.A. address, and guessing the event, planned a special evening. But I wouldn't go out that night, as year after year I had always gone to vesper service on the eve of my Saint's Day – Saint Elizabeth. My brother-friend, E. D., remained with me for a while and played with Tolia and Lika. All of us tasted Mother's cookies and jam, and then E. D. drove me to the church of St. Nikolas (Yavlenniy) on the Arbat, saying he would return after the service. E.D.'s devotion was rare. He told me that having looked into Mother's eyes just before the train left, he had given her a silent promise to be a faithful friend to her daughter. And so he was.

As I came out of the church a soft, fluffy snow was falling. I saw E. D. through the thick snow flakes which separated me from him and I felt like throwing myself into his arms and thanking him for something more than amiability, more than brotherly devotion, something I could find no words for. His Cadillac was no longer an open car; it now had a hood with celluloid panes through which we saw the streets as through real glass. Moscow became all white in no time. We drove slowly on the smooth surface of the first snow. The harmony inside and outside was so perfect that we did not speak.

A surprise was coming. One morning, without preliminaries, the landlady announced that I would have to share their living room with somebody else because the amount I paid for my corner was not sufficient. Wonderful, I thought to myself. This probably will stop their tea parties with another person in the room and my life will be more normal. "Is it a young or an elderly person who is going to share the room with me?" I asked. "It is a young man," was her casual reply. New government, new conditions, new points of view! "When is this person going to move in?" I questioned, hoping to be able to arrange some change in a day or two. "Tonight," she said. There was no time for discussion. I also knew there would be no use in trying to find something else. Besides, it was time to go to work; in fact, I had to hurry.

Upon my return, I found the living room entirely changed. The tea table was no longer there; the whole place was tidied up and in the middle of the room stood the many times requested and long dreamed of screen, dividing it in two. "Without misfortune there would be no good fortune," says the Russian proverb. Ironically enough, my corner seemed much more private now. I decided to go to bed early and sleep the entire night without any interruption for a change. I was almost asleep when I heard the door open. "I wish to introduce myself to my room companion," I heard a young firm voice say. "I am Alexander S. from Odessa."

"My name is Elizabeth Kraevsky," I said, "and I promise to respect your privacy as I am sure you will respect mine."

"Elizabeth Kraevsky?" he exclaimed. "How strange – we knew and loved your father. His death was such a loss for all of us."

"I am glad you knew my father. Thank you for your kind memory of him." Never was I disturbed by my new roommate. Never more was my nightly rest broken. Yet the harm of the lack of sleep in previous months was already done, and my health was seriously affected.

Shortly after, I found myself in the Moscow Clinic under the strict observation of a heart specialist. It was our American doctor who, during a general checkup, noticed some severe and rather menacing irregularities in the beat of my heart. No more Krassnaya Presnia! The transportation from there occurred as by magic. Through the solicitude of my American employers I was given the best room in the clinic, with windows overlooking the park which was dressed in white and silver of the first snow. During all these transactions no word of protest, not even a question, was allowed to be uttered by me and gratefully, I yielded, feeling it was all for my good. "Thank God, no more Krassnaya Presnia," I repeated, forgetting that only some really acute condition could have brought me here this quickly.

Sophia, my only roommate, was charming and beautiful. We understood each other well – both outwardly not too sick – yet forced to an absolute rest for an unknown length of time. We tried to give a feminine touch to our hospital room. There was the gentle scent of Sophia's exquisite French perfume (saved for years by very scarce use), fresh flowers sent regularly by E.D., and the large tin box of American cookies which I shared with everyone who came in. The doctors mentioned that our room was the coziest of all.

Twice a day they would come in with students to explain and demonstrate our cases to them, using Latin terms so we would not understand our condition. I caught up on my sleep and after two weeks of a severe regiment was allowed out for either a walk or a ride. E. D. either came himself, or sent his chauffeur, daily. Sophia was impressed by the attention given to me, but both of us enjoyed what we called our "luxurious outing in the Cadillac." Later I was told that had I not been taken care of at once, my heart would have had a permanent organic defect. Now I was out of danger. The change, the different atmosphere and the fact that I was well again, gave me a new outlook on life and new hopes. I rejoiced. The very moment that my mind began to generate brighter, happier thoughts, my outer circumstances became brighter and happier. My luggage was found and another wonderful thing happened – Mr. & Mrs. Kovaleff offered me a room in their new apartment – no more Krassnaya Presnia – never again. I couldn't wait to break all the good news to Mother. What freedom! What serenity came with the peace of my mind! The last week in the Clinic was a delightful holiday.

To live with the Kovaleff's, my old friends from Odessa, was ideal for me. Paul, a concert pianist and composer, practiced sometimes late into the night and I loved it. Lydie, born Eugelaine, French to the core of her being, was busy improving her new nest, working hard, with a constant smile on her face. With her delicate, beautiful hands she even chopped wood, for fear that her famous Paul might hurt his precious fingers.

There was a constant coming and going of our American friends from Odessa and new ones from Moscow. I continued to work at the American Relief Administration rather successfully, meeting new persons and getting to know Americans better. The girls who did not do so well and even lost their jobs were those who could not take criticism, or asked unnecessary questions. With them, the American employers, alert and brief as I found them to be, were most impatient.

For quite some time, sheltered by the American Relief Administration, I experienced the feeling of security, which helped me to look deeper into my own self and others. Still, I was not completely accustomed to living alone and on my own, and often in the tiny room of the Kovaleff's, listening to Paul's music, I cried for Mother. At other times, overcome by the deep, overwhelming Wagnerian music, I dreamed of some deep personal love not yet met. Christmas and New Year's passed, made as delightful as possible for me by E. D., the Kovaleff's and other friends. One party followed another from the White House to the Blue and Brown, mansions now occupied by the American Relief Administration staff.

With the news of Vala's arrival in Moscow, I had to work fast to find a room for two. It was in the old section of Moscow called Arbat on Bolshoy Rjevsky Pereulok, opposite the quaint little church called St. Nicholas on Chickens' Feet. The old landlady whose room we had to cross to reach ours was grouchy and since we were on the ground floor, we arranged to climb through the window for our mutual convenience.

I spent two years in Moscow. Vala and I had worked in the A.R.A. until it closed upon 48 hours notice from the Soviets, as a result of an unfavorable article which appeared in the New York Times' Sunday news section written by an official of the A.R.A. Many of the workers were transferred to the Joint Distribution Committee where they remained until the latter also closed. I shall never forget the kindness of Mr. Blattner and his wife, Rose, who, knowing that I had no job asked me to give them lessons in French and Russian, which helped me considerably.

The most outstanding event during this time was my mother's visit to Moscow. How happy we were together! Alone, in complete peace and understanding of each other, my little mother improved my dwelling, putting in a stove to keep me warm, fixing my clothes and cooking nice things for me. We visited ancient churches, museums, and some friends. We always had so much to say to each other, as though no chance had been given to us before to be alone.

After she left and Vala returned, I began to feel the futility of my life in Moscow, away from Mother – the greatest, the most precious person in the world to me. I felt that she, too, needed me badly. When I finally went home Mother looked rather pale to me, but seemed energetic and as good a pal as always. Together we examined our financial status and found that it was almost nil. The trouble with us was that we never were sufficiently businesslike. To find a job was most urgent for me now. Having worked only for Americans I wondered how it would feel and how the adjustment would be among the Soviet officials and their co-workers. Unhesitatingly, I wrote many applications to the offices where foreign languages were needed, as well as to the only American organization left in town called the Student Relief, connected with the Young Men's Christian Association. For weeks no response came. In desperation, I undertook to make the translation from Russian into French of a book of zoology – an urgent work for a professor of the local university. For three nights and three days I bent over this unfamiliar, purely technical essay. Mother urged me to sleep a little, but all I asked for was strong tea to keep me awake and going. Sadly enough, the work was poorly paid, and Mother decided to never allow me to make another scientific translation.

The reward for my diligence and tenacious efforts suddenly came. I was introduced to the Englishman in charge of the "Inter-European Telegraph" in Odessa, and the very afternoon my translation was delivered, a car stopped at my house and Mr. Walford came as agreed, to take me to a chamber music concert that was to take place in their home on the French Boulevard. There were not more than twenty people; I knew almost everyone. Captain Leslie Cook and Mr. Winn, not counting the most courteous Mr. Walford, made me feel at home at once. Our pleasant true friendship and association were well established from that day on and I could not begin to tell what oasis this association would be for me in the years to come. This first afternoon of music, pleasant exchange of thought, delicious dinner, and the intuitive feeling of being liked, cheered me for quite some time. Again, with the cheerfulness of my own mind and spirit, the door for more cheerful events was flung open and one morning in the mail, there were three different offers for positions: 1. From the Customhouse; 2. Maritime Agency of the Russian Mercantile Fleet and 3. American Student Relief. I chose the latter, although I knew it was not lasting, as I was subconsciously scared of the other jobs. I was accepted that very day by Mr. McNaughton, who had to leave urgently for Paris. He left me in charge of the office under the supervision of his Russian representative, Dr. K.

WORKING FOR THE SOVIET MERCANTILE FLEET

The year 1930 arrived and I greeted it with hope, pleased to see the end of the old one, which like all the others that had gone by in Russia since the revolution of 1917, had not been easy to live through. There was nothing to look forward to; but one must not give up hope. Besides, the figures 1-9-3-0 had fascinated me since my school days. January went the same monotonous way. I awakened before dawn in a cold room, with an almost irresistible desire to go back to sleep. But inner discipline prevailed. I jumped up, opened the balcony door, did some calisthenics, had a cold sponge, and suddenly was no longer a rag but a human being ready to start the day. When I had my hot tea with a little sugar and dry bread, the brisk half hour walk to the harbor was not an ordeal but a pleasure.

Not so, when my ration of tea and sugar was exhausted (it usually lasted only the first ten days of the month), nor on rainy days when I had to splash to work without galoshes, nor in winter when the freezing wind brought tears that froze on my cheeks. On such days I regretted not having made a cloak of the last warm object left at home, a scarf and several pairs of old stockings. The thirty-minute walk was an eternity in cold weather. Upon reaching the office, I rushed to take off all these rags in the washroom and put on my only decent pair of shoes and stockings, which I had to keep for the office, where we were required to be always presentable. At 8 o'clock sharp I was seated at my desk before piles of work, not knowing what to do first.

In the Odessa office of the Soviet Mercantile Fleet for servicing incoming and outgoing foreign vessels, my friend Marussia S. and I were typists and interpreters, both speaking four languages. The more you know, the more is demanded of you. We typed hundreds of bills of lading, deciphered code telegrams (Scott's Code, mostly), assembled the answers, translated foreign letters with complaints of damaged cargo, sea protests and other legal maritime documents, and attended to the many formalities necessitated by the arrival or departure of a ship, and all this in a small office crowded by the coming and going of captains, mates, even mechanics and cooks, and sick seamen who needed medical attention, or others calling for letters from home.

The captains often were talkative, but because it was dangerous for us to speak to foreigners we had to try hard, within the limits of politeness, to avoid conversation which might provoke the suspicions of the half-literate Communists assigned to our office to watch the non-party men and women in the agency. The foreign captains placed great confidence in me. "If Miss Kraevsky confirms it, we shall sign the statement," I often heard them say. This practice continued until, instructed by my bosses, I had to say, this is not one of my responsibilities.

Often Marussia and I would be invited out by the captains after work. "I would like you to spend the evening with me," a haughty German captain would offer. "Signorina, would you condescend to accompany me to the opera?" This from an elegant Italian captain, uttered while bowing gracefully. I had the same answer for all.

"Thank you very much, but I do not go out, I am in mourning."

Once, it did not work so well. A Hungarian master, just in from Fiume said, "What, again in mourning? You were in mourning two years ago when I was here last."

"Sorry. I still am." I was certain he understood my trick. Of all the masters, the Italians seemed the most cultured. Apparently, the educational requirements for the mercantile fleet in Italy were almost as rigorous as those of the Navy's.

Unable to converse with me in the office, some of the captains followed me on my way home. When far away from the office they would approach and shower me with apologies and explanations. I had to say: "You expose me to great danger by speaking to me on the street. We are not to associate with foreigners." Occasionally I had not enough will to reject a handsome young officer, seemingly of interest in me, eager to know more about me, and who apparently sensed my difficult situation. I would walk on with him, listening avidly to some good talk, so unlike what we heard every day, and it would bring back memories of visits to France, to Italy, and of a happier life.

On a rare occasion I would wander past my home to the very end of the town. Afterward, I felt choking anger at a government under which two young people, attracted to each other, could not walk together without fear. In this atmosphere I had slaved for five years, seldom going home at what was supposed to be quitting time, and often working very late at night preparing the papers for pre-dawn sailings. Strangely, though almost always half hungry, we workers sustained, outwardly at least, more cheerfulness than the well-fed, self-important communist watch dogs.

We had a real friend in Odessky, a harbor employee for more than twenty years, who knew more about shipping formalities and transactions than all the rest of the office. Several times he had refused promotion from his job as ship-chandler. Always ready to help, he cheered us most effectively through our stomachs. Never can I forget the sight of Odessky returning from a ship, his face a perfect smiling circle. This meant a gift for Marussia and me. Out of his wide, greasy pocket he would slowly pull a piece of foreign chocolate, nuts, an apple or tangerine – long forgotten delicacies. Instantly our mood improved and for a while life seemed brighter. Once, beaming all over, he announced: "Girls, you could never guess what I brought you today – something straight from America." He pulled from his pocket a large brown American envelope in which he had sealed a few rings of canned pineapple – his luncheon dessert on an American Export steamship. The juice had leaked through the envelope, soaking his jacket and had dribbled down his trousers and into his shoes. But our joy over the fruit seemed to repay him.

That very night the American steamer was being prepared to leave at daybreak. Captain Stuart, her young red-haired master, called at 11 o'clock while we were still working on his bills of lading. Learning that we had had neither lunch nor dinner, he stalked out. About midnight we heard the captain behind the closed door of our bosses office, shouting angrily. Then the door swung open and, red in the face, Captain Stuart strode into our room. He put some bars of American chocolate by my typewriter and some by Marussia's. "This is all I managed to bring you," he said. "I couldn't stand the thought of you girls working untill this time of night on my papers without anything to eat, and I had a big pitcher of hot cocoa prepared for you and lots of sandwiches, but I was not allowed to bring them. These inhuman rules of yours!" The customs guards were very strict about this rule.

Odessky had a particular liking for me. Jokingly, he would say, "If I have heart trouble, the cause of it is our Lizochka." He did have heart trouble. He must have known it was progressing and more than once, foreseeing the inevitable, would say, "Soon I shall go 'ad Patrem' and you will all continue to work without me."

"I shall not stay here without you, dear Odessky," I would say. "You must find an easier job and make me your assistant."

I worked conscientiously, feeling I was needed. Other agencies often consulted me on important transactions with foreign countries. At times I felt indispensable.

In the middle of January, Vala and I had a good time. We were invited for dinner by our old friend, Professor V. C., and a few days later to a party given by Dr. K. at the party I felt exceptionally well and happy, and danced all night.

As January ended, a rumor circulated in the city that the Government would once more search personal belongings with the purpose of confiscating all jewelry (except plain wrist watches and wedding bands) and foreign currency. Rumors were the usual thing, and Vala and I had become more or less indifferent to them, though we still had Father's gold watch and chain, his university medal, a few valuables belonging to my sister, and ten American dollars saved by Mother from the time I was employed at the American Relief Administration. There was also a new pound note, given to me by a captain for whom I had worked overtime, translating a French sea protest into English. The translation was difficult, and I did not feel like parting with the hard earned pound. Besides, I had never owned one before.

The morning of January 31st, I awoke with the feeling that something unusual was to happen. Good or bad, I did not know and as the hours went on, I throbbed with expectation. Vala, contrary to her custom, called for me after work, saying she had been worrying about me all day. We decided that the next morning I would take the watch, chain, and dollars to our trustworthy Odessky and ask him to sell them. He knew the ins and outs of such transactions. My sister went to bed at eleven in the little adjoining room, temporarily ours, while I continued to sit at my desk. After hiding Father's watch and chain in the pocket of my winter coat, I carefully pinned the ten one dollar bills to the lining.

INQUISITION AND ARREST

W hile cleaning the desk drawers, rereading and discarding letters, I came upon my crisp new English pound note. Folding it many times into a small square, I pressed it into a tiny metal surgical-needle box of my father's, camouflaging it with some ordinary beads, and left it in the middle drawer. More than once I glanced at the door, expecting – I knew not what. It was long past midnight now, and my mind was beginning to laugh at my heart for that senseless feeling of foreboding. Almost 2 o'clock. Nothing could happen now. This time my intuition had been misleading I thought, as I went to empty the waste basket and wash my hands. Stepping back into my room, I was startled by a sharp knock. Two o'clock in the morning!

"Who is there?" I asked.

"Does Elizaveta Kraevsky live here?"

"Yes."

"Open!"

"What is it?" I demanded, slightly opening the little window in the upper part of the door. I could see a green GPU hat, two armed soldiers and our janitor, Yvan. I opened the door. The GPU agent handed me an official order. Under my name I read: "Perquisition and Arrest."

"Some interesting work must have kept you up this late," said the agent, seeing that I was fully dressed. My throat was dry. I could not utter a word, but my mind was working.

All at once the room seemed crowded. Vala, awakened by the knock, insisted on being allowed in. One soldier went to the balcony door, the other stood by the entrance. The agent made me take a seat in the middle of the room and went over to the desk I had just finished cleaning. Vala, trembling all over, fell on the couch, feigning illness. Profiting by this, I asked the agent to allow me to cover her with my coat, and loudly expressing words of concern, I bent close and whispered in French, "Pull the watch out of the pocket! Before I could mention the dollars pinned to the lining, I was ordered back to my seat.

By the light of my pink lamp, the agent looked over my many manuscripts and correspondence. Everything written in Russian he put on the left side of the desk. Everything in foreign languages seemed to arouse his suspicion and was put to the right, undoubtedly to be taken along with him for inspection by higher authorities. Now he was opening the middle drawer. "My pound, my English pound!" I thought. "If he finds it, I am lost, lost, lost. At once they will accuse me of espionage! No! He must not find it!" My throat was scorched by the heat of fear. Suddenly, I began to pray like a child, "Lord, do not let it happen – protect me – You alone can – he will look and he won't see – he won't see! I believe!" The little metal box was in his hands. He opened it. He picked up every bead turning it in his fingers, lingeringly. My burning eyes watched him. "Oh, Lord, do not let – do not let him find it. He studied a large red bead longer than the others, and then closed the box and put it to the left.

My throat was no longer dry. Some magic key had opened a cool brook near my heart that freshened my mouth. I felt weak, but calm and happy. Relieved, I smiled at my sister. She smiled back, without knowing my anxiety over the pound note. The inquisition continued – two – three – four hours, a life time. I sat as though nailed to my seat. Books were taken off the shelves and examined. The agent ordered the soldiers to search behind the holy icona. They turned the furniture over and slit the upholstery. Then they moved the furniture into the middle of the room and tapped the walls. Not one spot escaped inspection.

In a little while, I thought, They will take me out of here to – to prison. My poor sister. She thinks the interrogation is all they came for. She will soon know. At 6 o'clock it was over.

"Get ready to go, now!" came the order.

"Get ready to go where?" my perplexed sister asked. Then she understood. Helplessness and grief clouded her face. She packed my little suitcase. I was allowed to take a tooth-brush, towel, a piece of soap, my doumochka (a tiny pillow), a little sugar and tea.

Sister was ready to hand me the coat when the agent issued the order, "Search the coat." A soldier pulled the tablecloth off, and the other soldier stretched the coat flat. The agent patted the cloth with one hand below the material and the other over it. I was breathless. Involuntarily I rose from my seat. I heard the crunch of the bills. I saw the pin stuck through the cloth. I could not stand it. I closed my eyes.

"ACCORDING TO YOUR FAITH IT WILL BE GIVEN UNTO YOU," said the small voice within me. I believe – I believe – magnify my faith. And though the body still trembled, the soul had thrown off all fear and believed.

"All right, get ready, now!" It seemed to come through a dense fog. Cold sweat trickled down my face. "Get ready, I said! What is the matter with you? Move!" It was 7 o'clock now. The agent was hurrying us.

"Here is your coat, Lisa," said Vala.

"Oh, no! I don't need it. Give me my blue spring coat and the green sweater." But she insisted upon my taking the heavy winter coat. What was I to do? In the last minute commotion, I made her understand that the bills were pinned in the coat, and the pound sterling was in the little box in the drawer. This and the gold watch would be all she would have to live on. I read astonishment in her eyes, and we both knew that miracles still happened. Forgetting the presence of the GPU, we blessed each other, making the large Russian sign of the cross. Vala was crying. "Cheer up, Vala," I said, kissing her. "Remember what happened!" I was escorted downstairs by the soldiers. Frightened faces of the neighbors peeped out of the doors. Some of the bolder ones dared to say, "Come back soon," and gratefully, I smiled at them. On the street I was no longer smiling. "Arrested! Arrested!" beat in my mind. The early February morning was dark and misty. The agent was no longer with us. It began to rain. "Could we hail a cab?" I asked the soldiers.

"Why not take a walk – and here, in the middle of the street," came the mocking answer.

"If it's a walk you want, let's have it!" I answered, boiling inside.

In a few seconds I was so far ahead that the soldiers had to run to catch up to me. Often in my life, when upset I would take a fast walk and it helped to calm me; but this time my indignation grew with every step. Arrested! Arrested! Arrested! How could my office allow this to happen and I thought I was needed.

It was close to 8 a.m. now. The young woman who registered me in the GPU office on Marasli Street looked at me with obvious astonishment. I must have been a sight. I felt my cheeks burning. My eyes probably were popping out. To her routine questions, I answered provokingly. She registered me patiently.

"Follow me!" came the command of a guard. "Sit here!"

In the next room I sat on one of the wooden benches that stood in a row like in a theatre. I tried to collect myself, but the pounding of my heart deafened my senses. More persons were brought in, all looking dazed, some crying. Soon we were led outside and made to climb into a truck. The morning of February 1st was still dull. I wanted to take a deep breath, but instead came a loud sigh. The other prisoners lifted their heads and looked at me. I saw grief on every face. The truck shook and we started on the long ride out of town.

Finally, the truck hopped through a gate and entered the gloomy yard of a large brick building. "Where are we?" I ventured, turning to the man next to me.

"This is the prison for men," he said. Yet all women as well as the men were unloaded.

My second registration took place, but I remember it vaguely. The fatigue was too great, and my eyes refused to see. I remember, though, that after being questioned I was given a large card and told it was a document for my new living quarters in the women's prison. With a small group of prisoners, I was marched under guard toward a building with a red roof that we could see from far away. We passed the cemeteries. Here to the left were Father's and Mother's graves. Had they been alive, how hard it would have been for them to see me now. My head was heavy, my feet dragged. Mechanically I kept in step with the moving group.

A tall hedge surrounded the building with the red roof. There were guards at the gate, then a square yard. Inside, I was taken to an office. There, in a small room, a fair haired man took my card and looked me over. He made me repeat the answers to the questions, though they were all written out on the large grey card I had handed him. Again he looked at me, then at my spring coat. "Isn't that outfit too light for this time of the year?" came the surprisingly sympathetic question.

"No, it isn't really," I answered, a little embarrassed by his concern, remembering the reason I was wearing it.

A tall woman in a dark uniform and men's boots stood by in a waiting attitude, clanking a bunch of keys. I did not see her face as she was looking out of a window with her back to me. "Come on," she said after I was dismissed by the man. Without lifting my eyes I followed her. The keys were now put to work. One door, two doors, three doors were opened and shut. The fourth door resisted. The woman bent down struggling with the tricky lock. It yielded but the door seemed very heavy. I tried to help her, but I could not. I was pushed back by a wave of putrid air, the stench of stagnant garbage – the odor of prison. I was so nauseated I lost my balance. The tall woman gently kept me from falling.

I looked at her. Instinctively I pushed her arm aside. I wished only one thing, to run from her as I did in my childhood. Yet stones seemed to be attached to my feet. I looked at her again. It was the woman who had appeared in my nightmares before every serious sickness of my childhood. The same woman was standing before me now. The doors, the keys, the woman. "Is it true, or is it another nightmare?" I wondered. "No, this time it is not a nightmare."

"Come on," she said, "only two more doors, that's all."

I followed her upstairs to a square hallway with four doors. She opened the door to the left on which was lettered "Political Corridor" and we entered a long, black hall. At its end, the last door closed behind me. I saw a grey prison cell, grey women wrapped in grey shawls, sitting on their bundles against the grey walls. I heard voices questioning me. Something sharp pricked my eyelids, and hot tears rolled down my cheeks.

"Have mercy, please. Let me pull myself together." But my new companions in misery were impatient.

"When did they come to take you?" "How long did the inquisition last?" "What did the GPU agent look like?" "Yes, yes. That was the one who searched my room also," said a round-faced, kindly woman, the most talkative of all. "Is Lisa Kraevsky your name? Of course, of course. Who wouldn't remember your father – a real doctor, a real human being."

I found out that this woman was Tania, a nun imprisoned no doubt for her outspoken opinions of the government. Another was M. S., an elderly homeowner. As a "non-working element," homeowners often were persecuted. A woman with a startlingly beautiful face told me her name was Helena G. She had been head of the city library.

A coarse looking prisoner boastingly told me this was neither her first nor her second imprisonment. She had been arrested this time for insulting a man who turned out to be an important Communist. She asked abruptly, "And what do you think they grabbed you for?"

"I have no idea," I said.

"It must be for the counter-revolution. As one of the offspring of the Russian Nobility, everyone with a face like yours is picked up for that."

Around noon I had an excruciating headache. Everything became meaningless except the pain. The prisoners hovered around me, trying to help. They spread my coat on the floor and I lay down, exhausted. I tried to thank them but was unable to pronounce the words. It was not until around 6 o'clock in the evening that a noise brought me out of my torpor. I heard my name called out. Someone nudged me. "Say present. Say present."

"It is the roll call," the nun said calmly. I saw the tall woman in uniform and two men, one of whom was counting us and checking the names on a large pad.

I was cold and the dampness began to go through me. The cell was dimly lit by one small lamp in the ceiling. Somebody discovered a nest of bedbugs and put a match to it. What a smell. If only I could fall asleep again. My head felt better, but I was very weak. Everyone began to prepare for the night by unrolling the bundles on which they sat. Bedbugs, but no beds, no mattresses, I thought. My companions fixed their beds on the floor as best they could. Where should I sleep? I had nothing but my little pillow. I looked around vaguely, waiting for the others to settle.

"You have nothing to keep you warm," said the nun. "Come here, next to me. My cloak will keep us both comfortable." She beckoned me to her corner where she was spreading a large fur cape. Kindness and love – by these we ascend the Mount and find our human divinity. I was touched not only by Tania's sharing her fur cape, but by her smile and the sweet expression on her face, her half-grieving, half-joking tone. All this moved me deeply, and I slept consoled.

Sleep, the little daily death that takes us away from life and at the same time protects us from it, was interrupted too soon by the prison routine.

"Here is your tea. Come on. Move! Take it!" I heard. Tania and I were next to the door. She rose, took a pail of hot water and some stale bread that were shoved in by a woman whose face was covered with cheap make-up.

"Can I wash up, first?" I timidly asked the woman.

"Wash up! Huh! Maybe you expect a private bath, all for yourself." She banged the door and locked it.

"Who was that woman, Tania?" I asked, "And what time is it?"

"It is five o'clock, my dear. They always wake us up at this hour. Women from the criminal corridor bring the water and our daily ration of bread. This one happens to be particularly rude and noisy."

"I slept so soundly I forgot I was in prison," I said. "Could I have a cup of this hot water now?" Shivering with the cold, I was surprised that none of my fellow prisoners made any attempt to take some.

"Better not. They do not open our door until nine, and hot water stimulates digestion. Nine o'clock in the morning, one o'clock and five o'clock in the evening are the only hours when we are allowed to go out to the washroom."

I understood. "But what do you do with this pail of hot water?" "We take turns and wash ourselves, and still we are eaten by lice."

"Lice!" A lump rose in my throat. What wrong had I done to go through this? I had only worked, worked and worked. Suddenly I remembered the wish I had made not so long ago on one windy, icy morning, going to work: "Let it be worse, only different." Different it was – and worse too. How quickly my wish had been granted.

At nine, twenty minutes were given to wash up, sweep the cell, and scrub the corridor. Turns for these chores were already arranged among the prisoners. We rushed to the washroom, only to find it already occupied by the criminal women. The ladies' room did not yield itself to any description. As I soon found out, here as in any other situation, the criminals had the upper hand. Hastily, we washed ourselves the best we could over the long grey sinks that looked like watering troughs for horses, trying to save five minutes for a stroll in the corridor to limber up. There I got acquainted with other prisoners, and found out there was an empty cell across from ours – a brighter one, from which one could see the entrance gate and, of course, the comings and goings. I told my cell companions about it, and we decided to try to improve our condition. To my surprise, they chose me to speak to the Chief of Prison.

It was amazing how completely this project occupied our minds. "Just think," said one, "the other side is the sunny side, and there is no mildew, no broken window." We let the dream of our future comfort go so far that three hours passed unnoticed before the midday meal of water and pearl barley was brought in. I was beginning to grasp the prison routine.

Soon after, Tania received a package. This meant there was communication with the outside world, I thought. It meant that Vala, my sister, might also come, and I felt the blood rush to my head from hope and expectation. And yet, she might not come. So Vala is here, probably somewhere around the gate, and I cannot even see her because of this cell. I could have, had we been in the opposite cell facing the entrance. How hard it is to satisfy a human being. A few minutes before, by some good fortune I received the package for which I had given up all hope. Now, hardly over my joy, I was already asking for more. But I could not help it.

"I will find my way to the Chief of Prison," I said aloud. "I will speak to him at any cost, and if not today, then tomorrow we shall be transferred to the opposite cell. We must rush while it is vacant."

"Good girl," exclaimed my cell companions, and after this we kept quiet and seemed to retire into ourselves.

At 5 o'clock, the last wash-up, the hastily shoved in dinner of hot water and barley. Then the roll call, after which came a total silence, heavy with the implacability of a hundred locks.

"Open! Open the door, quick! They must be waiting for me downstairs," suddenly rang throughout the corridor in a clear, beautiful, imploring voice. "I shall be late for my concert. Open! Open quick!

I shall be late for my concert. Open! Open!" We could hear the fists helplessly beating against some unyielding door. "The public is waiting for me. I must play tonight. Open! Please open."

"Rica is still hoping, poor child," said Tania.

"Who is Rica? I asked.

"Didn't you notice in the corridor a beautiful blond girl in a black dress? She came here the same night you did."

I remembered the pretty young face in an aureole of light blond hair. How could one help noticing her? Tania told me that the concert of the young pianist was due in the building of the Bourse that night, the second of February. She was arrested the night of the first. All day long she had paced the cell, wringing her hands, expecting to be released in time to play at the concert. She told everybody that the concert had to take place. For more than two weeks the announcements had been hanging all over town and no one could possibly replace her. Again we heard her plead, but after 6 o'clock no one would ever answer a prisoner's call, not even in case of sickness or death. "Please, please open – only half an hour is left. I must play tonight! Open! Open."

After this, all we heard was sobs.

The next morning everyone in the cell was unusually quiet. I noticed an intense expression of sadness on each face. "What happened to all of you? Are you sick?"

"Nothing at all. Nothing at all," said the librarian authoritatively.

I felt they were hiding something from me and finally the tough girl, the recidivist (repeater), broke the news. "Three women from cell number nineteen were taken after midnight to be shot, and you were the only one who slept through this night."

Indeed, by some sublime mercy I slept. I was spared the experience. I slept warm and cozy in Tania's homey pelisse while three persons – Oh, how horrible! No court. No way to protect themselves.

My mind, clear after the solid sleep, was ready to face reality. These women were arrested, put in prison, and now they had been shot. What had they done? I had been arrested and imprisoned. Was there anything I had done for which I could be killed? I did not feel guilty in any way. Unable to find an answer, and inclined to optimism, I dismissed these dark thoughts making myself believe there had been a mistake, and that one of these mornings I would be free again.

At this moment a pleasant voice reached us, and kind blue eyes sparkled from behind our little barred window. "You girls, do you need something? Aspirin? Laxatives?" This was the nurse on her tour through the prison. My cellmates needed all they could get, and the nurse in white uniform entered our cell like a sunbeam. "Is there a certain Lisa Kraevsky among you?" she asked.

"I am Lisa Kraevsky," I answered, happy that this lovely woman was inquiring about me.

"Odessky sends you his regards. I visit him in the Seamen's Hospital. He speaks highly of you."

"Thank you for passing his regards to me, nurse. And how is the poor old man?"

"Not too good. Not too good." Before leaving, her glance lingered on me and I felt her sympathy. Dear Odessky. He had heard about my arrest and wished to cheer me up. I had to wipe my eyes.

That day, returning from our walk, we came across the man who was first to check me into the prison and who had sympathetically inquired about the thinness of my coat. The Chief! The Chief of the prison. Here he is! Hurry up! In a split second I was beside him, presenting my request politely, but firmly. "There is an empty cell opposite ours, Tovarisht Chief, with no broken windows. Please do not refuse to grant us permission to be transferred there." Seemingly perplexed at my simplicity, he consented, copying something of my own manner. What a triumph! Everybody rejoiced. On the staircase Tania embraced me, almost knocking me off my feet with her weight. The cell across the corridor was brighter and warmer. From the window we could see the yard, the gate, and even the street. Tomorrow, I thought, I might see my sister, and planned to put my green sweater in the window for a signal.

We had started to settle in our new quarters when the lock sang its song and two new prisoners were brought in. One was old, almost decrepit. She sank to the floor with a deep sigh. The other was a young, red-cheeked country girl, full of health and strength. The old woman looked at us with eyes longing for sympathy, and between deep sighs, complained "Just think! No sooner did I manage to settle on my wooden box than that devilish truck jerked and I fell feet up in the air, hurting the back of my head terribly, terribly! Oh, it hurts – it hurts so." She pointed to the sore spot. "It hurts. Nobody helped me up. I lay there all the time. Such people, now-a-days. Such people..."

It was one of those tragi-comic cases, and the way and the accent in which the old Jewish lady presented it made it difficult for us to keep straight faces. "What kind of people, now-a-days? They almost killed me to death – no respect – no respect for the old age. How could they treat an old woman like that? A mother of three magnificent sons!"

I went to the pail of water, filled a cup, and after soaking my handkerchief, applied it to her bruise. Her tense expression was replaced by gratitude. "My name is Mrs. Broochis. And what is name, Barishnia?"

"Lisa."

"Married or not?"

"No, I am not."

"Well, God will send you a good fiancé you will see." A few minutes later she was ready to sleep and I covered her carefully with her old plush coat, wondering what could possibly have caused her to land in prison.

Then, my eyes turned to the other newcomer. Her name was Luba. She was caught on the Rumanian frontier, she said, trying to cross the border with a forged passport. She showed no emotion. She was very silent, obviously having no desire to talk.

During the roll call, Mrs. Broochis awakened and answered to her name. Then to our amazement, she spoke indignantly to the prison officials: "Putting an old lady, the mother of three magnificent sons, in prison! No respect. No respect at all!" Her voice rose – "What if I did sell some French powder and perfume and some silk stockings? Tell me not to do it, and I don't. Why should you drag me to prison? Why should you drag an old person to prison? Wait until my sons hear about it. They'll get me out of here, and quick!" When the officials were gone we complimented her on her courage. This pleased her greatly. Her remarks, intermingled with complaints, sparkled with humor. She was a good sport and from the first day endeared herself to us.

It was night. Everything was calm in our new cell. I was about to doze off when Mrs. Broochis called me. "Lisochka, Lisochka! Tuck me in with my plush coat, please." Trying not to disturb Tania, who had already begun to snore, I got up and covered Mrs. Broochis gently. "You will find yourself a lovely fiancé as soon as you are out of here, Lisochka. You will see."

"All right. All right, Mrs. Broochis. Thank you. Good night, dear," I whispered.

One morning all the prisoners of the Political Corridor were gathered into a large room for a lecture that, we were told, would clarify our situation. The lecture was given by a lawyer who told us we were suspected of being counter-revolutionaries. We could expect, he said, penalties ranging from three months imprisonment to capital punishment. It took time for me to realize that my imprisonment was not just a mistake. The putrid air, lack of hygiene, insufficient food, sleeping on the floor – these were the outer discomforts, more tolerable than the inner ones. Worst of all was the uncertainty.

Uncertainty! What for, how long, and why? Months of prison, forced labor, capital punishment, or freedom?

Uncertainty! Complete isolation from the outer world. The guessing, guessing and guessing at what might happen to you and your companions, while night after night, at the gruesome after-midnight hour someone was called out of her cell for the only certain thing – death.

Uncertainty! Fear before uncertainty. Its incessant gnawing. How adroitly it succeeded in shaking human nerves. How it robbed us of what is most needed by all – sleep.

When a doomed prisoner was to be called at night, the officials first visited every cell on the corridor except hers, stopping at each grille and asking in a low voice, so that the occupants of the neighboring cells couldn't catch the name, "Is Tovarisht so-and-so here?" By the time they reached the victim's cell the entire corridor had been aroused and there was no question of further sleep.

One night, after I had been in prison two weeks, our silent Luba's name was called. The lock creaked and she was ordered out. "May I take my things?" she asked.

"No!" answered a voice from the darkness.

"No!" repeated the echo of the Political Corridor.

"Are they going to kill her?" I asked. "They told her not to take her things along." "Capital punishment," confirmed a toneless voice.

I did not close my eyes. My thinking was intense and clear. I made up my mind that even if I had only one more day to live. I would live it the very best I knew.

Next day my energy was increased. I took charge. The loss of Luba, our companion, had a desolating effect on us, and I felt that I should try to pull the girls out of the marshes of melancholy. With this intention I gave them a talk (a friend later remarked that this must have been the beginning of my public speaking career). I told them about my night's reflections and about my decision, and succeeded in lifting the general spirit. We began to plan our common activities. Calisthenics, I thought, would do us good. "We shall rust if we don't exercise," I said. This remark was taken quite seriously, and right away we cleared a small space in the middle of the floor. One by one, encouraged by me, the girls stretched and kicked the best they could.

In a few days we had our personal routine well outlined: time for silence or prayer, time for exercise, time for general discussion about possible improvement of our existence, and also an hour for story-telling and laughter. We had to search our memories for something really funny, embarrassing or interesting. We became the envy of the other prisoners who, hearing our merriment, would ask next morning in the washroom, "What was there for you to be so happy about last night?" However, on the days for receiving packages, sadness would settle down on us, but we strived together to banish it. Newcomers were arriving daily. Now we were fourteen in a cell meant for two. Sleeping flat on our backs became impossible, and in order to have room for all we had to sleep on one side only, tight, very tight against each other. Still the spirit of our cell was that of courage and little complaining.

One morning I was called for the "inquiry" which meant an eye to eye talk with an agent of the GPU. I had no sense of guilt, and the reason why I was considered a political enemy of the state was unknown to me until this interview. From the first words of the young agent, it became clear that my correspondence with other countries has aroused suspicions. The agent acted as if I was highly guilty of some grave crime. I tried to explain to him that my correspondence with my schoolmates in Switzerland, France, and other countries was innocent, as anyone who censored my letters would know. I said that all my correspondence was done openly, and that I would be most obliged to him if at least one of the doubtful letters could be shown to me. I enumerated the names of all my foreign friends. I mentioned that many masters of foreign ships who met me on my job sent me postal cards with their regards, not only to the office, but often to my home, though I did not know how they obtained my address.

There was nothing threatening in the agent's manner. He listened to me attentively and our conversation was flowing smoothly until he asked, "How did it happen that in 1922 your mother was hiding such a suspicious character as Mr. R. from Switzerland?"

"How can you say such things about my Mother? You are terribly misinformed, Tovarisht. After the death of my father, the Soviet officials practically forced my Mother to rent Father's office to a man well known to them and absolutely unknown to her. All she could do was obey their order. Now that person is suspicious, you say. It was no fault of ours, especially not of my Mother. How could she have known anything about him?" Composed while the questions concerned me alone, at the mention of my Mother's name I lost control and wept.

"What is the matter with you? Why are you crying?" asked the puzzled agent.

"You should not have said that about my Mother!" I sobbed. "You should not !"

The black eyes of the agent were round with astonishment. "You better go back to your cell," he said softly.

Most probably these tears had needed release for some time and I cried for a long while in my cell, thinking only of Mother. My cell companions were upset by my tears, and in trying to assure them that nothing was drastically wrong, I somehow calmed myself down.

Soon after Luba's doom, a whole cell of Zionist girls, about six, intelligent and bold youngsters (who all stoically had gone through a seven day hunger strike) were sent to be on the Caucasus. Arrests were continuing. We all were sitting and waiting, dreaming about freedom. Every time the bolts were drawn, the heart would stop and the body tremble with an inner chill.

The second interrogation soon came. It was in the same vein. Obviously the purpose of the agent was to persuade me that I had committed some sinister political crime. The harder he tried, the more I resisted. I told him about my innocence and devoted work in the office of the Soviet Mercantile Fleet, to which I had given all my ability and energy; how in the evenings when we had no overtime work I rushed home to give lessons in foreign languages; and how precious for me were the few moments when I could sit down to read and answer the letters from my friends all over the world. I knew this agent believed every word I said. I felt his sympathy, his desire to set me free, if only it were in his power. I also had a feeling that I was being treated with more courtesy than others, for some unknown reason.

"What were your relations with Tovarisht Fursoff?" was his sudden question.

"Fursoff, you said? One of our Soviet fleet employees? I would be inclined to say none, none whatsoever."

"But you, yourself – have you anything against him? You, personally?"

"Nothing at all, really. Let me see – once he aroused my indignation by one of his actions – but then it was all forgotten."

"Now you do not hold any grudges against him at all?"

"No. I have dismissed him from my thinking." I thought I had, but I knew different the moment I returned to my cell. Fursoff, Fursoff – why was the agent asking me about him and nobody else? Fursoff, Fursoff – and the whole incident was resurrected, unrolling in my memory like a film.

At that time our foreign office was connected with the headquarters agency of the Soviet Mercantile Fleet. One morning we finished dispatching a boat which had taken more than fifty days to come from Argentina. For months the mail had accumulated, and when the ship finally reached our harbor I was happy to hand an immense pack of letters to Fursoff, our outside clerk, for delivery to the crew. Ten days later, when the ship had been cleared and was being piloted out of the harbor, more mail arrived and I rushed to Fursoff's desk, begging him to try to get a motorboat or tug to deliver these letters. The lower drawer of his desk happened to be open, and while speaking to him, I was horrified to see in it the whole pack of letters.

"Fursoff! Fursoff!" I screamed. "What is this? Why weren't these letters delivered?"

"None of your business!" he said, without looking at me.

"What do you mean, 'none of my business?' Look at me Fursoff! Don't you know these seamen had a fifty-six day crossing? Don't you know how anxious they are for news from their homes? Don't you know that?"

"This-is-none-of-your-business!" he said, clenching his teeth. "Look after your own work and keep quiet so that no fault will be found with it."

"Enough of that!" I shouted at the top of my voice, hitting the table with my fist so that all the papers flew up in the air. "I shall answer for my own mistakes, if any, but you – answer me right now! Why? Why? Why didn't you deliver these letters? You are inhuman, and your negligence unpardonable!"

It was clear to this coarse man that my actions seemed unpardonable, not his. In the silence of the prison's night, the angry face of this former workman in the American slaughter house appeared before me. Like a flash it entered my mind: Fursoff was the cause of my arrest.

After a month of insufficient sleep, inadequate and poor food, foul air, and isolation from the outer world, I caught a cold, followed by an excruciating toothache. I had gone to see a dentist just before my imprisonment, and he had started to treat the root of my tooth. This tooth now began to hurt intolerably. Soon the cheeks swelled and the pain increased. In vain I wrote one request after another for permission to visit a dentist.

I thought I would lose my mind and the nights were torture. Crowded together as we were, I was afraid to move, afraid to sigh, lest I wake up the whole row; and grabbing my knees tightly with both hands, I sat silent though the pain made me feel like howling. One night when the pain was at its worst, a sob tore itself out of my chest.

"Oh, Lord, why am I here?"

"You do not know why you are here?" I heard the voice of the most respected and educated of our companions, the librarian, Helen G.

Exhausted as I was, I could only look at her with astonishment. Could she possibly be mocking me?

"You do not know why?" she repeated. "What would we do without you? You are a Godsend to us."

Coming from her, these words gave me courage, somehow lifted me up. Even my toothache became more bearable, and soon merciful sleep returned to me. Gradually I began to feel better. The dentist was called to the prison and removed the cotton plug from the root of my tooth. The kind nurse tried to take care of my sore throat, though the inflammation and temperature persisted.

Around this time, because of a shortage of hands in the workshop for women, we, the politicals, were sent to make shoe boxes together with the criminals, thieves, murderesses, and procurers. The lack of workers occurred because recently a large number of prostitutes had been sent north to the Solvietsky Cloisters, from which the monks had just been expelled.

Our delight over something to do outside our cell was great at first, but the constant foul language of the criminal women soon became unbearable, and the avalanche of lice that fell from their sleeves at every move was far from improving our living conditions. After getting a little acquainted with us, some criminals began to show respect and force the others to guard their language. Two of them, one a thief and one a murderess, took a special liking to me and often at their own risk tried to be helpful. Pasha, the thief, would sneak into our corridor with a bite of spicy herring, cucumber or pickle, and hurriedly pass it through the bars, stipulating that it was for me, alone.

Early one cold afternoon in March I was called out with four other women from our corridor. A soldier escorted us to the men's prison, quite a distance from ours. It was nearly three o'clock, and the day packages were delivered. Sister Vala was standing by the gate with one for me. Joy and sorrow were never so close as they were when we looked into each other's eyes. Yet both of us had the presence of mind to restrain our emotions, so much so that the soldier didn't even suspect we were acquainted. As we prisoners began to move forward, Vala followed just as a casual passerby. I made sure she could hear me as I asked the guard "Tovarishy, are we going to the men's prison for an inquiry?"

He grumbled something in reply, but Vala already understood, and turning her head away from me, she began to sing on a very high note in French, "I shall wait – I shall wait – I shall wait until you come out of the men's prison."

The men's prison was even more depressing than ours; no wooden floors as we had, cement everywhere, black iron staircases, and high above our heads were black iron bridges connecting one side of the building with the other. We all stood quiet. My heart was throbbing. I remembered the young agent had said that he would pass my case to a higher official, and I was afraid.

A short middle-aged man with a hard square face called out my name and I followed him into a room that must have belonged to one of the wardens, with upholstered chairs, rugs on the cement floor and on the walls. We sat down at a table. "My name is Beltchenko," he said with surprising gallantry, "and I have good news for you, Elizaveta Antonovna. (Elizaveta Antonova – Elizaveta – daughter of Anton – the customary polite way of addressing acquaintances.) Suavely, he continued: "I have wanted to know you for quite some time. I have heard so much of you. Too bad your correspondence with foreign countries played you a bad trick, but believe me I am here to help you." He smiled to put me at ease, asked about a lot of prisoners, and seemed genuinely concerned over our less than primitive comfort. In spite of this I felt something unpleasant was coming and hardened myself to meet it. "No doubt you know that there is, outside the fact of being noble class, a whole series of accusations and adequate evidence against you, some of it extremely serious," he continued. "My mission is to help you."

"Thank you. You must know, then, that my correspondence is perfectly innocent."

"I couldn't put my signature to that. I know you are in great danger because of your correspondence."

"I simply refuse to believe it," I said. "I want proof of my guilt."

"Please do not get excited. It will not help. Just listen to me and try to understand. All your guilt will be forgotten and you will be free, if you consent to work for us."

"Work for you! What have I been doing? You certainly know that for years I have been working for the Soviet Mercantile Fleet, giving it all my attention and all my strength."

"Who is speaking of office work? I offer you a much more interesting position with us, and a very well paid one, too. With your knowledge of languages we could even send you abroad as our representative."

A shiver went through me.

"You see, we have watched you for many years," he went on in the most friendly way. "We have studied the effect of your personality on others. There is not another man or woman in the city who could instill such confidence, such total trust, as you do. Foreigners believe every word you say. You have unusual qualities, Elizaveta Antonovna, most valuable ones, and we are offering you a chance to use them for your own life's sake."

"I am willing to carry out any kind of honorable, open work."

"There is no reason to play hide and seek. You understand only too well what I mean. All you have to do is give your consent."

"I tell you that according to my nature I could not carry out any secret work whatever."

"Nonsense. You can't even imagine what future awaits you. With time, we anticipate sending you abroad, as I mentioned before, where you, with your qualities, will be much more popular than Mme. Kolontay. Just think what an honor we bestow upon you in spite of your guilt."

"Guilt! I have none. I have always worked energetically and happily and I expect to continue to do the same. But I could never carry out secret work."

"Of course, if you are not going to do it willingly, we know how to approach you differently."

"No matter how you approach me, Tovarisht Beltchenko, I definitely know now that your intention is to make a spy out of me, and that I would never be."

"You are being obstinate and for no reason whatsoever. You are not free, remember. You are accused of counterrevolution. You may even get capital punishment."

"I demand concrete proof of my guilt."

"You know your guilt. There is no use even to discuss it. We are through for today. Return to your cell where you will have ample time to think of the advantages of my offer. You will be called again and I warn you, no more obstinacy."

I left the false comfort of that room with a leaden weight in my heart. Outside, our little group of women lined up to return. Again, like a total stranger, Vala stood at a little distance from the gate, and when we began to march she was ahead of us, stepping forward arm in arm with another woman.

We prisoners began to exchange our impressions. I was walking in the first pair and was telling my companion, trying to make my sister hear every word, "Today a new agent by the name of Beltchenko questioned me." Then in French, "Il me force de devenir espionne. Qu'en penses-tu?" (He forces me to become a spy. What would you say?) I was testing her.

"Oh, mon Dieu, jamais!" (Oh, my Lord, never!) I heard the answer from my sister and I rejoiced that she thought as I did. Thus, unnoticed by anyone, she kept encouraging me in French, saying that she was doing her utmost to get me out of prison, imploring me to take care of myself.

"Ne t'inquiete pas, je suis calme. Pense a ta sante. Pense a toi," I chanted at the top of my voice. ("Don't worry about me. I am calm. Take care of your health. Think of yourself.")

Falling asleep that night, I prayed and the lead in my heart melted in the flame of my decision before God and myself, never to become a spy.

Day after day I expected the call of Tovarisht Beltchenko, but he seemed to be in no hurry.

Now more prisoners were crowding the already over-filled prison. The dark cells opposite ours were occupied by a flock of farmer women, arrested because of a valiant fight for their church bells, in which a communist had been killed. It had happened as a result of the order to take down all the church bells throughout Russia – from the church steeple direct to the foundry for metal. This operation, so painful to Russian people, was accomplished with fewer outbursts in the large cities than in the country among the peasants, who in some cases protested and then paid heavily for it. The anguish of the peasant women kept in our prison for investigation while their entire families were banished to the North, old and young dying en route of cold and hunger, was indescribable. It affected us profoundly. A beautiful young peasant, with blond hair and brown eyes, soon after hearing of the death of her baby, received news of the death of her second child, a five year old boy. Not a tear came from her eyes, but for days she did not move, utter a word, or eat. For others, many of them illiterate, we wrote petitions and letters, so many in fact we often had no time to wash up.

In those days the nurse, our "ray of sunshine," looked worn as she passed by our cell. We found out that one of the prisoners was about to give birth and that the nurse had spent several nights with her. The night before the baby was born, the mother almost lost her life, but with the nurse's attentive care, two healthy twin girls were born. There was nothing to wrap them in. We gathered up old towels, bits of material, handkerchiefs, and gave them to the nurse. The following day the grandmother of the twins came, with tears of gratitude, to thank us.

With Tovarisht Beltchenko's ignoble proposition constantly in the back of my mind, I had a nightmare. I saw his stubborn, square head, growing larger and larger by the second as it came closer and closer to me, uttering the decree of capital punishment. Next morning the girls said I cried out in my sleep, "Faith, faith! More faith!" – but

I did not remember. In spite of cold, toothache, and sharing the peasants' heartbreak, my morale stayed high while waiting for Tovarisht Beltchenko's summons.

"I am sure you bring me good news," were Tovarisht Beltchenko's first words of forced amiability. He smiled, not with his eyes, and his head really seemed squarer than before. "I gave you enough time to decide to use your good qualities for your own benefit."

"I consider these good qualities, if it be true that I have them, as a gift of God, and I am not going to sell them to you."

He jerked angrily, but quickly returned to his feigned placidity. "Who speaks of God? Quite old-fashioned for a young person. Quite middle-class for one so highly educated. It is about time to make it clear to you that I am giving you the chance to save yourself."

"I decline your offer."

"You are too hasty, Elizaveta Antonova. You may regret it."

"I am not hasty, but you, Tovarisht Beltchenko, are slow to understand. I am not fit for that kind of work. I will not spy on anyone, friend or stranger. 'No' is my answer." I got up.

"Wait now! Give it a second thought." His tone was harsh. His voice was hoarse. His poise was gone. I looked at him to make sure it was the same man. Yes, it was. His expression had become hard. "Better accept my offer now."

I did not reply.

"Now!"

"No." I was very calm. My decision was growing in strength. His face turned red with anger.

"For the last time, I advise you to accept my offer."

I managed to smile as though forgiving him his lack of understanding.

"Go back to your cell," was his terse order. "In three days from now at noon, you will report your 'yes' through the Chief of Prison. If not, blame yourself for the drastic changes that will occur." All his feigned gallantry had faded.

I was the only one called out to the men's prison that afternoon and now was the only one returning with a silent guard at my side. It was Friday – a day of no delivery of packages. The street was empty and quiet, the air invigorating, the snow sparkling. I started to hum an old Russian lyric, "My Soul is White as Snow," but then reproached myself for such sentimentality. Think of the 'drastic changes' passed through my mind. Instantly, fear attacked my whole being: SOLITARY CONFINEMENT – RATS SWARMING IN THE DARK – EATING ON MY FLESH! Suddenly there was no more sun, no more snow. Darkness fell a frightful darkness, until an authoritative voice shouted in me, "Afraid! You ARE afraid! You are a COWARD after all. Maybe you PREFER to be a spy?" Again I saw the white snow. Head high, shoulders straight, I walked ahead. Fear and self-pity disappeared. Never, never, never was the rhythm of my steps.

To our right was a white church. If only I could enter it, fall on my knees and give thanks for the renewal of my courage. We passed it, and now on our left were cemeteries – only cemeteries – the Catholic, the Lutheran, the Greek Orthodox. The last one, where my parents rested, was just opposite our women's prison. Many, many times, day or night, I knelt in spirit before the simple iron crosses bearing their names.

The fetid prison air again! I could not get accustomed to it. I rushed to my cell. In it was more than friendliness. There was love that transformed it almost into a home. I kept the sad news of our approaching separation to myself. Saturday and Sunday with them, I thought, and until Monday at noon. I fell asleep rather early. In the middle of the night I woke up. My tooth was throbbing and my throat was sore. Luckily, in the morning the dentist called me.

"Your tooth will be all right soon," he said, before dismissing me, "but watch your throat. It is in bad condition. Gargle with salt and water and don't work in the shop on Monday."

Thus the morning was gone, then the day. Again, I tucked Mrs. Broochis into her worn out plush coat. That night I hardly listened to her never-changing prophecy of a wonderful fiancé. I only thought of her, who would have to do without me soon. Once she had told me that her only happy moments were when I was bidding her good night. During that night the unwelcome visitor, fear, tried to possess me. If I dozed off for a while, a nervous jerk of my feet awakened me.

Sunday came, white and bright, with snow clinging to the naked branches as if trying to warm them. Every time I thought of the unpleasant insinuations of "Square Face," the cell became dearer and dearer to me. I looked at my companions, my new friends. I loved them all. I wanted to comfort them before leaving.

At 3 o'clock, Vala was waiting at the prison gate. Next to her I recognized old Zina, standing on her sore, swollen feet. It was her second visit, and God knows it was not easy for her to come. Vala handed two packages to the guard. Then, returning to her post at our window, she bowed low three times – the signal that meant that all was well. "Poor dear," I thought. "She tries hard to hasten my liberation, but no human being can help a political prisoner in Soviet Russia. She will be in panic when she comes next time and does not see my green sweater in the window. She will run from one prison to the other but – but where shall I be? Will she be able to find me?" Lost in reflection, I pressed my forehead against the cold window pane and saw her leave – smiling, waving, suspecting nothing.

Sonia, a newcomer and a former jewelry shop owner, was crying. For the first time she had seen her two little children at the prison gate. Someone in the corridor was sobbing.

"Lisa, you do not seem to be quite yourself," whispered Helena.

How wonderful it would be to share my anxiety with her. She could console me, approve of me, maybe – but better no softness, no pity. "I am all right, dear Helena Vladimirovna," I said, "really I am. But that tooth hurts again."

She looked at me still questioning, unconvinced.

Strangely enough, I had a most restful sleep again. On Monday morning the girls went to the workshop and I, by order of the dentist, was left alone in the tidied-up cell. I was alone for the first time in two weeks; how I needed this solitude. I looked around to make sure it was true, and saw nothing but fourteen neat bundles silently staring at me.

"Monday, Monday at noon you will report your consent through the Chief of Prison."

Yes, yes. The Chief was around last night. He also spoke to us early this morning. Could it be that he expected something from me when he said, "Are there any reports today?" Somehow at that moment I did not put two and two together. I saw it now; but I would not waver. I wanted to pray. I went to the part of the cell where no eye could see me. I prayed first like a child, the way I had in school, repeating all the prayers I knew. I prayed for fortitude, strength and health. I spoke to the Lord as to a father, asking Him to stand by me, to protect me, to love me. My spirit rose high and higher, to the realm where there is no injustice, no prison, no anxiety, no fear.

I came back to reality refreshed and full of joy unknown before. As I walked toward the window, on top of one bundle, I noticed a Bible that belonged to one of the girls, an evangelist. The urge to take it in my hands, to hold it tight, was overwhelming. I opened it at random and read: "Fear thou not, for I am with thee. Be not dismayed, for I am thy God, I will strengthen thee. Yea, I will uphold thee with the right hand of my righteousness ....For I, the Lord thy God will hold thy right hand, saying unto thee, fear not; I will help thee." (Isaiah XXXXI, 10-13) Again and again I read these words. Having been brought up on the New Testament I had never come across these lines before; and it seemed to me as though God Himself had answered, promising His help.

The girls returned from the workshop. "It was dull without you," said one. "Even the criminals missed you, and Pasha promised to bring you half of a pickle."

"How nice of her. I wish she would hurry," I said, hoping to have it in time.

"You look so rested and well," said Sonia.

"I feel very well, Sonichka, thank you."

A half hour later the Chief came and ordered me out. Energetically I began to pack, leaving some of my belongings and my food to the girls.

"Tovarisht Kraevsky! Do you understand I am not calling you out for freedom?"

"I know, I know, Tovarisht," I answered.

"Then why are you beaming?"

"Do I beam? Oh well, my heart is light, Tovarisht." My eyes met his, and I read sympathy in them. Ever since the day I entered this prison I had felt some kindness in him. Yet, outwardly, just as now, he acted sternly.

"Hurry. Hurry! Enough lingering. Get done with it, and quickly." Consideration pierced through his severity when he added, "And do stop this generosity. You might need every bit of it yourself."

"Goodbye, my dear ones. Goodbye. My how he rushes me. I have no time even to kiss you. Do not forget to exercise. Cheer up, now. Cheer up!"

But everyone had a long face, and some were crying. Helping me in that mad rush, no one said a word, and I heard Helena say, "Thank you for all that you did for us, Lisa. God bless you."

From the locked cells on my way through the corridor, I heard voices: "Doswidania, doswidania, put dobriy." which means, "Goodbye, goodbye," and then something like, "happy road."

"Where do they take you, Lisa?" shouted someone.

"We wish you luck. Goodbye, goodbye!"

I certainly had made friends. I seemed to fit in here, I thought, smiling to myself; and only then, I remembered that my moving was not such a happy occasion. But I was not afraid.

I followed the Chief into his little office. As he gave me my documents, he said most kindly, "We learned to like you, Tovarisht Lisa." He looked at me, and I noticed a nervous twitch in his lower lip. Later in life I forgot much of the cruelty and injustice that came my way, but never could I forget any expression of human kindness, and memories of these remain in my heart and bring tears to my eyes to this day.

My bundle, with a blanket, a pillow, and some other things Vala kept sending, had grown heavy. It was not easy to grip, and I dropped it repeatedly while crossing the yard. This time, the Chief himself took me to the other prison. The gate opened and closed. I stopped for a moment and looked back. In the window of my cell, the hands of my companions were waving like a flock of frightened birds.

"Come on," said the Chief.

I stepped ahead. It was so easy to walk. What had happened to my bundle? I looked around and it was on the shoulder of the Chief. The moment we passed through the gate, the kind man must have picked it up, and now was carrying it, stepping behind me.

"Tovarishtl" I exclaimed. "It is too heavy. I really can carry it myself."

"I am sorry I could not relieve you of it in the yard, but you understand there were too many eyes watching."

In the men's prison yard the large truck was waiting. "Thank God it is not the Black Raven," I thought (a black, closed car operating mostly at night, of which we were much afraid), but it was the same huge truck that had brought me two months ago. Many people were squeezed in it already, the majority being men, as usual. I climbed in it with ease in spite of its height, due to our prison calisthenics, I suppose, and almost fell into the arms of Rica, the most beloved young girl in our corridor (the pianist). She looked like a little fairy fallen into the midst of a group of sad looking, mostly unshaven prisoners. Beautiful, young, her cheeks blooming, her golden hair glistening in the sun, she embraced me.

"Lisochka! Thank God you are here! I hope they will not separate us.

What a surprise!" We both rejoiced over our good fortune.

"How cheerful you are. And both so handsome," observed a middle-aged man, distinguished even in his degradation and exhaustion, "How did you manage to preserve your 'joie de vivre?" he asked.

"We are happy over our meeting," answered Rica.

The truck rumbled over the wooden bar across the gateway of the prison. We were ordered to crouch down on the floor of the truck, where Rica and I held fast to each other. The soldier guards towered over us.

"I am afraid," said Rica, "I'm afraid we are turning to the railroad station. That means exile to the Far North. We shall die there."

"Wait, we don't know yet," I said.

"How is it that you are so calm? I shiver all over."

"Do not worry," whispered the man with the pale, aristocratic face, "Prisoners doomed for the North are loaded only at night or daybreak."

Everyone was quiet again. I managed to peep out. The railroad station was left behind and we were entering Marazlievskaya Street, unmistakably heading for the headquarters of the GPU. When back from France we had lived on this street in the house of Giburt Giburtavich. From here, Father left us to go to the front in the First World War.

Rica's eyes were closed. "Cheer up, Rica. Cheer up," I said. "We are still in Odessa by the Black Sea, not by the White Sea."

The truck pulled up to the back entrance of the GPU building. Inside we waited, all crowded under the staircase. A man, or rather a shadow of a man, led by two guards, passed by us. My heart tightened with pity.

Suddenly he looked up, and I recognized the pale, drawn face of a former lieutenant of the Imperial Navy, my co-worker in the American's Student Relief under Edgar MacNaughton.

The women prisoners were led to a very large, low-ceiling basement room. There were beds and at first it looked much more comfortable than the cell I had left. Questions, as usual, poured on us.

"Is Marussia I., still in the other prison?" "And how about Nina D.?" "And Anna S.?"

"How long did you stay there? Almost two months? It means that you are being brought here to speed your case. You'll see, you will be questioned very, very often," said one.

"Not necessarily," said another, "I was transferred here for that purpose, yet once I was here, they forgot all about me."

"Well, maybe you are an exception," said the first.

My eyes stopped on a delicate, Madonna-like face. "How beautiful you are," I exclaimed.

"Not any more," she said, "Not after my sickness. For three weeks I was in the hospital of the prison you just came from. It was better there. The air was good and the people kinder, I didn't want to come back here."

"And we are happy to be here," said Rica. "We expected something much worse."

"It would be hard to imagine anything worse than this. The smoke is so thick that sometimes we have to lie flat on our stomachs to let it pass over us through the open top of the window."

"But at least you have beds."

"We have beds, but none are vacant."

"Never mind," said Rica. "I have a little mattress. I shall share it with Lisa."

"One can see you are not too difficult to please," said the first, winking to her companion.

"There would be no use of complaining," answered my fair-haired Rica.

Rica and I were gradually adjusting ourselves. I wondered if these were the conditions "Square Face" was threatening me with. It was not worse, but better. The washrooms were modern, larger and cleaner, no criminals to rush us, the walking time twenty minutes, not fifteen, and not in a dusty, barbed-wire circle, but in a small, well-kept private garden which, surrounded by tall buildings, attracted all the sun like a hot house. Now, early in April, some leaves and delicate buds were breaking through the earth. From this garden, we could see between two buildings the gilded cupolas of the Church of the Trinity, which our family attended while living in this neighborhood. The room itself was like four of our prison cells, with six beds against one wall and six opposite, and a passage between where Rica and I were sleeping, unrolling her little mattress every night. True, there was much less air and much less light, but at that stage we were enjoying the novelty of the change. The other inmates often said we had brought them much needed gaiety and animation.

There were drawbacks. Deliveries were rare and the checking of each article was more strict – bread sent from home was cut in pieces, meatballs, also. We could write only one phrase acknowledging receipt of a package. But the worst was the total impossibility of seeing our dear ones from this basement cell, buried at the end of a yard inaccessible for them. The window of our basement was set deep in a cement pit, only its upper part being above the level of the large, stone yard. No ray of sunlight entered.

I was anxious to hear from Vala. Would she be able to find me? On the fourth day a package came from her and one from Rica's family. We celebrated the occasion by giving a surprise performance for our fellow prisoners. Even the soldier guard admired our improvisational medieval costumes. Rica wore white pantaloons and black stockings with bows made out of strips of rags at her knees and on her shoes. For the dance, she held in her hands an old flat basket instead of a hat. I had a blanket gathered around my neck, forming a ruff, and falling in a long train. In these outfits we danced an old-fashioned minuet to Mozart's melody, singing in two voices. This was a big success. Then I told some humorous stories that I had well-practiced on my former companions. A few duets were sung, and the waltz from the "Merry Widow" was danced, with everyone participating. The guards took turns looking through the peephole in our door, which could be opened only on their side, amused by the goings on. They had no objection, only asking us not to make too much noise.

With all this, we were far from forgetting sad reality. When the others were asleep, Rica told me her story. She was suspected of being a Trotzkyite. About half a year before her arrest, a former school friend asked permission to leave a printing press with her as he had no place for it in the tiny room into which he had just moved. Rica, whose father was a well-known architect, lived in comfortable quarters. She was only nineteen years old, and without giving the matter another thought, graciously consented to accommodate her friend. This must have been reported to the GPU, because one night their agents searched her room and found the Trotzkitie's secret press. In spite of her obvious innocence and the fact that she was scheduled to appear as soloist at a great concert, she was arrested. An artist at heart, the concert she was forced to miss seemed to be her greatest misfortune. At that point of the story, she gave in and cried.

I was trying to console her when the door was noisily unlocked, startling us and waking everyone up. "Tovarisht Kraevsky! Get dressed for the questioning. And no lingering!"

"Now? In the middle of the night?"

"Dress, Lisa," whispered the girl whose bed was nearest to our mattress. "Do not ask him any questions. We will tell you all about it."

I trembled all over. I did not know what to do first. "Wash your face," someone said. "You will feel better."

"Take your time, Lisa," another advised. "Look decent. It helps sometimes."

LOOK DECENT? I had only one blue dress. How glad I was that I had washed my white collar the day before. Rica kept quiet, shivering more than I did. They were all sympathizing. "Lisa, tell him about the smoke. Tell him we cannot live like this."

"Be brave," said the Madonna-like girl.

A narrow, steep staircase led out of the basement.

"Not so fast," said the guard.

In front of me stretched a huge, dark yard. Something cold touched the back of my neck and I tried to brush it off. "Hands down!" shouted the soldier, and the cold metal was pressed harder against my flesh. The yard left behind, the gate opened, and spring air filled my lungs. Only one whiff of it, and we turned and walked up the luxurious marble staircase of the former private mansion that had become the GPU offices. At the top of the staircase the soldier left me and I entered a well-lit and comfortable office. There was the scent of fine perfume. The office girl walked out and the – Oh! That one again! "Square Face," my "benefactor." A shock of disgust at first; then, overcoming it, I silently blessed myself and him and gained equilibrium. "Fear thou not, for I am with thee."

"You expected something worse than this, didn't you?"

I felt nauseated. If only I could escape from this conversation. "I expected nothing, Tovarisht Beltchenko," I answered. "I just live one day at a time, the best I can."

"You are quite a philosopher. I heard that, and quite a religious person."

"My faith in God is great," I said.

"I notice that you even look like a nun, with your deep blue eyes and pale face."

"I thought you called me here in the middle of the night for something very important."

"It is very important for you, Tovarisht Kraevsky, but we have all the time in the world. It is only three o'clock, the best hour for a heart-to-heart chat," he said, seemingly relaxed and in the best of moods. I remembered the fragile "Madonna" saying that here prisoners were questioned around three in the morning when their resistance was lowest, so I called upon my spirit to be high and not to fail me.

"If we have time, Tovarisht Beltchenko, then kindly allow me to ask you a favor. My co-prisoners wanted me to tell you about the smoke we have in our basement from seven in the morning till seven at night. You see, something is wrong with the kitchen next door. It makes us sick. Maybe you would help us."

"Of course I will," was his nice reply. "Maybe that is the reason you have become so thin and pale."

"Maybe," I said. "Thank you for the interest. But now, we better come to the point." I was surprised at my own words.

He came to the point, all right, and for more than an hour discussed all the responsibilities and work of a spy and all its advantages. I learned that in my case I would be sent to the gatherings of our former friends, professors and doctors, (Father's colleagues) to report their conversations. I was to try to make them express their approval or disapproval of the Soviet regime. A permanent pass would be given me for all the foreign ships, where I was to keep company with the captains and in my "special way," instill complete confidence, and "as usual," try to find out the opinions of each, and his country's attitude toward the USSR. I learned that I would enjoy much leisure at times, whereas at others I would work unlimited hours.

As though petrified, I listened, listened and listened to the revolting details of such a job, and only one new thought crossed my mind. If, through some of the tricks of their efficient mental torture, unconsciously I should consent to become a spy, my first conscious act would be suicide.

"You are not listening!" said Tovarisht Beltchenko.

"I am, Tovarisht – and very attentively, too, But I know that before accepting any job, one should measure one's strength and capabilities to fulfill it right. I never could become a spy. Please try to understand me once and for all. I could not – I would not spy for anyone; neither the Reds nor the Whites, greens nor yellows – not for anyone in the entire world!"

"Enough for this time. You look very tired, Elizaveta Antonovna. Next time we will discuss this in more detail. Goodbye."

I went down the stairs with another guard – a tall blond man. Alexandrovsky Park was across the street, and the aroma of the fresh spring night intoxicated me. Forgetting everything, I felt like throwing myself into this scented darkness. "Tovarisht guard, please allow me to stop here for a minute."

The soldier looked at me attentively. The expression on his face grew softer. I knew that his heart was softened also and without uttering a word, he stopped. Something wonderful filled my heart – ecstasy before the beautiful night, gratitude to the soldier, a stranger, but at that moment a being very close to me because of his kindness – and also joy, before a new surge of moral strength. Now, giving a sign to the patiently waiting soldier, I entered the yard. Though not having really seen the face of my guard, I shall never forget his understanding and delicate sympathy. Not only did he yield to my request giving me the momentary illusion of freedom, but he also did not hold the revolver against my neck. He carried it so that I would not even notice it.

I asked the guard on duty at our basement door to open it as quietly as possible, and I entered carefully, trying not to wake anyone. Only Tamara L. lifted her head. "Did you tell him about the smoke?" she asked.

"Of course, of course, and he promised to see to it."

Rica slept like a baby, tired after our minuet. I sat down carefully on the edge of her mattress.

My companions were right. They questioned us much more often here. I was called out almost every morning at two or three, yet never did I succeed in lingering again, even for half a minute, in front of the gate facing the park.

Soon it became clear that my case was entrusted to several GPU agents, of whom Tovarisht Beltchinko seemed to be the most determined to break me. I was coerced, I was accused – though the accusations always seemed to be built on sand. I was threatened, flattered as before, then reproached for my obstinacy which, they said, would inevitably lead to a tragic ending. At every new interview, Beltchenko said I was more sickly looking. Very often he monotonously repeated, "If you refuse to be with us, it means that you are against us." I was always glad when it was somebody else who questioned me.

I noticed that most of the agents began their questioning like lions and finished like lambs, probably because I showed no bitterness toward them.

Soon, no doubt was left as to the failing of my health. I felt weak and sometimes dizzy. Our meals here were less regular and deliveries from home rare. In spite of that, every time I was sent back to our basement without giving them any satisfaction, I felt stronger than before.

I was called out more than anyone else. "Someone is in love with you," joked my companions, giving me messages to deliver. "Ask for books or newspapers – even old ones would do." I never forgot to pass on their requests, and never failed to receive a promise. But no newspapers were ever sent to us, and the smoke was not abated.

"Next time you are called, Lisa," said Marussia L., "don't forget to ask for a piano for Rica. She must practice, you know." We laughed though the smoke was filling our eyes with tears.

Easter was approaching. Saturday of Holy Week, though of many different religions, we felt the solemnity of the coming Day of the Resurrection. We decided that all together we would break the fast at midnight. Those who wanted to sleep asked to be awakened a little beforehand. At midnight, we kissed each other three times.

"Christ is risen." And the response resounded throughout our room was "Indeed He is risen." Many of us cried. Then, gathered in a little circle, we broke our fast. One or two of us had something sent from home for the occasion. Someone had received six hard-boiled eggs and we cut them into enough pieces to go around. Vala had sent a little Easter bread and everybody had a bite. How close we were to each other. How united.

April was coming to an end. The GPU garden was all flowers: crocuses, hyacinths of all colors, blue, pink, purple, tender narcissus and tulips. Our basement seemed darker and stuffier than ever. We became more nervous, less balanced, and the talk about freedom more and more fervent. We did not care even for food. Freedom – freedom was our only need. Freedom – freedom was our only dream. I was hoping for the best and praying for the others as well as myself. At night I held my little golden baptismal cross tight in my hand remembering Mother's words: "None of the relatives were happy over your arrival, hoping for an heir, but your little star rejoiced and will shine and protect you throughout your entire life."

Consolation was so needed. Hope was so needed. "What date is today? April 29th! Oh Lord, three months in prison. Do you realize it, Lisa? Three months!"

"You probably will sit three more." said our poor, embittered Nadia. Her discouraging words had no effect on me at all and I went to sleep right after 7 o'clock.

"What is the matter with you, Rica? Why don't you let me sleep?" After a month of close friendship we had become chums, and I could scold her for disturbing me.

"Stop that! Listen to me!" she continued. "The soldier was here five minutes ago. What a job to wake you up. Hurry, now!"

"It is too cruel – much too cruel," I wailed. "Night after night – night after night." But having slept longer than usual, I got up feeling stronger than ever.

In a large room at a long table sat six acquaintances of mine, the GPU agents, each of whom had conversed with me more than once at the languid hour preceding dawn. A man unknown to me presided. There was an air of ceremonious solemnity. This is the time when I should make it all clear flashed through my mind. Blessing them, I decided to speak before they spoke to me. A surge of inner strength filled me.

"I am glad to see you all at once," I said, approaching the table and greeting them. Refusing the offered chair, I remained standing in the empty space of the room. "I am here to tell you my final word. Tovarisht, you know me by now. You have spoken to me individually. You understood me, though you made believe you did not. You also claimed to know of some stupendous crime I committed against the Soviet Government. Moreover, you have definite proof of it, you said. If so, what are you really waiting for? Capital punishment is simple and frequent now-a-days. But no, you do not want that now. You wish to grant me the privilege of becoming a spy first. In order to prove my loyalty to you, I am supposed to betray my old friends and other people who trust me." I took a breath. "I cannot do it. I can NOT do it! No flattery, no threatening, no exile, no life imprisonment, nothing can make me change my mind, nothing can force me to become a spy! Nothing, nothing!"

Fourteen eyes were fixed on me.

"You can – it is in your power to kill me physically," I said, "but you cannot – it is not in your power to kill me morally."

Silence fell. I stood erect. I felt strong. I felt triumphant.

"You can go now." I had never heard that voice before. The man presiding at the table must have spoken.

"You can go!" I heard again. But I could not move.

The struggle of getting back from the high realm must have shown on me for one of the seven ran to my side and offered to help me downstairs.

"Thank you," I said. "I do not need any help."

"I know you do not need any help," he said in a way which I shall never forget.

God was close, very close to me and I was close to God. In that brief moment of ascension of spirit, I knew that all would be well. Unfortunately, I could not remain on this high plane. Elated, I left the office of the GPU; elated, I glanced up at the stars and breathed in the cool air on my way back to the cell. Once there my mood, like the temperature of a sick person, plummeted into despair. From the sublime heights I sank into the abyss of self-pity. Why did I speak so boldly! What would they do to me now? I wept, asking God for His promised help.

The following day I hardly had the strength to get up and Rica was alarmed, thinking I was seriously ill. Only the walk in the blossoming garden restored me, reminding me that God is everywhere, and that with Him there cannot be any despondency, any weakness. In the cell again, I got busy at once. I repaired my dress and mended a few of Rica's things. I worked fast and well, my body rapidly bracing up under the command of my mind. Once more, I realized the peril of self-pity. I resolved not to give in to it.

Other girls took up their sewing also, and because that morning the air was unusually clear in our cell, the "Madonna" sang her beloved song, "Korabli" ("The Ships"). We were all singing when the guard entered.

"You," he said, pointing at me, "come on." "Why, Tovarisht?"

"Come on. That's all. Aren't you Elizaveta Kraevsky?" "Yes, I am. But how about my things?" "Leave them. Someone will take care of them."

This sounded ominous. Our room was dark, as always, with only the little electric lamp on. For a second I lost track of the time. Was it day or night? The girls were shaking, frightened.

"Why can't you take your things along?" asked one.

I pulled myself together. "Now, now. Come on, calm down. No one is shot in the daytime."

The cold metal of the revolver was not stuck against my neck this time, and the soldier who had escorted me more than once before ordered me to follow instead of preceding him. The yard, so dark at night, was light and clean.

"Where do we go, Tovarisht?

"To the secret agency, as usual," he said indifferently.

147

Yet, we passed the door I knew, then another, and through a third entered a small office. A man in civilian clothes was seated at a desk, holding a large envelope. "Is this your name?" he asked, turning the envelope so that I could read it.

"Yes."

With a strange, lingering gesture, as though caressing every sheet, he added some documents to the already well-filled envelope. I recognized my old gray prison card. Then he looked at me attentively. I held his glance, waiting, waiting ———

"Tovarisht Kraevsky," he said slowly, "be thankful to the First of May." He paused.

What does he mean? I wondered. What date is it? April 30th? Tomorrow is the first of May. I closed my eyes.

"You are one of the three women set free under the amnesty of the International Women's Holiday."

I opened my eyes. The man looked down at the papers, and then up at me again. "You are free."

"Free, Tovarisht? You said I am FREE? Is that what you said?" I felt like hugging this messenger of freedom, thanking and thanking him, but the expression on his face was harsh and cold. He wrote something on a square piece of paper, read it, and added something more.

I stretched out my hand to receive my dismissal, but this last document fluttered in his hand longer, much longer than necessary and instead of being handed to me, was thrust into the big envelope, my file.

THEY WILL TAKE ME AGAIN! Like a fierce animal, this thought leaped into my mind, but I pushed it away at the gate of freedom. Joy was the only emotion I could hold.

Outside the door I found my things, together with my diary and other notes written in foreign languages. Picking up the bundle, I hailed a droshky (cab). It took a little time before my eyes, accustomed to the darkness of prison, could look at the resplendence of this day.

Who would think that this year, the year 1930, which I had looked forward to since I was a child, would begin with prison! But I was too happy, and this day too intoxicating to dwell on anything sad. I loved everybody. I didn't hold a grudge against anyone in the entire world – not even Beltchenko. What if I had been in prison. Today, I was free! Yesterday was gone. Today I was happy – so very happy. Freedom! What a feeling! Only those who have been deprived of it can understand.

The cab turned slowly to the left, leaving behind Marslievskaya Street and the GPU. "They set you free, after all, Barishnia?" said the old cabman without turning his head. "How long did you sit?"

"Three months, Dedushka (Grandpa)."

"Dirty scoundrels!' he exclaimed, spitting eloquently. The rest of the way we drove silently. Russians seldom ask why one sits in prison. Usually, one does not know. We were passing by the Cathedral, two blocks from our home. The old man took his hat off. His white hair and long thin beard floated in the breeze. I looked at our lovely Cathedral, thankful to see it again, and crossed myself reverently. At this moment I remembered my fear, my weakness in the cell after the last inquiry, and felt ashamed and shocked that my faith was so fragile. "How could I," I said to myself, "How could I not grasp then, as I clearly understand now, that the sublime experience of spirit triumphing over fear starts a powerful activity toward all that is good and true, and that mortals, even the most ignorant and cruel ones, must yield to it, often unknowingly." The man at the desk had told me to thank the First of May, but I knew that it was God, the Power of all Powers, that I had to thank for my liberation.

FREEDOM

Wednesday – April 30, 1930: Home, home again. It is late and Sister has ordered me to bed; but I cannot let this day go by without writing down in my diary at least a few words about the joy that overwhelms me. My book and I are so happy to be home again. Accustomed to being handled by me alone, my book must have disliked the touch of strange hands and the glance of curious eyes on our intimate pages. But now we are together again under the pink shade of our familiar lamp.

Early this morning I was still "there" (I cannot force myself to even write the word) and very depressed. Gradually I overcame the depression and was ready to meet with courage whatever came; and the least expected, yet most desired, came – FREEDOM! On my way home, to the rhythm of the quick trot of the horse, I pictured myself flying up the staircase, hurtling through the door to surprise Vala. In reality, my feet could hardly move. Short of breath, I stood by the door a while, remembering the time when Mother and Father were here. I wished Mother would open the door and warm me with the tenderness of her anxious, loving eyes. Not boisterously at all, but hesitantly, my hand knocked. If only Vala would hear me first. And she did.

Vala, my frightened, emaciated sister, did not believe her eyes. She looked and looked at me. Then she looked down the staircase to make sure there was no one to take me away again. In our room, close, close to each other, we sat, unable to speak. So still was our silence one could almost hear our tears dropping upon our clasped hands. Little by little, pressing Vala to my heart, touching her hair, looking at her, I began to speak. I had to tell her all, from the day of our separation to the moment I came back home.

Later, my sister began to take care of me and my things. I would have liked to throw my old rags away, but we could not afford it, and we had to dust and air them on the balcony, and later put them "through fire and water," boiling them, drying them, and boiling them again. This time, Vala did not economize on soap. She washed and scrubbed me too, until it hurt. After that we ate what our friends (not knowing I was back) had brought to Vala for me.

Now happy, Vala slept her first peaceful sleep in months, being utterly exhausted mentally by fear for my life, and physically by the long trip she made almost daily to bring me food. I am going to sleep too, in a real bed – my own bed. I cannot believe it. I am so happy, so thankful.

Thursday, May 1, 1930: Last night, like a little child reassured by the happy ending of a fearful story, light of heart, clean of body, I fell asleep. I was wakened this morning by the strains of the "International." It was past ten o' clock. Crowds of people on May Day parade were streaming down our street. "Be thankful to the first of May!" Maybe some day I shall be thankful, not only to the first of May, but also to all that preceded this date. Today I could not summon the strength nor the will to do it. Today, in my memory, I followed another parade – the parade of the growth of my faith, as step by step, in these last three months, I was brought to a higher understanding and to a greater inner freedom. (At that time I wrote a poem in Russian which I later translated into English, titled "In a Political Prison, U.S.S.R.")

IN A POLITICAL PRISON U.S.S.R.

There is a limit to my memories,
a dead end.
The doom of previous happenings
is death.
You are no longer needed,
joyous memories;
only my latest misery
prevails.
Only you, my grief,
are truly cherished;
you, my dear, my near one,
fully mine.
Touch my face
with your course, sinewy fingers,
hold me close to you
and understand:
my path to happiness
is barricaded,
but I have grown through you –
now I am free:
the fear of life, of death,
has disappeared.
So hold me tight
and in this hard, dank corner
together we shall meet
the night.

We did not leave the house all day. I needed a little time for myself –
one has to become gradually accustomed, even to freedom.

Saturday, May 3, 1930: I was out for the first time today. We went to Zina's. What an experience to walk on familiar sunlit streets. I stepped cautiously as though on holy ground. This spring day was holy day for me and it was hard to make myself believe that for people rushing by, it was just an ordinary day. At Zina's, what a surprise!

I am home now, full of excitement and impressions, so much so that in order to calm down a little I think I am going to spend the rest of the day sharing it all with my book. The window and the balcony door are wide open. A spring breeze keeps me company and I can write and write.

Last night when thinking whom I should see first, the image of Zina stood before my eyes. I pictured her the first time she came to the walls of the prison, standing outside the gate, moving her hands in despair, apparently trying to persuade the guard to take her package. Her poor, swollen legs had not carried her fast enough from the streetcar to the prison gate, and she was considerably late for the regular delivery. But the guard accepted the package, and soon after, sent it up to me. What a superhuman effort she must have made, sick as she was, to have come twice, bringing her radish salad. It was the best we had ever tasted and each one had a spoonful. Of course, my first visit should be to Zina.

This morning I woke up early. After three nights of peaceful sleep, I felt much stronger. Everything was quiet and there was no need to hurry. I looked at my grey and white cotton dress, laid out on the chair by my bed. I love it. It has a wide skirt, a narrow waist and a lovely neckline. I did not have it with me in prison. Winter is gone, I thought; May is outside, and I can wear it. On the other chair I saw my grey coat, "coat de gala," the one made out of the blanket Dr. William Russell Smith of the American Relief Administration gave me when, in 1922, soon after Father's death, I went from Odessa to Moscow in search of a well paid job. I have always cherished that coat. I could count the times I have worn it in the last eight years. It is still a beautiful coat.

I thought of William Russell Smith – of his sympathy for us after our great loss. Where is he now? Practicing medicine in some lovely office in

New York City? How were all those nice, free, happy Americans who, moved by their hearts, found in themselves the desire and the will to come with the American Relief Administration under Herbert Hoover to help our unfortunate population, dying by the thousands of hunger and privation.

We knew them all quite well and also some of the officers of the United States Navy, the young men of perfect upbringing and refinement who, much to our regret, stayed only a short time in our harbor: George Merrick Dusenberry and Lieutenant McAutree from the Destroyer Childs 241, and others from Destroyer 222. (The U. S. warships were circulating around the Black Sea ports for the protection of the U. S. citizens in Russia; no diplomatic relations existed at that time between the two countries.) I was lost in recollections when Vala called me to breakfast.

Dr. Anton Kraevsky, Mrs. Olga Kraevsky,
and daughters Valentina and Elizabeth

Teenager Elizabeth Antonova

Elizabeth Antonova in early 20's

Martin H. Feinman in early 30's

Elizabeth Antonova in early 30's

Vala in early 30's

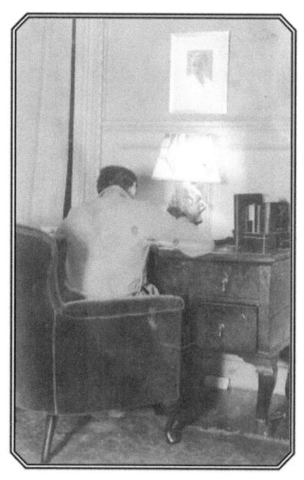

Martin in New York writing letter to Elizabeth
(her photo on wall above desk)

Martin waiting for letters from Elizabeth

Honeymooning in Yalta

Elizabeth waiting for her passport

Captain Harry Grimson

Elizabeth in her 40's

Martin in his 40's

Elizabeth and Hans Mose 1955

Feinman and Mose family reunion in Denmark in 1955

Natasha, Elizabeth, Martin, Olga and Tania 1965

Olga, Elizabeth, David Melin, Tania, Natasha and Martin 1975

Elizabeth in Russian dress

Martin at dinner in his honor

Left to right – Tania with daughter Tammy Rae,
Natasha with daughters Lisa and Tatiana,
Olga with daughter Gina – early 1970's

Left to right – Olga, Natasha and Tania, 1979

Martin and Elizabeth in her early 90's

MEETING MARTIN

We left the house at noon. Walking out of the front door I couldn't help remembering the gloomy February morning when I marched down the middle of the street with soldiers at my sides. How furious I was then – how glad now to walk on the sidewalk next to Vala, chatting gaily.

Zina's white chickens, in a homemade pen which she kept by the door, greeted us first. We went down the steps to her basement, still as neat as a Swiss chalet, and through the open door saw the dear woman busy in the kitchen at the sink.

"Lisochka, Lisochka, you are back! What a joy! Thank God, thank God," she cried. With her wet hand she crossed herself, then kissed and hugged me. I tried more than once to praise her delicious salad, but she didn't listen. She seemed to have something else on her mind. "Too bad Nikita isn't home," she said. "I wonder where he is. You surely came at the right moment to help me." She kissed me again, and a certain tense expression on her face disappeared. "You see," she went on, "a man, a very well dressed man, just came in – I would say a minute or two before you did, and asked for Nikita. All I understood was Nikita's name. He said something else, but it was not in Russian. You, Lisochka, know all the languages. Go and ask him why he needs Nikita. He is waiting there in the sitting room."

At first glance I thought he must be French, because of the little mustache he wore, but then, no. "You must be an American," I said, quite sure, yet half questioning.

"You speak English! What a surprise! Yes, I'm an American. You guessed it right. My name is Martin Feinman."

How interesting, I thought. Isn't it strange that this morning I was remembering my old American friends, and this very afternoon I come across another American? I introduced myself as a friend of the hostess. We shook hands and before he could make another move I picked up a chair from the other side of the room and sat next to him.

"Sorry I didn't help you with the chair," he said, "but you move so fast."

"Do not apologize, please," I replied. "Here, we forgot about chivalry long ago," and we both laughed. Somehow, right away, I felt at ease with this tall, attractive American. He had a most agreeable smile, a sensitive face of delicate contour, a high forehead, intense, yet kind, blue eyes and expressive lips.

I asked him to explain the reason of his visit to Zina, adding that she seemed to be rather puzzled by it. As he began to talk, I drew my chair a little closer, afraid to miss a word. I found out that Martin Feinman, an extensive traveler, had arrived with a group of other American tourists on a month's visa. He had already visited Leningrad and Moscow and had a special reason for his trip to Odessa. It was the city where he was born and which he had left as a child. He also wanted to see his father's old friend, Nikita, and bring gifts to him and his wife. After hearing this, I ran out to comfort Zina with the good news and returned right away to resume the conversation in English. I enjoyed myself thoroughly and felt the American did too.

When Nikita came, the real excitement began. The old man was beside himself with joy. He laughed and cried at the same time, brought out a long-hidden bottle of vodka and announced that we had to drink to this double celebration: "Lisa's freedom and Martin's arrival from

America." His toasts succeeded each other in Russian, German and a bit of English.

In no time a little lunch was served. We ate and drank to the endless toasts of Nikita. Then the presents were given out: a wristwatch for Nikita and some tools which he must have asked for long ago, lovely sweaters for Zina and material for a heavy coat. The last gifts were American records and an American phonograph put to work by Nikita. Soon the music of a fast fox trot resounded and Martin and I danced like old partners. I forgot about the past and future, fully enjoying this hour.

Soon it was time to leave. The young man wished to take us home in a cab, but this, I explained, was impossible and Vala and I left alone. All the way home we spoke of the interesting foreigner. "He seemed to like you very much," said Vala.

"I liked him, too," I admitted, "but what of it? As a matter of fact, I ought to be afraid even to think of him."

At that moment I heard someone call my name. It was Nikita who, together with the young American, was passing in a cab, greeting us enthusiastically. The fervent glance of our new acquaintance met mine, and I'm almost sure I blushed.

"They should be more reserved," said Vala, "more careful. You are being watched."

"Never mind, Vala, never mind." I said, feeling carefree.

That was all. Not much, maybe, but I derived endless pleasure from this afternoon. I danced, I spoke English, and I really could not get over it. It was wonderful, and he was so nice. He had a captivating smile and his blue eyes were full of laughter and full of thought.

Sunday, May 4, 1930: We went to church. From there we took a trolley to the cemetery. I leaned over the grass hills of the graves of my parents. I could not help crying, but these were tears of thanksgiving, not grief. Across the road was the prison, the building with the red roof, reminding me of the recent past.

On the way back we walked until we reached the Seamen's Hospital. Odessky had been much on my mind. I was anxious to see him, but oh, I found him so very, very sick. Yet, he recognized me and rejoiced over my freedom. I thanked him for having spoken about me to the lovely nurse. He said she liked me and that he knew all about me through her.

We are home now. Vala and I have just had tea. The last sun rays fill our room. The little that is left of our former furniture – the oil paintings, our crystal vase, the clock that hung in our dining room when we had one, the 'trumo' (full size mirror), and some other objects in our only room, seem luxuries now. Prison has changed me; my evaluation of things is different; I could get along with much less than before.

I am thinking of my companions in both prisons, wondering who else was liberated on the First of May. The man mentioned that I was one of three. Who were the other lucky ones? For those who are still there, the evening is the saddest time of the day when, after roll call, everybody quiets down before the uncertainty of the oncoming night. Is it true that I was there – that night after night I lived through the same anxiety? How strange that after all this, after having been persecuted for corresponding with foreign countries, no sooner do I get out of prison than I meet a foreigner, a person whom it would have been better for me not to have met at all. But I met him, and now and then, I catch myself thinking of him.

Right now I am sitting at my desk. Three months ago a man in uniform sat in this very place, searching my drawers, examining my papers. Here it is, my little metal box, a few beads still in it. I touch everything with gratitude for the Divine help received at the very beginning of my trying experiences.

Same day – 9:00 P.M.: Around eight o'clock Nikita came on an errand for his young friend. "He has been waiting for you since early this morning," Nikita told me, "hoping you would drop in for the pink scarf you left behind yesterday. Now he sends me to ask you kindly to come as he has something important to tell you."

I told Nikita that it was impossible and did not go. Too bad, it would be nice to see him again.

Monday, May 5, 1930: We are at the end of our resources, though Vala says that the money she obtained for Father's watch and chain, the ten dollars, and the pound sterling have stretched, and are still stretching, rather miraculously. However, it is time for me to take the necessary steps to be reinstated in my rights, and then apply for a job. Therefore, this morning we both went to the courthouse, quite a distance from home, to file a petition to that effect. I filled endless 'anquettes' and also wrote a personal letter with a request to speed the delivery of the much needed document. I am so glad I did.

Tuesday, May 6, 1930: Rica is also free. This morning when she entered my room we both nearly died of surprise, but preferred to fall into each other's arms instead. How dear she is to me. Is it not strange? We were taken to prison, transferred and liberated the same day. After a long chat about those days, I told Rica about my new acquaintance and then we went to her home. They still lived in their own apartment which has remained completely intact, her father being a talented architect much needed by the government.

I liked Rica's room; it had white fluffy gauze curtains, an old fashioned dressing table with valance and fringe, and a bedspread of white lace. She seems to be part of that whiteness, to belong there. To think of the place where we met a few months ago – what a 'koshmar' (nightmare)! I haven't been in the cozy atmosphere of a home for a long time since most families are reduced, as we are, to living in one room.

Wednesday, May 7, 1930: It is eight in the evening. Nikita has just left. He was here again with the same request. As gently as I could, I explained the situation to him and asked him to make clear to Martin that meeting him would be most dangerous for me. Yet, Nikita continued to plead, "Lisochka, dear, please have mercy! Martin doesn't look like himself any more. He waits and waits for you."

But I did not relent and now I feel sad. I am sorry for Nikita, sorry for Martin, sorry for myself. Fear seems to overrule all my other feelings. What has he to say? I should have gone, maybe. It might not be so terribly imprudent. Well, it's all over now. He probably will feel offended. Never again will he send Nikita for me.

Friday, May 9, 1930: Apparently people with unwavering thoughts do not get offended, but clearly see their goal and move toward it. Last night Nikita came, but I was at Tetia Tonia's. Tonight as soon as darkness fell, the old man knocked at my door. "What is it now, Nikita?" I asked.

"You know, yourself, Lisochka." He looked at me imploringly and I felt ashamed.

Did the prison succeed in making a real coward out of me, I thought. I, who always was rather bold, have I forgotten how to take a risk? "One cannot die twice," says our Russian proverb, "but one death is unavoidable." I could not keep on hurting their feelings. I told Nikita to return home, promising to follow him a little later.

While dressing, I thought of Martin's perseverance. So many times he had sent for me, sitting there in Zina's basement, waiting, waiting. What could be the matter? Why such insistence? I combed my hair, pulling it straight back from the temples, dressed myself with special care and, proud of my courage, left the house.

I greeted Zina and Nikita cheerfully, and could not help noticing the extreme pallor of Martin's face. We sat down and the old people disappeared. "Forgive my persistence," he said, "but I could not help it. From the moment I saw you, I knew you were the girl I'd been looking for all my life. I'm no youngster, I've seen much of life. I thought I'd never marry because I've witnessed too many unsuccessful modern marriages. Then I saw you – please understand that I would never have allowed myself to disturb you except that I have something of great importance to tell you." He stopped and looked at me, his glance reaching deep into my heart. "I had to see you to ask you whether you could ever consider becoming my wife."

How earnest he was, how sincere. Oh Lord, if only I could find words that would not offend him, I thought. As sudden, as unexpected as it was, I could not take it for a joke, nor laugh it off. "I am touched by your utter sincerity," I said. "I like you too, but under existing circumstances we cannot even think of letting this feeling grow – and for reasons that would be hard for you to understand. It would be best for you to forget this sudden fantasy and never try to see me again." Tensely he listened while I went on. "I will be frank with you, Martin. Your sincerity deserves sincerity in return. You have no idea what we have lived through here in Soviet Russia. After my latest experience in prison I feel that something in me has changed. I am no longer the same cheerful person and I could never be the right companion for you who are so free, so spontaneous. Moreover, I could never become your wife because after months of imprisonment, I shall never be let out of Russia."

"Is this the only reason? Oh, well, it could be arranged, I'm sure," he said, the color returning to his cheeks. "Let's inquire. You probably have some friends who could make it all clear to us. I'm sure there must be a way."

He looked so hopeful that I had no heart to let him down. On the contrary, I felt actually swept into the tide of his enthusiasm. We got up, ready to go, neither of us knowing exactly where. "Well, let me see," I said. "Maybe Rica's father could help us."

"All right, let's not waste time. Let's go," he urged.

At that moment, the owl-eyed faces of Zina and Nikita emerged from nowhere. "Aren't you afraid to walk out together?" Zina asked. "Aren't you afraid?"

"No, Zina," I said. We walked through the faintly lighted streets of the city, Martin's hand clasping mine. Where am I going? What shall I ask about? What is it that I wish to know? Not taking time to answer these questions, I kept walking as though I had a definite aim ahead of me, and not just the idea of not destroying right away the hope of this unusual and sincere man who thought he loved me.

"If we marry right away, say tomorrow," Martin continued, "I know they wouldn't be able to keep you here, since you would then be the wife of an American. The person you're going to, your friend, will probably confirm this. He'll know all about it, won't he?"

"Oh, yes, he will," I said, sustaining his hope. He quickened his step. We walked hand in hand until we reached the street where Rica lived. In my sudden predicament, Rica and her family seemed to be the only ones I could go to for advice.

"I'll wait for you here," Martin said.

"All right, I'll be back in fifteen minutes. Do not stand in one spot," I added. "Try not to be obvious." That familiar fear. It is there no matter what.

The door opened. Rica's blue eyes were questioning. We spoke. "Is it that serious?" she asked. I told her how much easier it would be if it weren't, if he were not so real, so utterly devoid of affectation. She said. "Of course, the best thing would be to consult my father."

In a few minutes I was called into her father's workroom for the verdict – a rather pessimistic one, but the one I was prepared to hear. Not only now, but even after complete rehabilitation, a person with a prison record would never be allowed to leave the country. He also added that even through marriage no Soviet citizen can automatically become an American, but must wait until the Soviet government issues a passport. Suddenly I remembered that this was something like a strategy, a desire to be diplomatic and delicate for Martin's sake.

I rushed back and told him: "Nothing encouraging – nothing at all. I shall never be let out."

A moment of dead silence and we continued to walk side by side, persons from different worlds. The pressure of his hand became firmer as he realized the real obstacles facing him. Yet, he didn't give up. He mentioned the names of some important Americans, then spoke of what seemed to him a possibility right here. I listened, amazed at his imagination, at the colossal heights of his spirit, which I could feel even in moments of silence. How did this all happen? Is this what little old Mrs. Broochis prophesied in prison, night after night, when I was tucking her in? As we walked on my heart, unaccustomed to such emotion, eagerly listened to Martin's free and bold heart, ready to break down all barriers.

"I never knew I could love anyone as I do you – never thought I could live through the days of anxiety, waiting for you to come. I'm enthralled by you alone. Nothing else is of importance. Such feeling, I'm sure can overcome all difficulties. I love you, Lisa."

Quietly, I listened and thought, "I will not disappoint him today." We were approaching the corner nearest to my house. "We must stop here," I said. "You cannot go any farther. I will see you at Nikita's tomorrow afternoon and speak to you then. Good night, Martin." Taken, not so much by the expressed as by the hidden force of his feeling, happy over something wonderful I was living through, I got on tiptoes and putting my arms around him, kissed him, mentally parting with him forever. For a moment he held me in his arms as though puzzled. Then he looked hopeful and happy again.

It is long after midnight now and I am still writing. I feel perturbed. Why did I kiss him? He loves me. I like him. We could never be together, and I, like a heartless teaser, went ahead and kissed him, giving him hope where there is none at all. I was wrong. What an evening it was, making me happy and unhappy at the same time. Part of me is thinking logically, completely down to earth; part of me giving in, not to my own will, but some other which is stronger than mine.

Saturday, May 10th, 1930: I hardly slept last night. I looked for the words I would use to cut our romance short, but could not find them. I was nervous entering the old people's house.

"How wonderful of you to come! Good news, I hope," said Martin, stopping the Victrola and coming towards me.

We sat in the same chairs as at our first meeting. "You mean you still have not given up the idea," I joked, gaining a little in poise. Ah, the look on his face at my remark. How could a man seem to have so much love, so much devotion after such a short acquaintance? Maybe this is all my imagination. No matter what, I thought, I must not weaken. I know exactly what to speak about. This morning Vala reminded me of the danger of our meeting. Martin didn't seem to be in a serious mood. With humor he spoke of what he called "my first apparition" in Zina's place, of my firm handshake, of the chair I lifted like a giant and carried across the room. He amused me and I was laughing. Yet the purpose of my visit stayed in the back of my mind all the time. Zina, in her soft slippers, came in noiselessly to water her beautiful geraniums and walking out, winked meaningfully at me as she closed the door.

Martin was still smiling when I resumed. "As happy as we are, Martin, we must – we simply have to become a little more serious."

"What do you mean?" he asked.

"I mean all that happened yesterday – you seemed so hopeful, and yet there is no hope at all. I shall never be let out of here."

"If you can't leave, then I'll stay here," was his quick reply. "Nonsense," I said firmly. "This would mean moral ruin for both of us."

"But I cannot leave you here. This is no life for you." He got up and began to pace the room nervously. "Nikita told me just a little of what you've lived through and it was terrible. There's nothing I wouldn't do to see you safe and happy." To listen to him was torture to me. He sat down again and took my hand in his. "Every minute I love you more, Lisa. A man who loves so much must succeed. You mean more to me than my own life – more than anything in the whole world."

I felt worse and worse. "Martin, dear," I said, "somehow I know – I feel – I am sure it is true, and I know you would like to prove it, no matter what. But believe me, it will not be easy for me to say what I find myself obliged to say."

"Say it, Lisa," he said.

"Leave tomorrow and never try to see me again." (I still wonder how my lips uttered it.) For a long time neither of us spoke. "With time your feeling will wear out, Martin," I continued. "It is all consuming now, but also very new."

He shivered all over. "Don't say that – please, don't! It never will."

I took both his hands in mine. "Time will show," I said. "You must understand that right now, to see each other is to expose us, Vala and me, to a danger far greater than the one I have just lived through."

He squeezed my hands very hard, and then dropped them. Gravely he said "I'll do as you say, Lisa."

I thought "Happiness knocks at my door and I, a hunted frightened creature, refuse to lift the latch. So our interest in each other must die, like a seed that has no adequate ground in which to grow."

"I'll leave tomorrow," I heard him say. "I understand I should not see you any more?"

"That's right," I replied.

"You'll allow me to write you, though?" "Better not, really," I said.

Disturbed and nervous again, he got up. "Please don't take this only link away from me. I'll write to the address of the old people and they will pass my letters on to you."

"All right, Martin." I replied, getting up and turning my head away, trying to hold back my tears. But he pressed me close to him.

"I leave you because I love you," he said and I felt it in his farewell kiss. The room was whirling.

Sunday, May 11, 1930 -7:00 P.M.: His train left early this afternoon, and I did not see him again. No doubt it had to be so. A feeling like his had to be answered by the same dynamic feeling. Therefore, the sooner we parted the better. We are persons from different planets. It all came and went like a thunderstorm. I am sure he will be able to master his feelings – his life is colorful, his impressions rather kaleidoscopic. As for myself, putting my short dream aside, I will think only of one thing – a job.

Wednesday, May 14, 1930: Spring this year is a magic one. The May storms rage only at night, and days are sunny, scented and fresh. Every day I go to the courthouse for the promised document, but in vain. I have decided to be tireless until I tire them out. If I miss one day, they might think I'm not interested and not give me a document at all – and I need it so badly. Often I catch myself thinking of Martin. I shall probably remember him all my life. Will he be able to forget me?

LIFE GOES ON

Evenings, Vala and I sit on the balcony, remembering our recent separation. My imprisonment was hard on her. Rumors were constantly filling the city about new exiles, new 'rasstrel' (executions), and one day at the end of March she went as usual to the prison at 3 o'clock, but her basket of food was not accepted. "Why?" she asked.

"She is not here anymore." the guard told her.

"Where is she?"

"How could I know?" replied the guard.

Timidly she asked if he could inquire inside the prison.

"I already have," was his answer, "but they, themselves, do not seem to know."

Vala could neither eat nor sleep until two days later, she finally found out that I was in the prison of the headquarters of the GPU. I knew it all and felt her anxiety. For hours sometimes, we would sit and remember, then reproach ourselves for living in the past.

Nikita just brought a postal card from Martin – greetings from Moscow.

Thursday, May 15, 1930: Today we buried Odessky. I could not and did not want to restrain my tears. We lost a kind, sincere man, a friend. He was one of the few who always sympathized with us in the office. He never was stingy with his time and although his day was over, he would stay with us, helping to translate letters, dictating bills of lading, giving us the chance to go home earlier. He was always joking and never was mad at anyone. Poor, dear Odessky! It seemed as if all the employees of the Soviet Mercantile Fleet of Odessa were at his funeral. There was not one person in the harbor who didn't know him.

Many of my former coworkers greeted me joyfully. Some Communists registered astonishment on their faces, as though to say, "Incredible! How could they let you out!" Many, for self-protection, did not recognize me at all. This hurt me for a moment, but right away a happy thought entered my mind! What are they to me? Their actions are their own affair. What I truly possess is my own inner joy, which no one can take away from me. God, Himself, took me by my right hand and led me out of prison. Is that not enough? After this, I continued to walk in the procession, relaxed and at peace with myself and the world.

"Elizaveta Antonovna, Lisochka, the same smiling one, still the same bright one. Look at her! She is even more beautiful than before." With these words, the manager of the Exportkleb office, V.V.G., mysteriously led me aside from the road and told me that there was an opening for a typist-secretary and that he would be glad to recommend me. I thanked him most sincerely, told him that I would be happy to work for him but that I had to offer my services to my former chiefs first.

He scowled. "Let them go to Hell! Excuse my expression – but don't even go to them. Don't go!"

"Why?"

"Well, just don't go. Better come to us."

I thought it would be wonderful to work for V.V., a good employer, an intelligent, well-bred man – here is hope for a job, and I wished the document was already in my hands.

May 17, 1930: No success. I was waiting in line for two hours. I hope there is no complication of any kind—

Passing by the house of my old friends, I dropped in to see them. Nikita was about to go to my house with two letters from Martin, and a telegram from Berlin.

"EXPECT TO BE BACK IN TWO WEEKS (STOP) IF NO OBJECTION ANSWER IMMEDIATELY AMERICAN EXPRESS PARIS – MARTIN."

It was a shock. I hardly exchanged a word with Zina and Nikita and ran to the telegraph office. The answer was prepaid. "RETURN IMPOSSIBLE LETTER FOLLOWS," I wrote. A few more words could be used. I added "BEST WISHES LISA." His telegram is right here before my eyes now. What is the matter? Could it be that he did not understand me at all?

May 20, 1930: Hurray, hurray! The document is in my hands. It reads, "In view of the absence of crime, the case of Elizabeth Kraevsky, etc., is closed." Thank God, thank God! It is quite early – only 11 o'clock, and I decided to go home, change into my best clothes and run to Sovtorgflot (Soviet Mercantile Fleet – my former employer).

I reached home quickly, so overjoyed that even inanimate objects seemed to cooperate. I changed in no time and didn't walk, but flew toward the harbor, stopping only to open my pocketbook and make sure that the document was there. But my mood was not transmitted to the chiefs of Sovtorgflot. Four hard eyes looked at my beaming face. "You instilled too much confidence in every foreigner, don't you think so?" sarcastically remarked one. "We did not expect you." said the other. "For three months we managed without you and will continue to do so. You troubled yourself for nothing, because we do not need any suspicious element."

"I did not trouble myself, Tovarishti. I considered it my duty, after having obtained the document of my complete rehabilitation, to offer my services to my former employers first." I said it politely, with surprising poise and left the office. God Almighty, I thought, people not knowing anything about your experiences, your problems, your triumph, speak to you as if you were a criminal. I found out that the office of Exportkleb was upstairs in the same building. There amicably, almost sweetly, V.V.G. listened to what I had to say.

"I told you not to go there, didn't I?" he said.

I was sorry to have disobeyed him.

V.V. explained the nature of my future work and told me to report for duty June 4th at 9 A.M. Precision helps one's balance immensely. I forgot the disagreeable chiefs of Sovtorgflot and on my way home planned to sell some things that I no longer needed and use the money for a two week vacation. I knew how badly I need physical and mental rest before I began to work.

May 28, 1930: Lustdorf – I have been here since the 24th. The sun, the sea, the flowers – all are mine. I feel as though life has just started. The sky, the sea, the earth and I are one. This comes to me as a revelation and with humility, I accept it.

The grass here is a rich green, and the flowers – how did it happen that I never noticed the intricate design on some, especially one, the name of which I do not know. It looks like a white lace doily with a perfect little ruby in the center. And the flame of the poppies, the meekness of the bluettes! Father loved them. Often, half hungry men and women of the village walking heads down, brighten up at the exuberance of my greeting because they feel that I love them. Sincerity cannot deceive. Never before did I meditate at length on the great gifts freely offered us. Now I realize that all, all there is in the world is for us, and that with true, unselfish love, with only the divine spark in us, we can make this world even more beautiful, even more perfect.

May 29, 1930: I love my tiny room and will be sorry to leave it. Daria, the wife of the post office clerk, in whose house I live, is kind and feeds me as best she can. For three days I have been going down the high cliff to the beach to swim. Geook, Daria's Shepherd dog, walks with me to the beach and watches my things while I swim. He doesn't like me to stay too long and after ten or fifteen minutes begins to express his dissatisfaction by coming to the very edge of the water and barking until I come out.

May 30, 1930: I appreciate every minute of my stay here. Thirstily, I drink in the invigorating air of Spring – for me, the air of freedom. Only Vala and some of our nearest friends came to see me once for a couple of hours. I need to be alone, my whole being craves it. I spend my solitude rejoicing – rejoicing over every petal of the flowers, every blade of grass. This joy is born of peace within me attained through new experiences and new strength given by the All Powerful Source of Good. This strength, I know, is indestructible and mine forever.

June 18, 1930: I am already on my job for two weeks. My diary is more and more neglected. I am working most conscientiously. I do my best to prove my gratitude to the kind V.V.K. He in turn, pays me back by sending me home earlier on days when all the work is done.

Some of my former pupils have resumed their lessons in French and English and more requests for lessons are coming. In short, I find myself pretty busy. I had a couple of new personal impressions, but find no time to write about them. Besides, they are really of no importance.

Martin continues to write.

The end of May and June brought many letters and cablegrams from Martin, my devoted American tourist; first from Germany, then France, and finally the U.S.A. None of these messages showed any cooling of his feelings. Instead, every line revealed that his feelings were growing in strength. What was I to do? I knew that after having been on the black list I would never be let out of Soviet Russia, and I decided that I should try again to make him realize this.

In the meantime, many of my former admirers had reappeared. There was an architect from Moscow, quite sure of his ultimate success. Also, an important Soviet employee from the city of Samara-on-Volga, returning via Odessa from a spa in the Caucasus, determined to win me with his "new look". They probably thought that the months in prison would have taken away some of my independence. I did not like them before and did not find any reason to like them now. As kindly as I could, I made this clear to them. Of course I was polite. After all, I understood that it could not be so pleasant for any man with the best of intentions to be refused twice. None of it affected me much. My greatest concern was neither they nor I but the future of the charming and kind Martin whom I liked and who loved me at first glance, and whom I had to persuade to forget me. What was I to do?

I thought and thought, then wrote a stern, unsentimental letter, laying all the cards before him. I ended by saying that because of obstacles far beyond our control, we must consider our friendship merely a pleasant interlude and put an end to it. This letter went off the first of July. I blessed it on its way, hoping I had done the right thing, realizing only now that I was more concerned with his happiness than with mine. I calculated that it would reach him by July 15th. He would probably answer it at once, and his reply would come toward the very end of the month. I prepared myself for the answer that would bring the end to our brief romance. I wanted it to be final, yet I could not help daydreaming at times of what it would be like to be free and happy in America.

Every day in the office I worked with intense concentration. At home I wanted to be alone. Sometimes, not wishing to meet anyone, I walked through the empty streets of the suburbs where people went to bed early. Once at dusk I found myself facing a broken gate. One side of it was almost erect, the other hanging pitifully on one hinge. To the left was a small guard's house. This entrance seemed familiar. What was it? Where was I?

Of course I knew! This was the gate through which Mother had brought us to school every fall for many years. It was long – so long ago. As a child I had expected this year 1930 to be an extraordinary one. I had such hopes, even on New Year's Eve. Now, half of 1930 was gone and the only gain had been a new spiritual happiness attained in prison.

"Who are you looking for?" A tall young man towered over me, hands in pockets. He probably had come from out of the little house to the left.

"I am looking for no one, I am just looking around." Then noticing his friendly smile I asked, "Could you please tell me what this building is now?"

"What do you mean now?" He smiled again, quite forgivingly. "It is and always was the Workmen and Peasants Technological Institute."

"Oh yes, of course," I said blankly, with no intention of informing this youth, product of a new generation, that not so long ago it was a fashionable school for girls of Russian nobility.

Every Sunday I went to the final resting place of my parents. There, I felt I was communing with Mother. I told her about my letter, about maybe giving up my last hope for happiness. I knew that her spirit was much closer to perfection than mine, and I asked her to pray so that the right thing, the right outcome of events would take place, so that he whom I had given up would not be too hurt, and I who had to remain here would gather new courage to keep on living.

I tended the flowers on the graves of Father and Mother, watered them and some others nearby, and late in the afternoon when all was quiet and the intense July heat had subsided, I sat on the stone enclosure I had built for them and listened to the silence. Sometimes, through the thickness of the trees my eyes would unwillingly catch the sight of the red roof – the roof of the prison. A shiver passed through me and I would remember the desperate days spent there; then quickly, I thanked God that this was in the past, grateful for having been given the strength to live through it. Closing my eyes, I would return to the silence. It cleared my thoughts and emotions. Peace was the reward for it. I was sure that I had done the right thing. My heart was lighter.

Letters were coming from New York as before. Most were dated before the end of June. Old Nikita was faithfully bringing them to me. He, his wife Zina, and my sister were the only ones who knew about this correspondence. People lived in such fear that they would try to keep a secret even from themselves if they only could.

On Tuesday, July 29th, I received a telegram, not from America, but from Leningrad. Leningrad! I had to sit down before opening it. My heart was beating fast, and I had a feeling that the message would be a perturbing one. "DEAR LISA," I read, "I AM IN LENINGRAD ARRIVING ODESSA AUGUST FOURTH VIA MOSCOW LOVE – MARTIN."

I passed the telegram to my sister. "Oh Lord! It means he is coming here! What shall we do? They might suspect you again. Oh, it is so dangerous!"

"Of course it is," I said. That night I couldn't sleep. The comforting serenity I felt during my long calm had disappeared. I was overwhelmed by the news. I could hardly believe it. I was afraid. The GPU is still on my track, I thought, and here he sends me a telegram directly to my address and informs me that he will arrive on the fourth. What a child! What a child! He knows nothing of our fears, of the precautions we must take at every step. I was afraid. I had not expected him! I had expected a letter, a sad painful letter, confirming the inevitable. Instead, every minute was bringing him nearer and I could not stop him.

During all of July I had remained in a semi-sentimental mood, tinged with sadness that far from taking away my inner peace added to it, knowing I had done the right thing thinking of his good. Now there was no more peace. Why did he do it? Why didn't he return my letter? Why didn't he ask as before, whether his return would be welcome?

In the office I could not work well. Thoughts of Martin's return obsessed me. How should I meet him? What should I tell him? How terrible! He was coming from so far away just to go back again. Nervous and excited, I forgot even to pray. Only on the day of his arrival did I compose myself. I felt more calm and trusted that God would help me make the right decisions.

In the afternoon Nikita, whom I hadn't even informed of Martin's sudden return, appeared very much out of breath, to inform me that Martin was at his house and that they both would come to see me at 8 o'clock that evening. Without as much as a thought for any other plan or arrangement, I calmly said, "All right, Nikita, let him come." Around 7:30 I was nervous again. I hoped that no one would see him come up our staircase. Vala was not at home and I waited for the man whom love had brought back to me from so far away. I searched for joy in my heart on this occasion, but fear leaves no room for other emotions.

I heard quick light steps on the sidewalk below. Nobody walks like that in Russia anymore. Watching from the balcony I saw two men enter the house. Three flights of stairs and he would be here. Martin entered smiling. He carried a large box of candy, and his light gray suit created an aura of brightness. We held out our hands and looked at each other. His joy met my sadness. "Martin, Martin," I said, "why did you come?"

"Your letter made me come, Lisa," he said. "I could not decide this question by mail." I looked at him. My brutal question did not seem to have disturbed him. He was all vivacity, all eagerness, all love. His eyes were of a deeper blue, his hands trembled. "I couldn't stay away from you any longer, Lisa. I couldn't bear the thought of you being over here all alone without protection. I couldn't sleep, thinking you might be in danger again. I couldn't eat. I came in spite of your discouraging letter to tell you that no obstacle will be too big to overcome, if only I can hear a 'yes' in your sweet voice. If not, I'll leave at once without urging you anymore."

There was no sound in the house or in the street. The same little lamp with the pink flowered shade which six months ago lit the intense scene of my arrest was calmly watching us now. Martin looked at me and I understood beyond any doubt that I meant life and happiness to him. I saw in his eyes something for which, as he said, obstacles did not exist. I read love strengthened by respect, supported by courage and determination.

My tenseness suddenly gave way and I couldn't control my tears. Martin pressed me to him, and lulled me as one comforts a weeping child. The little pink lamp shone on us in each other's arms, solemn in the moment of the shaping of our destinies – too solemn even to kiss.

Then we spoke of ourselves, deciding that we ought to know each other better and trying to determine how to arrange it – Martin definite, even daring in his projects, I still cautious, planning every step.

Poor old Nikita had waited in the corridor to escort his American friend back to the hotel. When we opened the door he was fast asleep in a chair.

That night when Martin left he took with him much of my fear and confusion. His desire to make me happy and free under his and his country's protection was so strong that I borrowed from it some sense of security. In peace, I fell asleep.

The next morning I was more alive, more alert. I rose earlier than usual and before work ran to see an old family friend, Mme. Boulgakoff, who lived at the very end of Lassal Street, close to the harbor. I told her everything from the day I met Martin to the previous night when Martin and I had decided to see her in the evening, if possible, and ask her advice about our plans. Mme. Boulgakoff, or Tetia Tonia as I called her, loved me as her own daughter, and I was drawn to her with my problems. She scolded me for my secretiveness and then, gracious as usual, said that she could hardly wait until 8 o'clock, when we were to come.

Mme. Boulgakoff, pretty and charming, had lived in luxury for a great part of her life. During the Civil War her son Kolia died tragically; and in 1926 Captain Boulgakoff died just at the time I lost my mother. Our common grief brought us closer together. Immediately after her husband's death she was ordered to vacate her comfortable place and move into a one and a half room corner of an apartment. The Captain had been active to his last days in the Soviet Merchant Fleet, and his widow received a small pension, which she supplemented by selling many pieces of rare jade and ivory bric-a-brac brought from China by her husband. Her relative, Vassinka, an elderly lame man, served her devotedly. She had a cot for him put in the tiny half room that also served as a kitchen. He did the shopping and the cleaning, managed their small finances, and even cooked. Though close to sixty, Mme Boulgakoff was still beautiful, rather ageless. Not only Vassinka, but everyone felt it a privilege to wait on her. She was slightly plump, had very fair skin and lovely blond hair, beginning to be streaked with gray. Her eyes, when she was not complaining of her trifling ills, were rich brown, vivacious and playful.

We went to Mme. Boulgakoff's separately – I at eight sharp, Martin a few minutes later, as agreed. The little rooms looked crisp and fresh as on an Easter day. The hostess wore a lacy white blouse, not her usual black, and looked prettier and younger than ever.

"Where is he? Where is he, Lisa?" she demanded.

"He will be here shortly, Tetia Tonia. We could not take the risk of being seen on the streets together, you know."

"Of course, of course. How foolish of me! Of course you couldn't!"

Vassinka's greeting was to kiss my hand as usual. He was my silent but permanent admirer. When he looked at me, his eyes were two question marks, eloquent enough, and no word was said. The event seemed very important for Tetia Tonia, and he knew it would be better for him to let her do the talking. He must have worn himself out with all the preparations for receiving the American!

Mme. Boulgakoff took Martin's hand in both her tiny ones, and kissed him on the forehead. I could not help thinking that she received him cordially and more sweetly than I had the previous night. "Well, well," she said, "you come from America to see my Lisa, and I do not blame you."

I translated her greeting, word for word; Martin smiled and nodded. "Yes, nothing in the whole world would stop me."

We sat in the large room. The sofa and the few armchairs had white slip covers – immaculate, though carefully patched. Tetia Tonia clung to the old habit of putting slip covers over her furniture in the summer, the season when we also covered our oil paintings with thin white gauze stretched over the frames. An ebony screen with a design of ivory encrustation divided her room in two. Behind it was her neat bed. Vassinka brought tea on a tray, with fancy homemade cookies and jam. We felt most welcome.

"You are a wonderful hostess, Tetia Tonia," I said. "Even in these gray days you make everything look brighter and everyone feel happier."

"But wait a minute. Just think whom I am receiving today." Our conversation began, warm and natural. I felt that I had nothing to worry about.

Tetai Tonia's tea spread a fine aroma. It was a special tea served on special occasions (usually kept in a round Chinese box). Now it filled the room with a scent no perfume could surpass, increasing in everyone the sense of well-being and ease. The wheel of destiny must change, must go upward, I thought. I expect only good to come my way from now on.

"How perfectly charming he is, how perfectly charming," Tetia Tonia whispered more than once. She did not take her eyes away from Martin, and I felt his glance constantly on me. We told her all of our immediate plans. "Well, then," she tried to summarize it all, "do I understand that day after tomorrow, the seventh, you will register in SAAKA (equivalent to a United States City Hall) as husband and wife, and after that you, Lisa, will have the marriage certificate at hand for your safety, especially when you are with Martin?"

"Yes, Tetai Tonia. This way I can meet Martin without fear. He will no longer be just a foreigner to whom GPU agents might think I would pass some information, but officially my husband, though for us only on paper." Tetia Tonia smiled a little mischievously."You see," I continued, "this will give us the chance to know each other better, to judge whether or not we have some common points of view, common interests, hopes, and aspirations."

"I am sure you have," she interrupted.

"I am glad you think so, but if not, we will go back to the same SAAKA to get a divorce and Martin will return to America. It is very simple to get a divorce now and cost something like two and a half dollars in Martin's money."

"But this, my dear Lisa, will never happen!" Tetia Tonia suddenly became very excited. "You will never dare to reject him because if you do I shall not know you anymore." She spoke very emphatically. "Just watch him a moment. He looks at you with eyes of a father, a brother, a husband, a lover. Why, the greatest, all-embracing love is in his eyes. Let me tell you, he will be your guardian angel all your life. You might as well know if you do not marry him, I shall refuse to know you or be your friend, no matter how painful it may be for me."

"Oh, please, Tetia Tonia, do not make yourself sick about it – do not get so excited."

"How can I help being so excited? I have lived long enough to know a good, kind, reliable, loving man when I see him. As things go under this regime, where do you expect to find anyone half as good?"

"I understand, my dear Tetia Tonia, you do want my good, but please calm down."

"What does the lady say?" Martin asked, no doubt wondering all this time at our extraordinary animation.

"I'd better not translate it for you word for word, it might spoil you. Mme. Boulgakoff praises you so very highly."

"Is that all? All right, I won't insist." He smiled and winked. "Please thank her for thinking well of me, and tell her that I find her most charming and am very happy to have met her."

All this time Vassinka was silent and only when bidding us goodbye he said, "Well, it looks as though we are to lose our Lisa, our last sunshine," and a mist covered his eyes. I left first and walked with an even step all the way home. The night breeze was fresh. The streets were empty. Alone, relaxed and at peace, I walked in God's world and felt guided by Him.

When I reached home Vala was already asleep. I had hardly seen her during the past week. Little Shoura, our former maid's daughter and Vala's pet, was sick, and Vala spent days and often nights with her in the hospital. Not until the next day after work did I have a little time to chat with Vala about Martin and me, and she helped me to realize that such a personal problem should be decided by me alone. She left for the hospital telling me that the child was feeling much better. I sat down to repair a simple old dress I liked and wanted to wear for our tentative wedding. That night I was not supposed to see Martin who had many relatives to meet.

The next morning was lovely – not too hot, with clouds that were like huge snowballs in the rich blue skies. I saw Martin from far away and instinctively walked faster. "What is your hurry? Where are you running – and why? You will never be out of this land." I was nagged by a pessimistic voice within me. "Never mind – go ahead – have courage," contradicted another more authoritative inner voice.

Martin looked rested and happy and so utterly different from everybody on the street. He complimented me on my appearance and then hailed a passing cab. The driver was an old timer with a thin white beard. "I had better hold you tight," Martin said. "You might fall as these Russian cabs have no backs."

"Wait a minute, wait a minute," I said, pushing my large straw hat over my face. "I cannot risk being recognized in the arms of an American whom I have not yet married." We laughed heartily and without restraint. I had not laughed like that for a long time.

SAAKA (City Hall) was near the opera house which we were now passing, a graceful circular edifice. Climbing up the hill were the tall red flowers that blossom so richly towards autumn. They looked like flaming torches set around the theatre for some special festivity. The registration and other formalities did not take more than ten minutes. I knew the girl at the matrimonial desk and she expedited matters. I registered as a typist and Martin as a workman, so that the authorities' attention would not be especially drawn to this certificate. Soon the document was in our possession.

"Our first important step," Martin said, pressing my hand. The morning was still young, the air cool. The same old cab man beckoned to us with both hands.

"To the main post office," I said, "and stop in back of it."

"Ladno, ladno!" (all right, all right!), he said and beamed, lifting his hat a bit. For a brief second his face seemed familiar. On Lassal Street we stopped to get a few bottles of cold Borjom, a fine mineral water that Martin had been advised to drink instead of city water. The bottles fitted perfectly in the little suitcase I had taken along, and we went back to our cab.

"I am just thinking, Martin," I said, "today is the first time that I have been out with you in broad daylight. With our marriage certificate I don't even care whether they are watching me or not."

"I hope you will never again be in danger, Lisa." he said. Just as he was saying this I saw a group of men in green hats – agents of GPU. I felt a spasm in my stomach, but kept quiet.

Two more blocks and the cab stopped. Much to our surprise, the old 'isvoshtik' (cab driver) jumped off his seat with great swiftness and taking off his hat, said, "The Holy Ghost be over us. Allow me to congratulate you. I guess you must be husband and wife now. God bless you generously." It was good to feel his course, broad hand, hear his simple words of blessing, and look into his sparkling eyes which seemed to jump out of his kindly, wrinkled face.

And suddenly something clicked in my memory. "But dedoushka (grandpa) – I think I know you – yes, I do. You took me home in your cab from prison last May."

"The Holy Ghost be over us! Of course I did! I recognize you, Barishnia – Barinia (Miss, Mrs.), the moment you and Mister stepped into my cab, only I said nothing." He stood in front of us, putting all his weight on one foot, then the other, turning his hat in his hands, eyes down. "Once more," he continued, "God gives me the joy of serving you, and this time on a happier occasion. The Holy Ghost be over us!"

"Bless you, dear, dear man," I said. "I am so happy you spoke to me and helped me to recognize you."

Martin, who understood that we had been congratulated, stood quietly by. We almost forgot to pay the man, but when Martin remembered, he put in his hand much more than was due. While we were crossing the street, I began to tell him of the surprising coincidence. As we reached the opposite curb, the suitcase burst open and the three bottles tumbled out and broke with three explosions. "Good sign, good sign!" shouted our cabman from across the street. "It means you will be happy all your life!" And we shouted, "Spassibo!" (thank you) back to him.

This time Martin saw me to my door, and as I was due back to the office at 1 o'clock, we agreed to meet after work. For the next few evenings we took whatever conveyance we could, to reach the seashore where it was delightfully cool. We went to places that were once elegant summer resorts, such as Little Fountain, Big Fountain, even Lustdorf, which was farther away than the others and full of memories for me.

On the way we saw much destruction. The once gorgeous villas lay in ruin, their wooden parts having been used for fuel during the revolution.

We usually went by train or street car, and hearing us speak English, people looked at us with curiosity. That year (1930) American tourism was encouraged by the Soviet Government which needed dollars, and we were both taken for Americans who did not know a word of Russian. Never before had I heard such outspoken, impartial opinions of myself. The comments on both of us were mostly favorable, and I translated those for Martin that were amusing. "And she", said one very observant man, meaning me, "She could pass for a Russian." It was hard for me not to laugh.

Though Martin knew these days could decide his future, he did not try to put on airs to impress me, but was simple and natural – always himself. At first we did not speak much of ourselves, only once when I talked of my childhood, of Mother and our great love for each other. He said, "I shall try to replace your mother." This took me by surprise and though I wondered his words were like a warm current flowing through my being.

Our certificate of marriage, carefully folded, was always in my pocketbook. Every night I said goodnight to Martin, as to a new acquaintance, and he went to his hotel and I back home where, in the peace of the night I went over and over the recent events. I still could not get over the shock of his return. Is it true, I asked myself, that he, who according to my letter, should have definitely given me up, is here? That he, whom I never expected to see again spent the whole evening with me, his warm hand holding mine? I tried to sleep, but the train of thought continued. I never could have imagined that all the rather sad but logical and convincing proofs of the impossibility of my becoming his wife, explained in my letter, would be completely disregarded in the face of his overwhelming feeling. And now he was here, with a bold determination to overcome all obstacles if I would give him only a word of encouragement.

Was I ready to give him that word? I did not know. Suffering had developed hesitancy, timidity, and a certain lack of decision in me of which Martin had none. Suffering had taken away from me the spontaneity in which Martin was so rich. Even if I said yes, I thought, we could not become husband and wife until, by some miracle, I was out of Soviet Russia and safe in his free country. All the official and semi-official information stressed that now it was very hard for a non-communist to obtain permission to leave the country, but a person of Russian nobility with a record of political imprisonment – absolutely impossible. This was the stumbling stone, the obstacle that Martin did not fully size up and, therefore, believed he could overcome. Eyes open, I thought and thought—If we decided to unite our lives, he leaving when his visa expired and I remaining here, could we stand the separation and live on the fragile hope of possible reunion? And later, if all our hopes collapsed, could we bear it?

"If they refuse to let you out, I shall become a Russian citizen and live here, where you live," Martin had repeated on the day of his return.

I had replied that I would prefer to suffer alone.

Things were happening as if dictated by forces beyond my control and I instinctively yielded to them. Very soon I would have to decide my destiny in one word. Tetia Tonia had pointed out to me, when she dropped in, that I was no longer "sweet sixteen," I was not a glamorous beauty though, as she put it, loving me and exaggerating of course, I had a charm that few girls possessed. After prison and so much privation, I was nearly exhausted and should welcome a loving and helpful companion like Martin, ready to walk with me on the road of life, be it bright or stormy.

"Where do you expect to find another man like that," she demanded, "who crosses the ocean, crosses many lands to look once more into your eyes with the hope of maybe finding a little spark of love for him, and if so, ready to turn the whole world upside down for your mutual happiness?"

"I do not expect to find any other man at all, Tetia Tonia, but I would not allow myself to make this particular man miserable by jumping on his neck, saying, "Here I am, my troubles are over, now it is your turn!"

She laughed. "He would not object to that, silly girl," she said. "On the contrary, he would like it. There is nothing he would not do for you.

Nothing frightens him, he loves you. Don't you understand? He is crazy about you. All you have to do is to say 'yes' and leave the rest to God."

I was thinking and thinking. My eyes were getting heavy. Remembering this conversation with Tetia Tonia I finally fell asleep, her last phrase still ringing in my ears. "Leave the rest to God – leave the rest to God."

Time was going on and hour after hour Martin was winning me with his natural directness, his unlimited devotion, and his quick humor. A designer of modern furniture and a business man, he was at the same time interested in music and literature and arts of every kind. There was no writer ancient or modern in French literature, whose work he had not read in translation. He was equally well acquainted with Russian literature, and had read Gorky, Dostoyevsky, Turgenev, Tolstoi and Chekov, and could discuss their work with sharp intelligence. During our long walks conversation never lagged. His thoughts were strikingly original and he always had the right word on the tip of his tongue. In the most human, yet fascinating way, he told me of the deep impression my letter had produced on him and how, in spite of all the obstacles raised by me, he had felt that I liked him and that there might still be hope for him, if he could but speak to me face to face again. He sailed the day after my letter arrived and an arrangement was made to receive his second Russian visa in Stockholm. He had a gentle manner, and yet never was he too sweet or over-sentimental.

On Saturday, we reached the seashore early and were admiring the sunset. Remembering our first meeting at Zina's house, I casually asked, "Martin, do you think you liked me because I spoke English?"

"I liked you before you spoke," he said gently.

The three evenings spent with Martin by the sea were good for me, as usual. I felt stronger and looked much better, so I was told. The Black Sea was my friend. To be born by it, to have taken my first steps on its shore, and to have known it all my life created a tie that could never be broken. How many times in the past it had helped me to regain my peace, my poise. It always cleared my thoughts, and in these last years it invariably returned lost strength to my body. I remember how I missed it when I lived in Moscow and how I longed for its healthy air.

That night, August 10th, we went to a place called Arcadia. I had found out that one could dine there and looked forward to my first dinner with Martin. Things seemed to come our way. The street car was waiting for us as though especially ordered, and we had two front seats so that I could see the road ahead and recognized many places. "Look at this ruin," I said to Martin. "It was the villa of our friend Coronelli. I used to go there and spend weekends long, long ago, soon after we returned from France. We played tennis. I remember the court was here. See, here to the right."

"Do you still play tennis?" he asked.

"No, Martin, I don't. I have no one to play with anymore. I also have no racket. I give French and English lessons almost every evening after work. But let's forget about that! How about you? Do you play tennis?" I learned that he was an all around sportsman, and that tennis was his favorite game, in which he had won a championship at nineteen.

It was surprising how carefree I felt that evening, how I succeeded in forgetting where I was and who I was, and didn't let even one thought darken my mind.

The Arcadian dinner left no impression on our stomachs nor on our minds. We were glad to leave the crowded, noisy dining hall and take a long walk along the rocky coast. Here there were many more signs of reconstruction than in the other seashore places we had visited. Some buildings were completely repaired and some were in the process of rebuilding. The weather was splendid and the sea was very calm. We had fun hopping from stone to stone, trying to keep our balance. Soon darkness fell and we sat down on the ground in a spot that looked like a bench of sand. The Black Sea at our feet was telling its ageless tale.

We watched the moon come up to seek its reflection in the waters and soon a wide, golden road, starting right from under our feet spread and sparkled all around the sea, losing itself only far, far away at the horizon. We did not speak. The golden road stretching ahead of us was like a way of salvation. Millions of golden ripples glittered and danced before our eyes. I felt dizzy and leaned against Martin. Eyes closed, I sat protected and secure with his arms tightly around me. It was a supreme moment when the mind interrogated the heart and heard its reply. I opened my eyes and saw the ocean still pointing to the path ahead. Moving away from Martin a little, I sat erect facing him. His smile questioned me. "Martin," I said, "I do not think I feel like going—" His smile faded. "I do not feel like going back to that place for a divorce."

Like a torrent kept too long from flowing, his restraint broke free, and taking me into his arms, he kissed my eyes, my cheeks, my lips. Hardly able to catch my breath, I said, "Martin, do you really think you love me?"

This silly question of mine was too splendid a chance for Martin's rich humor to miss. Assuming an expression of sophisticated indifference, his mouth moving from side to side as though taking time to think it over, eyes full of the devil, he said, "I really do not know."

It takes courage to face an enemy. It takes courage to face death. It also takes courage to face love, which if crushed by circumstances, may never blossom. Just as fear attracts its own and brings forth doubt, depression, hatred and ultimate defeat, so love brings forth its own – hope, good will, trust and faith. Faith! 'The assurance of things hoped for.' Mobilizing my faith, I began a new chapter of my life. Let it be, let it come, I thought.

Even if our joy cannot be full, even if it may not last, let it be, let it touch us now. Even if the happiness of our future days proves to be only an illusion, even if we have to pay a great price for the little we may have, let it be, let it come now. I did not ask for it. I did not call him back from America. All I did was to plead with him to keep away from me and from this country, for his own good. He came, I did not call him; it was not my will. Maybe it was the will of God.

The tempo of my heart changed completely and the major reason for it was Martin's all-conquering joy, sweeping away like a strong wind, all the debris of fear. With a provocative note in my voice, I would say, "Down with fear! I have had more than my share of it. I am going to be as cheerful as you are, Martin," and I was. I laughed louder and heartier, and didn't care whether a "green hat" (Soviet Police) or any less obvious agent of GPU was on my track or not. We began to make plans. I wanted to have the blessing of the church. I explained to Martin that since my parents were dead, this was even more important to me and that without it nothing would seem right. I also told him that according to the Russian custom, our children, if any, should take the religion of the mother. Martin agreed, on the general principle that whatever I believed, whatever I wished, whatever I did – was right.

We went to see the Archbishop who, sick and emaciated, had just returned from a concentration camp near the Caspian Sea where the summers are torrid. Apologetically, he refused to marry us, to be of any help whatsoever. "I am old, children," he said, "very old and weak. To help you, my daughter, child of a nobleman, to leave Russia, might mean for me to be sent back to the place I have just come from. I could not live through that again. Forgive, children. I am too weak, too weak." We understood, of course, and could not blame him.

Father Nicolai, a younger priest whose baby son became ill and had been treated successfully by my father, took it upon himself to arrange a church ceremony as quietly as possible. No one but our dearest friends could be present. The date was fixed for the 12th of August at 9 o'clock in the evening in a private chapel on an abandoned estate. It was on the way to the summer place called "Little Fountain," some distance from town with mostly uninhabited and destroyed houses around.

Three days were left and we had to hurry to get something for me to wear – something white and lovely and new. What an experience! I could not remember having bought anything new for twelve or thirteen years. Now one of my recently married friends, Verochka, guided us to the same people who though no longer in business, had helped her with her wardrobe. They had a few rolls of material saved from the time of their private salon. There was little variety. I had to select from what was to be had; a dress in one place, slips in another, shoes in a third.

I was a very awkward shopper, terribly embarrassed by the fact that an American gentleman was paying for all these things. Verochka made fun of my embarrassment. She tried to put sense in my head by saying that from then on, all that was his would become mine. I knew that, and yet I blushed every time Martin opened his wallet.

No wedding bands were to be found and, according to the Russian custom, we had to have one for each of us. We heard of a former jeweler, now a workman, who would make the rings if we supplied the gold. Sister suggested Father's university medal, the only thing of value we still had. For eight years I had saved it as a precious memory. It was a rather heavy oblong golden plaque with a fine vignette in bas relief bearing Father's full name and the date when he finished his course at the University of Kiev. At first, the idea of melting this medal seemed wrong; but then I thought that Papa needed it no longer and would enjoy giving us our first and most important wedding present.

We had to go twice to the modest dwelling of our jeweler. He lived in a tiny room at the end of a long courtyard and worked sitting on his bed, having only one other piece of furniture – an old table. An old icon, an image of St. Nicolas, hung in a corner of the room, the kind face of the saint and the silver halo brightening the place. He took the measurements of our fingers, and discovering that Martin was an American, showed a special interest in our bold attempt to unite our lives. The last time we went he seemed sincerely delighted to see us. "God loves brave people," he said, returning Father's medal transformed into a pair of simple wedding bands. The transaction was almost finished and I still held the two rings in the open palm of my hand when the man resumed his speech. Looking at the holy image, then at us, then at the holy image again, he said, "I shall pray for you and ask my saint to bless you on all your ways."

I pressed Martin's hands. "He is blessing us. He is kind," I said, and leaving him I felt more hope in my heart. At night now, I no longer lay awake but completely relaxed, thanked God for His nearness, and slept.

Tuesday morning, the 12th, even before dressing, I ran to look at my new things. They were so lovely, especially the dress which was pure white silk with a Grecian design in relief bordering the neck, sleeves and skirt. It was not the wedding gown girls usually dream of with a veil, train and expensive laces, but for me it meant much more. It was like a sacred gown I had been given to wear, led to a ceremony which not long ago I had not even dreamed.

At 6 o'clock sharp I was back from work. The hour of our semi-clandestine marriage was approaching. Verochka met me at the door. She informed me that everything was ready for the evening, and also that tickets were reserved for our excursion to Yalta the next day with two other couples. She advised me to rest, and having no special preparations to make, planning to wear my hair plain as usual, I obeyed her and rested with a surprisingly mental calmness.

A harmony of magnificent voices filled the air as Martin and I passed through the threshold of the secluded chapel. How majestic and melodious was the bridal song, different from the usual one I had expected to hear. Father Nicolai had arranged everything in a unique way. A man of rare musical talent and exceptional voice, he knew what the qualities of a choir should be. He trained his own singers, and here it was, his great joy, the superb Capella whose expression of art and feeling would stir anyone. Here it was, Father Nicolai's rich and yet delicate wedding present to me – his choir.

I was deeply stirred. The blood rushed to my heart and for a second, I saw nothing. The choir sang. It seemed that in this beautiful coordination of men's and women's voices, there was not only talent and skill, but there was also love. A delicate scent of flowers delighted me.

When I could see again, I was amazed. The chapel was a garden of roses and carnations through which the gold of the candles gently gleamed. A few times I looked at Martin, feeling that he needed my moral support. He stood very straight, a bit pale, but apparently peaceful, eyes aglow, only now and then reaching for my hand. I let go of all tension, and though physically participating in it all, mentally I was transported to a higher realm. Father Nikolai put the rings on our fingers. Before kissing me, Martin hesitated for a moment. His glance meeting mine was a gift of his life to me, and we kissed for love until death.

When the ceremony was over, our friends surrounded us. I pressed Vala close to me and told her that if one day I should become an American, she would become one also. Tetia Tonia had much to say. Her congratulations were effusive. She was proud of us, she was happy for us, she knew we would be the happiest couple in the world. Vassinka stood silent, trying to smile. Zina and Nikita felt very important and they had full right. Was it not in their house that we first met? Mlle. Dreving, my school 'dame de classe', the one we nicknamed 'the Saint', now quite elderly, had not stirred from her prayerful attitude, standing not straight but somehow on the bias like the Tower of Pisa. It was most comforting to have her with me on such an important occasion. She united the past with the present. I approached to kiss her and she blessed Martin and me. Our former maid Angelina, Shour's mother, was crying. Verochka was beaming. Marussia, my dear friend and office mate for many years, careful as usual, had not dared to come.

Father Nicolai joined the group and said an informal word of congratulation and blessing. As though reading my thoughts, he added that in spirit my parents were with us also. Father Nicolai had conducted the whole ceremony beautifully, and our wedding was an unusual religious concert in an atmosphere of flowers, friendship and love.

When we left, the little chapel sank back into silence and desertion. The moon was already high. We looked to the right, and from the high coast of the "Little Fountain" where we were we saw the wide golden road across the sea, the same road that had opened up before my eyes previously in Arcadia. We stood in admiration of the splendid view: Vala, Tetia Tonia, Vassinka, and Verochka and her husband. Verochka was the happiest and most talkative one. She was raving about my looks in church, could not get over Martin's absolute composure, and the harmony of the ceremony in general. She wanted to know whether Martin was pleased with the flowers that decorated the church which she had chosen upon his request. I knew nothing about this and had wondered where the magnificent and costly flowers came from.

"And so you already begin to do things behind your wife's back, Martin," I said. Looking at him I could see he guessed how much I appreciated his secret surprise.

We chatted for awhile and then judged it more prudent to separate before our group was noticed. "Tell Martin," said Tetia Tonia, "that we actually are victims of circumstances, victims of historical changes. Not so long ago it would have been unheard of that after a wedding there would be no reception, no champagne."

"Please tell Tetia Tonia I understand the situation very well and that no reception, not even one with champagne, could make me any happier."

"Thank God for that, and keep that happiness forever, my boy. I would greatly enjoy giving you a real old-fashioned reception," said Tetia Tonia, kissing Martin. Then we all went our own way.

At home, still dressed, I sat at my desk, scribbling with my pencil. Tetia Tonia had said it, we were victims of circumstances. There was always a mist of fear coming from one direction or from another. How great of Martin to try to understand it all. One would think it strange that after the civil marriage and now after the church's blessing, husband and wife were not together, did not even plan to be together, but had gone separately to their different homes. But Martin understood. Having been convinced at last that I would not be allowed to live with him, but would have to undergo alone all the formalities of the Russian bureaucracy which meant waiting and waiting – he knew that we could not take the risk of having a child born in Soviet Russia, nor of my being prevented from traveling because of my possible condition.

Tetia Tonia was shocked at the first mention of our mutual agreement, but Martin's great heart was generous in everything. The arrangement for the company of two other young couples on our trip to the Crimea would make more of a picnic out of what should have been a honeymoon cruise.

The steamship Krim, recently built in a Dutch shipyard, floated smoothly on the calm Black Sea as if conscious of being the most beautiful, the most modern passenger vessel in those waters. The night came. Martin and I were on deck. He hummed a song I liked and tried to memorize – "Let Me Call You Sweetheart," and then another, "Ah, Sweet Mystery of Life". For a long time I had not heard any American songs but I knew how catchy they were from the time when I worked at the A.R.A., "I Wonder Who's Kissing Her Now?", "Yes, We Have No Bananas," ragtime and Charleston music were most popular. These songs were different with more melody and more feeling.

By now we were over our disappointment that Verochka's husband, having been retained on his job could not make the trip, and of course, neither his wife nor the other couple felt like going without him. I would have been inclined to think they had just played a trick on us, wishing us to be alone and would even have suspected Tetia Tonia of being mixed up in it some way had I not seen Verochka's tears of disappointment.

"I am sorry for Verochka," I said to Martin, "but after all, maybe it is for the best. We have only a few counted (precious) days to be together. The only trouble is that this way it will be much harder to part."

"I wonder how I'll have the heart to go and leave you here," he said.

"Do not speak of it now. Do not even think of it. We are on a pleasure trip. We are both Americans, you and I. Nobody suspects that

I am a Russian. I feel as though I had never had any worries at all. I am free and happy with you on this lovely boat." We waited until the sparkling road on the sea became its widest. The ship seemed to cut through the very center of it. "Right now," I said, "I must get all the fortitude, gather all the patience, because after you leave and before we meet again I may have to stumble over many obstacles. I shall trust my little star, though – and I told him Mother's comforting legend.

"It certainly smiles at me through you," he said. We stood at the rail facing the bright road. The feeling that God Himself had sent this kind, fine man for my protection and my happiness did not leave me. Martin felt how highly tuned my spirit was and responded accordingly. In our cabin after I had gone to bed he came and knelt at my berth, passing his hands over my hair. Then he kissed my forehead and left.

The next day we were in the historical city of Sebastopol. We had enough time to see the town and take pictures at the famous monument erected as a memorial to the Crimean War. Leaving Sebastopol, the most graceful coast of the Crimea appeared before our eyes. The green hills in the distance seemed dropped from the very skies. The nearest slopes were covered with orchards. Vineyards and rare parks surrounded the rich villas and palaces, some of which used to be the winter residence of the Tzar's family, all transformed now into rest homes for workers and peasants where it was not so easy to get a place for an ordinary non-communist citizen. There was one palace of Moorish style, another with a Moslem minaret of pure marble; and here, there, and almost everywhere the stately yet somber cypresses lifted their summits high into the sky.

I was telling Martin all I knew of the Crimea of the early time when some of the ancient navigators settled here briefly and left their traces in the vestiges of one of the very oldest ruins in the land, the Genoa Tower near Theodosia. For a long time the majority of the population had been Tartars, a tall and slender race with exceptionally handsome men who before the Soviet regime charmed the fashionable ladies coming here for the winter season, and served as guides on their trips through the mountains. Many a story was whispered about the irresistibility of these attractive men. (I might mention that these Tartars, who became a separate Tartar republic under the Soviet regime, later fell into disgrace and right after the German invasion of World War II were transplanted from the warm Crimea to the far north and cruelly annihilated.)

I told Martin how much I liked the narrow winding streets of Yalta, and how glad I was we were going to stay there and not go farther to Theodosia, Novorossisk and Batum. As we came nearer and nearer to the coast, Martin could not help but see its resemblance to the French Riviera. He spoke of Nice and his artist uncle, and I remembered the time Vala and I had visited there and at Monte Carlo with our 'dame de pension' Mme. Dolores when we were on a tour through the south of France and Italy. Soon, we reached Yalta.

It was remarkable how many privileges were given to us as American tourists. Even the people in the crowds seemed to want to please us. "Let them go through! Let them pass first!" I heard. "They are Americans, very quick, not accustomed to wait." We were among the first to be let off the ship. On shore, we were driven in a special car for tourists to the best waterfront hotel, where Russian travelers could obtain a room only if it were not occupied by Americans. I understood that the Russians in this hotel were accepted only on condition that they would vacate as soon as another party of Americans arrived on the boat coming from Odessa, or on its way back from Batum.

Our room, a combination sitting room and bedroom on the third floor, was spacious and elegant, with three little balconies, two overlooking the sea and one overlooking a narrow and picturesque street. The whole room was carpeted with a rug of deep red with a symmetrical design of French fleur de lis. The furniture was of fine mahogany: a large dressing table, two dressers, a writing desk, a full-size mirror in a wardrobe, a few easy chairs, and twin beds. I felt like a school girl on vacation, ready for adventure.

"Remember, Martin," I said, "we both are American tourists."

"I wish we were," said Martin. "It would make everything quite simple."

Having unpacked and changed into lighter clothes, we went out on the balcony. It was a splendid day. The vast Black Sea, reflecting the sky, was of Mediterranean blue. Down below on the pavement of the long narrow tree-lined promenade, lights and shadows were jumping and catching one another as the sea breeze made the autumn leaves tremble slightly. Along the street was a line of cabs with fringed linen tops which looked like awnings from where we stood. Quite a distance to our right we saw a small, sandy beach.

"Wonderful!" said Martin. "Let's go for a swim." "Not now, sir. First things first. Did you forget?"

"Oh-h-h, yes. The telegram to my dad. There wasn't time to send it from Odessa."

"Come on, quick," I said. It seemed to me that my feet weren't fast enough. I wanted to run and skip all the time. We took the nearest cab.

"This cab is more comfortable than the ones in Odessa. At least they have a back," said Martin. "They remind me of those in St. Augustine, Florida." I was ashamed not to know anything of St. Augustine, Florida, but I learned much of its history listening to Martin on our way to the post office.

The telegram was sent signed, "LISA YOUR NEW DAUGHTER AND YOUR SON THE HAPPIEST MAN IN THE WORLD."

From there we went to the garden around the stately church of St. Alexander on the Neva. On the outside in the niche, was a full-size image of the warrior saint in mosaic. I went close to look at this masterpiece when Martin called my name, and the result of it was a lovely snapshot of the saint and me which I still cherish. Martin's camera was the latest model, unknown to us in Russia. Photography was obviously his hobby and he got so enthusiastic about it that we were late for the hotel lunch which was meager anyway. We could have skipped it entirely without any loss. Both Martin and I were hungry and he, the provider of the family, went out in search of food. I changed into my new bathing suit of blue linen and approved of it, looking into all the mirrors in our room. Martin returned rather alarmed, having been unable to find anything to eat. "No bread, no cheese, no cookies – nothing without a ration card."

"But what is in that large package?" "Grapes. Just grapes. Ten pounds of grapes."

"Ten pounds! For the two of us? A Crimean grape cure, I guess."

After swimming, not satisfied with grapes, we hurried back to the hotel to be on time for dinner. The menu was not very promising but the waiter remarked that we could order as many portions of black caviar as we wanted. Famished, we each had two portions to start our dinner and at the end two more with our tea. It was really delicious. The bread they served with it was freshly baked for the party of Americans expected in the morning.

"Too bad they do not serve lemon," I said.

Martin got up with his usual speed, excused himself, and disappeared. A few minutes later he returned and began to slice a beautiful, juicy lemon. I didn't utter a word, my mouth watering. I was waiting for a slice for my tea and another for my caviar sandwich. This started a general commotion in the dining room. The waiters had to run from one table to another, telling people that we were not privileged characters, but that the lemon was a personal belonging of this particular American.

Obviously we had become a sensation. To share our lemon with all those around us would have been impossible, so we sat trying to make believe that we did not notice what was going on. "Now, tell me, where did you get it?" I asked Martin, translating for him what I was hearing about the lemon.

"Tell me first how you like it."

217

"I never enjoyed anything more, believe me I have not had a lemon for years."

"Well, I like it too. But it took foresight." He winked at me. "Last time I was in Russia I missed lemons a lot, so this time I brought some right from little old New York."

"Hurray for your foresight!"

After dinner I wanted to stroll again through the streets of Yalta, but soon realized it was too much. I could hardly lift my feet on our way back to the hotel and was asleep before I knew it. In the middle of the night I woke up. The moon was practically in our room. My eyes followed its rays through the wide open door with the view on the sea. I heard the noise of a chair on the balcony. It was Martin, sitting alone at that late hour. I was surprised and somewhat sorry for him, but I did not stir, nor did I call him. It would not be right, I thought, and yet there was something wrong in not calling him.

"How come my dear little wife fell asleep without even saying goodnight," said Martin the next morning, making me believe he was terribly offended. I thought to myself that there was more truth than joke in his pretended offense.

That day we went to Gursuff, a village not far away from Yalta. We saw the remarkable Grotto of Pushkin, named after our great poet who lived here and dedicated quite a few poems to this Grotto. One enters it in a small canoe and is amazed at the phosphorescent green and blue of the water. Our guide said its only equal is in the Blue Grotto in Capri. No wonder Pushkin was inspired by it.

The afternoon was to be devoted to letter writing. Our room, being very bright, enabled us to take snapshots of the interior. Then, sitting on the shady balcony, we wrote postal cards to Martin's numerous friends and also to some of mine, both in Russia and abroad. The first friend I thought of was Captain Harry Grimston, who I knew would rejoice over the news of my marriage and possible change of address. The evening was approaching and long shadows were spreading on the street, deeper was the gamut of colors before sunset and darker the blue of the sea. I finished with my mail and was contemplating the beauty of the Crimean twilight. Martin was still writing "some long neglected business letters," he said.

"I am going out for a stroll," I said. I waved and motioned for him not to get up. I walked, moving ahead without destination, walking for the sake of the walk I thought, not really knowing that it wasn't the stroll I needed, but solitude – a long and sincere chat with myself. Ever since I had seen Martin sitting alone on the balcony in the middle of the night, I had felt disturbed, and I wanted to face the reason for my disturbance. I kept on walking and then stopped, finding myself in familiar surroundings. Indeed, it was the garden of the Church of St. Alexander Nevsky. I sat down on a bench and thought of Martin and me, the unnaturalness of our self-imposed abstinence from each other, or was it imposed by me alone I wondered. I wondered whether Mme. Bulgakoff was right and I was wrong. I tried to analyze myself to find out whether it was my cowardice or my selfishness that had put limitations on our happiness. What a good actor he must be I thought, or does he love me more than himself; outwardly he does not seem to mind the incompleteness of the days he dreamed of. Am I right or am I wrong? Am I a woman or am I a monster, to calculate so closely, to be so worried about what might happen to me should I become pregnant? People were entering the church. Vesperal songs resounded on the air. I went in and stood and listened to the prayers and songs, not thinking of anything at all, not even praying.

Martin stood outside the hotel, nervously looking around and I called him the moment I saw him. He ran, put his arms around me, and in his eyes, in his embrace, was all the anxiety, all the love a man could hold. Suddenly I knew that no fear of the future difficulties, nor anything else, could create an obstacle to our complete happiness.

We had three more days in Yalta – happy days darkened only by the thought of their short duration. The air of my native country was good for me. I loved the splendid autumnal weather, daily swimming, long walks in the scented Yalta hills and boat rides on the motionless sea with the man I loved and trusted, a man who had no calculation, no other reason to love me but for what I was, a poor heavily tried human being undefeated only in spirit, and alive and happy through it. We had ample time to discuss the recent not too pleasant past and to dream of our future. Having discarded my previous hesitancies and apprehensions, my growth in self-respect added much to my happiness.

The boat that was to take us back to the port of Odessa was to leave at midnight. We checked out of the hotel early and by the time we boarded the steamer Martin was very hungry. He asked for food but was told that the dining room was closed and that he couldn't possibly get anything at that hour. Martin would not take no for an answer – though not able to speak Russian he made himself well understood by every employee of the ship from the captain to the sub-cook. Quietly I was observing the development of this scene without participating in it. I knew he would win. Never in all the years of starvation in Russia had I come across a human being fighting so passionately for the satisfaction of his hunger. He knows what he wants and how to go after it, I thought. This seems to be his principal trait. There and then I knew for sure that with such a temperament, accepting his offer to remain in the U.S.S.R. if I were not let out would be folly.

Martin disappeared for awhile, returning excited and triumphant from the kitchen and the pantry. "In a few minutes they are going to send up something for both of us."

"Wonderful! What a victory! You deserve a medal!"

Half a large loaf of black bread and a dish of salt were brought into our cabin a while later. Martin, normal and happy again, tipped the surprised ship's boy generously and without anymore words broke the loaf in half, handed one part to me and devoured his with the greatest relish.

Odessa. A few friends met us upon our return; among them was Vassinka, the lame grey-haired errand boy of Mme. Bulgakoff. He brought greetings from Tetia Tonia and an invitation to supper that night for Martin, Vala and me. Here again, was Mme. Bulgakoff's typical perseverance. She couldn't rest until she had arranged some kind of a party for us.

It was a lovely supper. Martin was amazed at the way the table was arranged and at the elaborate menu. Of course, having lived elegantly for two-thirds of her life, Mme. Boulgakoff hadn't forgotten any of it and Vassinka was ready to execute all her orders. The cloth on the round table was of the finest embroidery. I knew it was the only one left as she had shown it to me once, thinking to sell it one day. Tiny individual crystal salt cellars artistically placed on red and yellow autumn leaves looked like diamonds in a topaz and ruby setting. Vodka infused with some rare herbs was served with tiny canapés of chopped herring and egg on black bread.

Then followed a clear soup with hot pirojki (meat cakes), a delicious stew with potatoes prevailing, tea, and of course her unique cookies.

Tetia Tonia, charming as usual, combined formality with informality. At first, very stately, extending her tiny hand to be kissed by Martin, and a few minutes later she was trying on our present – a pair of cute Tartar slippers, which she wore for the rest of the evening.

In Odessa my heart was not as much at ease as it had been in Yalta. The shadows of the not-so-distant past grew taller as the twilight of our brief happiness was approaching. Only two more days and I would be alone again. I had every minute planned. Next day we were to go first to my parents' graves. We started early for the cemetery, a rather sad road to take for more than one reason. Passing by the Seamen's Hospital, I told Martin about Odessky and his constant kindness to me, of his helpfulness in our office, of the nurse by whom he sent his regards to the very prison, so that the kind woman would notice me and maybe somehow be of assistance to me; and of his death soon after Martin's first departure. "Thus," I said, "neither he nor I ever returned to the Foreign Maritime Agency of the Soviet Mercantile Fleet, as we had once promised each other."

Pointing out the red roof of the prison, I spoke of Mrs. Broochis my cellmate, the old lady whom I had lovingly tucked in every night. The funny little Mrs. Broochis, who like a kind sybarite, had predicted a "charming fiancé" for me – which, I said smiling at Martin, "turned out to be so very true." For this, he kissed me right in public, right there in the trolley car.

At Father's and Mother's tomb I prayed aloud. We both knelt, asking them to bless our life together and to protect us. There was a passport picture to be taken and a few more friends we were to see, all closely tied with the memory of my parents and my childhood. To visit them with Martin was for me a case of conscience. We stopped to see Mrs. Stoyanoff, an elderly Romanian lady who had known my mother since Mother's childhood days in Yassy.

"She certainly doesn't look her age, this nice person of eighty," remarked Martin.

"Her vivacity and general awareness are really remarkable." I said, "She is a brave old lady, never complaining."

"But what was that drink she offered us?" "Didn't you like it?"

"I'm sorry. I couldn't stand it!"

"Thank God you did not show it. That was the usual Romanian refreshment – water with jam. Every Romanian housewife takes great pride in her jam."

We were walking slowly towards our house. "Let me ask you a question," said Martin. "How old is the next lady we are going to visit?"

"Please don't expect me to introduce you to some young fascinating beauties," I joked, "because I won't."

We had a bite and in the afternoon went to visit "Maman," my adored school directrice. She, also, had been in prison briefly, probably because she was an aristocrat. They kept the stoic and beautiful lady only a few days. A feeling of sanctity filled me now as it always had in my childhood when I came into her presence. The grand lady, one of the last of her kind, "Maman" to me now as before, was seated in a comfortable old chair knitting, her feet covered with a warm shawl. She kissed me on the cheek and I bent to kiss her hand as we did in school when she condescended to kiss us. Strange, but somehow I was still her pupil, and she my beloved school "Maman."

"I am glad you came to show me your husband," she said, "and I must tell you right away that I am favorably impressed and compliment you on your choice." This was said in Russian, and then to Martin she said in English: "I am happy to congratulate you on your marriage. You certainly are a lovely couple." Then she turned to me. "It is a pity that your mother is no longer with us to see you loved and protected, and to know that there is hope for you to live in a free and just country." "I often think of her," she continued, speaking of my mother as one of the most graceful of women.

Maman's daughter, Olga Vladimirovna, handed us cups of hot tea. The evening was approaching. Martin was engaged in an animated conversation with Maman.

Olga Vladimirovna left the room and I sat aside, close to the window, looking at the cameo face of Maman. Like a motion picture film the school years passed before me and I realized, as never before, the great role she had played in my life by her example of justice, poise, dignity and charm. Here before me was the school's Maman who, after I had spent seven years in her establishment, blessed my first steps in life, giving each of my classmates and me a little gospel for guidance. Now, so many years after, the same Maman was speaking to me and my husband, wishing us happiness at the beginning of our married life. "What an experience to know such a person," Martin said as we walked out.

Nikita met us at the corner of our street. His head was low and I knew that his last attempt through some private acquaintanceship to arrange our departure together was in vain. He handed Martin his return ticket for the next day's afternoon train to Leningrad via Moscow, and said that Zina was expecting us for an early supper. A warm and sweet gathering it was. Even Zina's crying over Martin's departure was not taken too seriously.

Long into the morning hours Martin and I sat writing the addresses of my numerous friends to whom he wished to send parcels from America. "Do you realize, Lisa," he said after we had finished, "that only a little more than two weeks ago, right here in this very room, the happiness of my whole life hung on a thin thread?" I only listened. Later, "Remember that under any circumstances, Lisa, I love you, and I will stop at nothing until I have you safe and happy in America." My eyes were moist. "Those eyes must shine," said Martin, kissing me. "They must always shine with the light of your little star. No past sorrow shall dull them."

"My sorrow is not of the past, Martin, but of the present – the sorrow of parting with you," I said.

The last day came. A few hours were left before his departure, then one hour, and then only a few minutes. The more I felt the sorrow of separation, the greater grew the courage to stand firm on my own feet until the day of our reunion. We said goodbye at home, not at the railway station. I could not stand the thought of bidding goodbye to Martin in public. Only now I fully understood why Father insisted on saying goodbye to us in our own home. Now I disliked a public farewell just as he did. Martin left at three in the afternoon. It was a clear and cool day. At that hour the sun was at its brightest in our room. I sat alone. The sun rays were of spectral hues as they passed through the prisms of my crystal vase in which Martin's gift, long stemmed red roses, were gleaming. Gently the sun touched my forehead. I felt it on my eyes, my lips, and looking down, saw it reflected in the gold of my marriage ring.

LETTERS

W ho was this person who had just experienced seventeen tumultuous, yet enchanting days? Was it I, or someone else whom I had watched closely, wondering at the happenings? I continued to go to work at the Exportkleb as before, giving lessons in the evening and falling asleep before any thought could torment my mind. The first week or ten days after Martin's departure, I lived day by day, unable to size up the events of the last month. On the whole, the city, the streets, and my work were the same. The days fell into their former routine, yet everything seemed less somber and was less disturbed by the uncertainty of our life, probably subconsciously visualizing myself free and happy on some future day, and considering the present as a temporary inconvenience.

I wore the silk shirts that Martin had bought for me; one light blue, the other beige, and walked the streets of Odessa with a sure step, the privilege of one not possessed by fear. Some girls, total strangers, stopped me and asked where I got these ravishing shirts, and I answered as casually as possible, "In America." Some of my acquaintances, not knowing about my marriage, complimented me on my looks; they thought I had just returned from a vacation, and of course, I let them think so. The less said in Soviet Russia, the better.

My elated mood did not last. I missed Martin more than I had thought I would and began to write him almost every day, starting with the first of September. My husband saved nearly all these letters, and I am sorry that, afraid as we always were in Soviet Russia, I destroyed his with the exception of one or two hidden in my diaries. I copied my letters as they were written, and hope my readers will notice that since then my English has improved a bit.

LETTER #1 Odessa

1 Sept. 1930

My dear Martin,

I received your cards from Moscow and thank you very much for them. Soon I hope to have word from Riga.

In the constant rush of our last days together, I forgot to tell you many things I wanted to say. Martin dear, you are far away again, and you can only write to me, but do write. Speak to me, tell me all your thoughts, encourage me; I need encouragement. I miss you. Don't think I am weak. Oh, no. Not at all! But how could I explain it to you? You see, I am a little lost about myself. Your companion of those last days, your Lisa, was new, not only to you, but to herself. Now, having returned to my ordinary life, I am surprised at many things – how this new Lisa could so easily leave the other one far behind, so that in reality you did not know much of that other Lisa at all. Yes, I see it now. I did not speak much of myself. I did not try to make you understand me better and thus, though very near, I am afraid I remained far. You, also, it seems, spoke so little of yourself that sometimes I wonder how well I know you. So, let us try at least through letters to understand each other better—

Good night, my dear, sleep well. I miss you.

Your Lisa

2 Sept. morning

P.S. I just received your parcel from Moscow. Thank you very much, dear Martin, but I would prefer you to have the sweaters along with you on your way to Riga. I am sure you felt cold. We had many cold days even here in Odessa. I had to put on one of your sweaters. Thank you, I like it. It reminds me so much of you, I shall put numbers on all my letters, please do the same with yours. I am waiting for the photos.

LETTER#2 Odessa

Thursday, 2 Sept. 1930

I have sent you my first letter yesterday and in the afternoon I received your letter from Riga and the card from Köln. I was really glad to have your good news. So you left Riga behind and traveled safely farther—

Thank you for all the information you give me. Let us hope there will be no obstacles to our plans. As yet I have received only a letter from the consulate in Riga, and I read it here on my job after office hours.

We also passed through Koln once in our life, and admired its wonderful silhouette, and the famous cathedral—

Martin, how are you? Here, we are still upset by the sickness of the little girl, and Vala has had no rest at all. Our house is in a turmoil. Everything would seem brighter with you around—

I am still glad we said goodbye at home, and not before everybody at the railway station.

We have a bright autumn day here in Odessa, a glorious day. But I am far from being happy, yet I know I must be brave.

Same day, 11:00 P.M.

The Yalta photos arrived. I looked at them at least a hundred times, and will do so again and again. Everybody finds me rather natural in most of them. Which one do you like best? Tell me. The captain of the steamship Krim and his tremendous wife will be glad to have one. Do send me some for them and also some to send away to friends. It is so nice to have such a vivid recollection of Yalta!

It is getting late, but never mind, let us talk a little more.

Martin, darling, when thinking of our future little home, don't forget the bathroom must be one of the best rooms, rather bright and large. I am a little bit crazy about bathrooms. Before that flat we always had beautiful bathrooms. I do not give any other order, but please do not forget this. Oh, my, my, my! I dream of it now, but I am afraid it is too early even to dream.

Your large photo is in front of me. I look into your eyes and ask you many, many questions which it is impossible to ask you in letters. You keep quiet, but your glance is kind. I remember you once told me that any of my thoughts and deeds, anything I like is dear to you. I thought deeply of that phrase of yours. It helps me to answer my own questions. You said very much by it, and in moments of sadness or uncertainty, I remember these words and they help to brighten my mind—I have faith in your words, Martin, I do.

But, Darling, it is time to go to bed. Please send me away, it's enough talking. Goodnight, my dear. Do you wear your wedding band? I do, but not at work, only at home and at night.

Sleep well,

Your Lisenka

LETTER # 3 7 Sept. 1930

My dear Martin,

I am free today. I shall go out into the fresh air and take along "THAIS", the book you left for me. It will be quite an experience to read Anatole France in the English translation.

I shall try to go far away to the seashore, probably to Arcadia, where recently we were together. Vala wishes to stay home. She really lost too much strength with the little girl's illness. I hope you are enjoying your stay in France. I am sorry now I didn't ask you to buy Mother's and my beloved perfume, "Apres l'ondee" of the Fabrique Guerlain.

So many things I did not do when you were here. I cannot look now without being angry at myself, at some rare old editions I wanted you to take along and save for me, also Father's beautiful silver glass holder, out of which you could have drunk your hot tea with lemon, like a Russian, without burning your hands as you did in Yalta. So many other portable things—Well, never mind.

I often think how on the day you left, you said with great conviction that "Everything is going to be all right." I do trust it will be.

Love L.

LETTER #4 Odessa

11 Sept. 1930

My dear,

I received lots of things, a card and an envelope with the photos from Nice. The little note from Paris was no doubt written very much in haste. Sometimes later I shall tell you what funny mistakes you made in it. Your card informs me that your uncle, the artist, has added much enjoyment to your stay in Nice. I am very glad. I always imagined Nice is a town where nobody worries.

It is the 11ᵗʰ of September. Since you left I am going regularly to my job and sometimes work very late in the evening. As for myself, sorry I cannot say I have no worries at all, and they might turn to be some quite serious ones.

At home, things are going better. The little Shoura is recovering and is going to be taken home from the hospital by her mother, and Vala will rest and think a little more of herself—

I am writing again from the office. I imagine you will be at home tomorrow. All this distance covered so fast and without difficulties – without obstacles, from one country to the other, this seems incredible to us here—

I know you are happy to be home. How did you find your dear father?

Is he well, was he annoyed by your long absence?

Regards to all,

L.

P.S. It is now the 12ᵗʰ of September. Just a month ago, do you remember this day? Or rather evening, in Odessa?

Sept. 29 – 30

My dearest Lisa,

I was about to answer your third letter when your fourth arrived. There is no more satisfying pleasure to me than the sight of the familiar envelope with the familiar handwriting. You do not know how happy I am.

I did not open your letter upon receiving it, but will wait until I have plenty of leisure. During this time I am in a state of pleasurable anxiety and imagine to myself the things you might have written. Then I run off to some lonesome corner and open the letter very slowly and swallow the lines greedily. Dear Lisa, if you wish me to be happy, please write, write and write.

I am brave and have all the courage and inspiration a young man can possibly have, all due to you, my dearest.

My desire was to do something in honor of your arrival, so I leased a store on the most important street in New York (Fifth Avenue). I am sure that when you come you will be proud of it. All my efforts are being put into making this new establishment a place of beauty, art and culture. My brain, for the past two weeks, has been occupied with designs, financing and construction. Beginning tomorrow, I shall have to contend with carpenters, painters, electricians, architects and city officials. Not until this project is finished will I have time to rest. I find endless pleasure in doing this work, for I am working for you, my most precious lamb—

Beginning October 1st, I shall live at a new address. I have moved into a home not very far away from my business. It is a large, comfortable, pleasant room with an open fireplace and a spacious bathroom. When you arrive you will see whether you wish to stay here for awhile or seek a new apartment to your liking. I feel you have just as much right to decide in this matter as I have.

I have purposely moved into this old-fashioned house with large doors and windows, instead of into one of the new apartments being built in New York today. I am sure we will be happy, planning our own home together.

I, too, have your picture before me. I smile and am proud of you. I talk and sing to you, and kiss you. Oh, if only I could embrace you. I pledge my fidelity and honor to those beautiful and sad eyes of yours. No, no, my dearest dove, I ask no questions of you. My love is too great and pure for questioning. I kiss your letter and smell the perfume. It reminds me of you. I kiss your eyes, your lips and go to sleep dreaming that soon you will be in my arms again.

Your Martin

LETTER # 5 Odessa

16 Sept. 1930

Darling, if your travel without me seemed unbearable to you at times, my stay here without you is often unbearable. If only you could know how sometimes I wish to have you here, near me, to speak to you, to hear your voice, to ask you to take immediately off my poor heart the burden which is too heavy for it. My dear, the thing I feared so much came. One doctor said I am going to have a baby. After this, I went to another, a specialist, who assured me that there was no sign of it. I do not know whom to believe. What should I do, Martin? I am waiting for your news. I received your dear telegram informing me of your safe arrival. I carry it along with me because its kind words do me good—

L.

LETTER # 6 Odessa

18 Sept. 1930

Thank you very much, my dear for thinking of me. I need it now more than ever—

I had my fifth free day yesterday (we were given every 5th day off, the employees being rotated so that the office was always kept open) and at the request of a friend of mine (the thin Verochka you know) I went with her about 5:30 P.M. to the S/S Krim because her brother was sailing on it for the first time as an Apprentice. I saw the Captain and gave him the photos. He was very pleased and sends you his regards. Though I did not feel very well, I am nevertheless very glad I made an effort and went there; it was nice to see that boat again and sad at the same time. An hour after I came home Nikita arrived. I was glad to read these words of yours giving me some unexpected hope.

Goodbye, my dear. I shall write very soon.

L.

LETTER # 7 22 Sept. 1930

Dear Martin,

There is nothing good to tell you. I am doing my best to be courageous. It is impossible to write all about my worries. I can only say I was somehow not prepared for it at all. As yet I had no opportunity to speak to the specialist; he is too busy. I cannot succeed in making an appointment with him.

Be well,

Elizabeth

LETTER # 8 25th Sept. 1930

I should so much like to speak to you personally, dear Martin, to be able to tell you many of the thoughts that cross my mind. It is so difficult to write about them—

Needless to say this is not a time for new complications ... I so greatly need quiet and I have none. I know I must not be nervous at all, but strong and balanced. I think of my dear mother. What would I give to have her with me.

Write to me, Martin, tell me everything will be all right. Do you think of me? I wish you all the best, my dear.

Elizabeth
Odessa

30 Sept. 1930

I am waiting for your answer, dear Martin. I cannot add anything about my state of mind. You must understand it well enough yourself. There is nothing certain with me, and incertitude is the most dreadful thing.

My dear, this question occupies all my being, it is so serious, so very serious as nothing before. I find myself perplexed, do not smile anymore. I know I need great courage, but temporarily I am saddened by being left alone with more worries than before.

My dear, it is to you to help me with your letters and advice.

I am waiting for them.

Would I only know when it will be given to me to see you again.

I kiss you, darling, and ask you to excuse me for my letters which grew, against my will, nervous and worried. Please confirm them all, it is important.

Elizabeth

After the 4th of October when I wrote the letter to Martin about the baby, I regained my equilibrium and began to think of others. I still waited anxiously for the letters in Martin's firm, unpredictable and rhythmic hand. I never had enough of them.

One morning the humble R.R. told me about her husband, a general who had fled with the White army and had been living for many years in Paris. He had just lost his job as a scrivener because he was over 55 years of age. Now penniless, he was living on scraps of bread that he begged from a restaurant, to feed his non-existent chickens.

Having just received a cablegram from Martin with a prepaid reply of more words than I needed, I at once added the general's address, emphasizing his desperate need, and having done it, felt very happy.

IMPRISONED AGAIN

How well I remember this day – Monday, the 13th of October. In the afternoon I finally had the appointment with the renowned specialist, and felt rather sad when he confirmed his previous doubt about my condition. Disturbed, I went to visit the ailing Zina. She reminded me that this was the eve of the feast of The Protection of the Holy Virgin (August 30, Julian calendar), and urged me to go to church.

I went in spite of the late hour and stood in the place where in previous years I often used to stand with Mother. People were beginning to leave, and I noticed the figure of an old man kneeling in front of me. Although I could not see his face, his back was evidence of bitter suffering. The neatness of the threadbare coat covering his bony shoulders, and his carefully combed gray hair bespoke dignity and misery. I prayed for him and him alone, more ardently than I had ever prayed for myself.

The service over, a beggar reached out his hand to me where I stood and not at the door as was the custom. I gave him some change. Bowing low, he disappeared. When I reached the middle of the church, again a beggar approached me. I felt rich, as the wife of an American, and gave him alms also. Again, at the church door, a beggar pushed his fellows aside to reach me. Only when he took the money did I realize that all three were the same man, who had camouflaged his appearance: at one time limping, at another holding one arm stiff, and so on. Amused by his versatility, I laughed at my gullibility.

Walking home, I thought of the man for whom I had prayed in the church and, for reasons we humans cannot fathom I was certain that he would get up from his knees with greater courage.

In the street there was an appetizing odor. I looked around and to my surprise saw a man selling waffles right on the sidewalk. I hadn't tasted waffles in years. Unable to resist the temptation, I bought one for myself and one for Vala, and started eating mine at once. I was hungry all the time.

I hurried home for fear I would start to nibble on my sister's waffle, and was almost running up our stairs, proud of my will power. I was holding her waffle in my extended left hand, when I heard quick footsteps behind me. Looking over the banister, I saw the top of a green hat on the flight below.

If only I could reach our door and lock it behind me! I pushed it open, got inside, but I could not close it. Two strong hands prevented me.

"You are arrested," said the man in the green hat, brusquely grabbing my pocketbook, "and by surprise, just as we planned."

"It can't be! I am free of any accusation, officially reestablished in all my rights. The paper is there in my pocketbook."

"Never mind the paper. You are arrested!"

Something quivered in me as if I had been struck a blow. I was stunned. I don't know whether I sat or stood. I don't know who searched my room, nor for how long. Everything was a thick mist, out of which my forgotten premonition of five months ago emerged. "They will take you again."

The mist was beginning to clear. "Write to Martin, Vala dear," I said. "He must know – oh yes, I mustn't forget. Where is my purse, Vala? Did the man return it?"

"Here it is," she said.

"See if my marriage certificate and the other paper are still there. I shall definitely need them."

"Yes," she said, "they are."

Walking out, I stumbled over the waffle, which must have fallen from my hand in a desperate leap through the door. The crushed waffle helped me to link up my thoughts: eve of the holy day, the church, the kneeling man, the beggar, the waffles – the green hat.

Suddenly my mind was extraordinarily clear. "Vala," I said turning back to her, "Vala, do not worry – I am going now – but I shall return on the fourth of November – my name day and the feast of the Holy Mother of Kazan…" I heard the slow monotone of my own voice with surprise, as if listening to a stranger.

It was the same dark, smoky cell of the GPU on Marasli Street that I had left last spring on April 30th at noon. At times, in that dark basement, it seemed as if I had never left, as though the five months of freedom had been a dream. In my confusion, I often looked for my fair-haired companion Rica. I missed her, wondering where she was, then remembered that for the last three months she had been living in Moscow. I rejoiced over her absence; yet soon after, forgetting again, I felt lonely and called to her.

The other girls, almost all new, were kind but not close to me. By and by I adjusted, rehearsing in my mind the sequence of events that had led to my return to prison, and began to concentrate on one thought. Why? Why here again? I had plenty of time to wonder. Days and nights, a week, then ten days passed without an answer.

My health was not the same. I was not only restless from the uncertainty, but dizzy and nauseated. The happiness of August seemed to have befallen that other Lisa – my happier double.

I escaped the nightmare of my days only in sleep, when I dreamed of Martin – walking with him through the streets of Yalta, eating luscious grapes, swimming—

Among us was a middle-aged woman, arrested on her way through Odessa to her native Kiev. She knew no one in Odessa. Having a delicate constitution, she weakened on the prison rations so that she could not get up without help. We shared with her what we could, but her weakness persisted.

Luckily one day Dounia, a country woman, was sent a large bag of garlic together with other edibles. She issued two cloves of it to each of us daily, and it was surprising how much vitality it gave us. After two weeks of spicing the prison's rations with garlic, the sick woman felt strong enough to walk. The generous Dounia's magic food was rubbed on our bread or crushed and mixed in the watery soup. The soldier who had to open our door to let us out three times a day nearly smothered from the aroma of garlic coming out of our cell.

I, too, began to feel a little more vigor, and the dizziness and nausea were less frequent. During the hours of relative physical ease, I would try to take account of myself. While pretending to sleep I lay silent, thinking. Though in prison again, and ignorant of the reason for it, I was thankful for Martin's love.

The discomfort I felt every morning was puzzling. Though I had been persuaded by a doctor whom I had visited just before prison that there was nothing the matter with me, I wondered if he had not been mistaken. Instinctively, I knew that my body was trying to adjust itself to some new condition. Often, even during daytime, I sought refuge in sleep. I had never been able to do that before.

Three weeks went by – three weeks of languishing in the dark stuffy room. More and more I felt the need of some elementary guidance about my symptoms and longed for the lovely nurse of the other prison. Here, there was no nurse. One morning though, a doctor came, dashing through our heavily scented room. "Doctor, doctor!" I said in a very low voice, attempting to attract his attention. "I must – I have to ask you something – privately."

"Privately!" he roared. "Nothing to speak to me privately about. Do you want me to sit where you are? Privately! Forget about it!"

Oh, I felt horrible, horrible. I went away from him quickly and as far as I could. Tears were choking me.

That night my heart was calling for Martin. If he knows where I am, what grief it must be for him, I thought. I had expected many obstacles before our reunion, but not this, even though subconsciously I had carried the thought: They will take me ——— They will take me again. My mind now cried: Martin, Martin! It is prison again. But this is not all – there is something else – something within me – for which I have more concern than for myself.

One night I slept alone, stretched full length on the narrow bed previously shared with a strange, sad girl, whom I was afraid to disturb even in my sleep. She had left us that noon "for freedom," the guard said, and though we noisily rejoiced over her good luck she expressed no emotion at all and said goodbye to us, cold and passionless as ever. With all the other girls squeezed two on each cot, I felt privileged having so much comfort and decided to profit by it fully, well knowing that it would not last.

Out of all the nights, this had to be the one when I was shaken out of a dream of my voyage to America, to the reality of a trip through the dark familiar yard into a cold wet October night – destination unknown. The guard did not turn as usual to the left. Instead, he crossed the street and walked by me on the sidewalk along Alexandrovsky Park. I trembled with nervousness and chill. The weather was restless, dead lulls replaced by gusts of wind which tore the last black leaves off the trees or whipped them in bunches from the earth. In their whirling flight they struck me in the face and I smelled humidity and death.

The soldier walked with an even ordinary step, saying nothing, farther and farther toward the end of the park. I was about to ask him where he was leading me when a horrible suspicion intruded. Don't ask him now came the half-mocking half-benevolent thought. You will know it soon enough. Walk for awhile in peace. But there was no peace.

The girls had spoken of the cliff at the end of the park where people were shot. Oh, no! Not now, dear Lord. Not now when I have so much hope. Not now when I am no longer alone! As we left the sidewalk my feet dragged heavily on the muddy path of the park. If it is to be so – help me Father – give me courage. My life from childhood on unrolled before my eyes. Mother and all my loved ones were with me, but Martin was closer than anyone.

Oh, Lord, help me! If it were for nothing else but the tears I shed over the stranger kneeling in church whose face I did not see – for my trust in You. Beloved Father, help me!

Steps, steps, steps, steps – no more thought, no more fear, no more sore sorrow – steps, steps, steps.

At a house by the curb of the park, the soldier stopped and looked at the number. He scratched the back of his neck and then took off his hat and scratched his head vigorously for quite some time. "I guess I'm out of my way." he finally said. "I thought this was the house."

"Oh, Lord, this is not the end – they are taking me to a house. I still have a chance! Returning as though from death to life, I managed to speak to the soldier. "I can help you find the place," I said. "I know this street very well." He gave me a piece of paper and I read the number. Eagerly I led him back, out of the mud of the park to the sidewalk and across the street to a row of houses among which I quickly found the one he wanted. With every step I took up a queer spiral staircase, my passionate desire to fight for life and happiness grew. At the top, a short man of healthy complexion, in a uniform different from any other I had come across in the GPU, reprimanded the soldier.

"Why is it that you took so long to come?"

The soldier hesitated, so I took over, asking brusquely, "Why is it that I am here at all, Tovarisht?"

He opened the door, let me into an office, and pointed out a chair at a desk with a soothing green lamp. He sat down opposite me. "What do you mean, 'here at all'?"

"I mean, Tovarisht, that after my absolute clearance of any guilt, it seems most inconsistent that contradicting itself, the GPU deprives me of freedom again, and makes me languish in a prison basement for two weeks without giving any reason for it."

I handed him my valuable document. He glanced at it and then disinterestedly said, "This document doesn't mean a thing. You are no longer under the jurisdiction of the GPU, but under the Speztroika (Special Three) Committee, which will decide your fate."

Come on, come on – fight for yourself, urged my heart. "I still cannot understand one thing," I continued. "During my previous imprisonment, my correspondence with foreign countries was held against me. Since then, I have not corresponded with anyone but my husband."

He lifted his head and looked at me attentively. "Your husband?"
"Yes, my husband, Tovarisht."

"This cannot be true," he said, moving restlessly in his revolving chair, riffling the papers before him with the tips of his fingers. "I studied your file for four days and nowhere is it indicated that you are married."

"Here is my marriage certificate, Tovarisht." How glad I was to have it!

He took time to examine it. "And may I ask who your husband is?"
"He is an American."

The rich red of his cheeks turned to plaster white. "Why on earth was this marriage not reported?" he exclaimed angrily, as though speaking to himself. I felt that I was gaining in position. Why was he so perturbed? He pushed his chair closer to his desk and chin on fists, asked, "How did it happen?"

"I do not mind telling you how, Tovarisht, provided you will believe me. But, weak as I am, I cannot afford to waste my strength in telling you something you may have decided not to believe at all."

Eyes directed on me, he said, "I shall believe you. But wait a moment; I think you will be more comfortable here." He motioned to the other part of the room. I sat down in an armchair on one side of a round table, and he on the other side. I closed my eyes for a moment.

Then I related my story, bringing out the high points – speaking simply, yet judging by his interest, rather movingly, until I reached the day of my arrest. He settled more deeply in his chair and rubbing his palms together said, "Well, well. This certainly would make a splendid subject for a film."

At that moment, my thought of Martin was so intense that I almost felt him close to me. I heard the agent move his chair and hurriedly stopped him from getting up. "Please wait a minute, Tovarisht; I have to ask you a favor."

"Go ahead," he said, reclining again.

"There is a time in the life of every woman when, uncertain of her condition, she must see a doctor." He listened attentively. "Would you arrange for me to see one? The doctor who rushed through our cell the other day had neither time nor desire to listen to me."

"I shall take note of that, Tovarisht Kraevesky," he said. Then, picking up a napkin that covered something on the table, he passed me a low vase filled with grapes. "Help yourself," he said. "They will do you good. We just received a shipment from Crimea." He stopped, then added, "Yalta."

This was far too much for me. It would be a sacrilege to eat Yalta grapes now, here with him. I was about to refuse when, looking at him, I caught sincere human kindness in his expression and smiling out to it, I took a bunch of grapes. He took one, too. Nothing more was said. The night was over and a pale dawn was peeping in. Leaving, I saw the first snowflakes silently falling.

I had not long to wait. On the morning of the twenty-seventh of October, I was told to be ready for my former prison. I was glad. The agent with the red cheeks had kept his promise. Good for him! If only the same nurse was there! At 8 o'clock Masha, who had regained her strength and I stood in the yard facing an empty truck. Very soon a grey crowd of men came out of a door and, matching their steps moved toward the truck. "Bundles down!" a voice commanded. "Into the truck." The prisoners, young and old, about forty of them, climbed into the high truck, the more agile helping the others.

"How many women?"

"Two," answered our guard.

"Climb in!"

A prisoner's strong hand helped me up. Masha took a little more time to lift herself, but she made it, and we all stood pressed close to each other for lack of space.

"Get down!" we heard. We tried, but it was hard – too many people, not enough room.

"Get down, duck!" The command was thundered.

The knees and the elbows of the men jabbed us in the back and in the sides. A boot struck heavily between my ribs. I screamed with pain. Some ducked, some hung awkwardly, half in mid-air. Then, something like a hail of stones began to fall on our heads. Our bundles, mostly wooden boxes and metal kits, were thrown as though into an empty truck. "Oh, Oh! Oh! Oh! Oh! Oh!" came with each falling box. A man was badly cut near the temple. I held my hands over my head. Treated worse than animals, I thought. I rode in a prison truck before, but it was not like this.

We had almost finished adjusting ourselves when soldiers with bayonets, taking their posts in the corners of the truck, pushed themselves through the tight load of people, and another commotion started. The boot in my rib, which I had begun to tolerate, changed position. Oh my! Some knees were seeking more stability. Without making a move, I was pushed away from my only woman companion. Now I was hit in the back, now in the chest. I felt ill, completely beaten even before the truck started. When it began to jounce, everybody inside grew very sick. Many moaned. A man cried out, "I'm dying! I'm dying!" I felt faint and lifted my head, longing for air. "Heads down!" ordered the guard, and I sank back, probably hurting those around me as I was hurt by them. I remember nothing more of the trip until I heard a shout, "Jump!"

I looked around. The truck was empty. I sat up and remembered. "No time to sleep, sister. Hurry! Jump!" "Please give me your hand," I begged.

"No hand. Jump!"

I tried to jump and fell on the granite pavement. Something terrible had happened, I sensed. Yet, in my mind I refused to face it.

"Cell 6B. Temporary, for doctor's checkup," said an unfamiliar voice. It must have been about seven in the morning. My spirits were very low. In this familiar prison I wished to see or hear someone I knew, but recognized no one. A buxom woman soldier in boots bigger than herself took me to new quarters: Cell 6 was crowded with women, old and young, asleep on the floor, heads to the wall, their feet leaving a small, empty space in the middle.

"This cell seems overcrowded, don't you think, Tovarisht?" I said to my clumsy guide.

"There is room enough for you, though," she said calmly. "Right there in the very center. You will be all right."

I stood in that uninviting space, unable to force myself to sit down and by some strange analogy remembered a part of the ballet "Gioconda," once seen in Moscow. The Prima Ballerina, representing the hand of a huge clock, stood in the center of the stage. Twelve dancers, whose lovely heads were supposed to be the figures on the clock, lay gracefully around her, their glittering ballet shoes gathered in the center by the clock hand. The prima, extending her arm, brought them, one by one to a standing position, after which each danced a fantasy of the hour of the day or night with the lighting effects changing accordingly. This charming picture flashed and faded. I was not the prima, and these were not the ballerinas. Putrid air reached my nostrils. My knees gave way and I plunged down, closer to the poor, dirty feet that I could no longer imagine in pink ballet slippers. I thought that ten minutes would be more than I could endure to stay. I looked around. A woman was sitting on crossed legs, combing her black hair. She smiled at me.

"Couldn't that window be opened – just a little?" I implored.

"I shall try," she whispered, "if the others do not object. It was cold last night and we fought about closing it or leaving it open. Too many wished it closed." She got up, stepped carefully over the sleeping bodies, opened the window a tiny bit and a cold wintry breeze sprayed the room.

Relieved, I settled down as best I could, arms around my knees, letting my head rest on them as though on a pillow. I wished to sleep, to forget the truck – the cell – all, all of it.

The woman, her long hair tidily braided in two tresses, helped me up when the routine of the day took all of the prisoners from the cell. Returning, I found the room more inviting, the floor had been washed, the bundles in order. I hardly had time to exchange a few words with a girl or two when the Chief of Prison – the same blond, blue-eyed man, entered.

"I was not in when you came early this morning. You shouldn't have been put in No. 6 at all."

My mood was picking up. Tonight – another cell, thank God!

A doctor whom I had never seen before examined me, and with a shallow, professional smile said, "False alarm, lady. False alarm. All that worry for nothing. You surely stirred us all up, though!"

"I'm terribly sorry, doctor. But I didn't know – and I had some symptoms—" I was not only embarrassed, but ashamed of myself.

The doctor must have noticed it, for opening the door to let me out, he generously remarked, "Think nothing of it. Young married women often let their imaginations rush ahead of them. Soon you will have definite proof of your false alarm."

I said, "Thank you very much, doctor. I am so very sorry I disturbed you."

"Not at all, not at all," he said, a little more personal, a little more friendly.

Going out I practically stumbled over the dentist who had been so helpful and understanding during my first imprisonment. "Hello, there!" he said. "Fancy seeing you again. How are your beautiful teeth?"

"Who is she?" I heard another man ask.

"A famous recidivist, if you please," the dentist joked. Then turning aside he continued, seriously, even indignantly, "A wonderful girl – daughter of the late Dr. Kraevesky. She couldn't possibly do anything wrong! And here she is, in prison for the second time!"

Forgetting my embarrassment in the doctor's office, relieved of my feeling of added grave responsibility and comforted by the dentist's kind compliments, I returned to my cell altogether a new person. But the feeling of relief did not last because of a certain physical malaise throughout my body. I tried, without success, to overcome it mentally. My body seemed broken, useless, pulled down by limbs that weighed a ton. I was excused from the fifteen minute walk in the circle and slept a little, but did not regain my strength. Doubt began to creep in. I recalled how I had felt during the past three weeks, and remembered the doctor's "false alarm" this morning. Infallible woman's instinct! The red-cheeked man, who was probably following my case, might think I had made up a story....

The girls were back and the one with braids, seeing me so limp, advised me to catch up on my sleep and even saw to it that I was comfortable. Doubled up, trying to keep my stomach warm, I slept.

The Chief woke me with his threatening order: "Elizaveta Kraevesky, to the isolation cell!" The girls were frightened, but I knew. The isolation cell happened to be the same that had sheltered me the first few days of last February. The window was still broken and it was as cold as before, but there was only one girl in it, sitting on the floor crying, forlorn. "There will be nobody in this cell but you two," said the Chief, and I thanked him, hoping for a restful night.

"Do you know what time it is?" my cellmate asked me immediately, in an almost childlike voice.

"About 2 o'clock," I answered.

The hour of package delivery was approaching and I was sure that Vala, quite experienced by now, would find me. With this hope and even a greater one – that she might walk around the building to the north side of the prison in search of our signal – I stuck my green sweater into the broken window, then tried to chat with my new companion.

She was a half educated little woman with a face as childish as her voice. Her name was Jenia. She was "sitting" here because of having given shelter for one night only to the sister of a White officer for whom the Government was looking. The imprisonment was very hard on her and she poured out all of her misery to me. "...... and Ivan, my husband, warned me not to take her in," she sobbed. I knew that at this point she was inconsolable and let the torrent of her tears wash away her grief.

I got up. The window, like a magnet, attracted me and I stood by it, looking out. It began to snow. The sentinel, apparently not minding it at all, marched back and forth like an automaton. On the other side of the wall, a dog on a chain crawled quickly into his shelter. Farther out, the cemetery lay bleak under the shroud of snow. No garden, not even a tree around this gaol – nothing but cemeteries on all sides. The people who chose such a location for a prison must have been true sadists.

After my recent nap, watched over by the sensitive, kind woman in the other cell, I felt a little stronger and, of course, longed for freedom. I wished to walk aimlessly in the softly falling snow. What if they do not let me out at all? Did Vala inform Martin of my helplessness? Dear Martin, do you know that I thought I was with child – but no, it was a false alarm and I am told there is nothing the matter with me. Maybe it is for the best – still, I am confused – if only I could straighten it all out in my mind. What is happening to me, really?

A package from Vala and a note. Excited, as usual, I read: "My dear, I am sending you things – a change of underclothes, a pair of warm stockings, a book of Maikoff and a copy book. Food – a jar of compote, ten slices of bread, one quarter of butter and milk. How are you, my darling? Vala."

This was the first written communication from the world for so long. I hadn't received any on Marasli Street. Tears at my throat, I wrote an answer: "Vala dear – Clothing and food received. Thank you for everything. Do not worry. Your Lisa."

Back at the window, I stretched the green sweater a little wider and let one sleeve float outside. If only Vala would think to walk around! My eyes pierced the distance. It is getting late, I thought. I saw nobody, heard nothing but the bray of a donkey from behind the cemetery. One glance at Vala – only one. Suddenly I saw something move under the black and white web of trees in the abandoned cemetery. I heard branches creak, and strained my eyes. I could hardly believe it! Vala and Verochka were slowly moving toward the wall. Verochka tried to climb it. They had found me! Now they waved and threw kisses! Once again, joy and grief were so closely intermingled that they were practically one.

I watched the sentinel. He turned the corner and profiting by that moment, I waved back smiling, hoping to give the impression that I was not unhappy – that things were not too bad with me. It was almost dark now – not safe for them to be here. The prison dog barked and I thrust my hand out of the broken window, signaling them to go away. They left, bending low to crawl under the branches of the thick trees, then waving to me through the grey veil of early night. I stood there peering into the distance long after they were gone.

All was quiet. Only once in a while the air was torn by the sad voice of the donkey. I turned to Jenia, still sitting disconsolate on the floor.

"I just saw my sister and my friend," I said, and told her my experience by the window, drawing the story out as long as possible. I wanted to rejoice over it, to hold on to it for a long time, but there was no use fooling myself. The truth was, I felt sick and sad.

Six o'clock and roll call. Three prison officials came to check us present and this time wished us goodnight. In the corridor it was quiet. Nobody laughed, nobody cried. Jenia lay down fully dressed on the naked floor, with a jacket over her shoulders and a basket for a pillow. Her nerves a little calmed, she fell asleep at once. I stretched my blanket on the floor and took my doumochka (pillow) out of the small suitcase that had kept me company before. It was the same one out of which the bottles of Borjom had fallen and broken so noisily on the sidewalk the day of our civil wedding. The old droshky (cab) man had thought it a sign of good luck. Happy memories. Patting the suitcase, I covered it with the little pillow. With a scarf over my head and coat and sweater on, I tried to sleep. But sleep did not come. The floor was very hard and deathly cold.

I thought of exercising to keep warm, but I was too weak. All I could do was pray. Prayer is the only thing one can do always and everywhere. I thanked God that I had seen Vala. I thought of her and the gentle, yet determined, young American who, two and a half months ago had become my husband. Strange, all that had happened – his immediate, all-absorbing interest in me the moment he saw me at Zina's. Mrs. Broochis had predicted it. Where was Mrs. Broochis? I wished I could tell her that her prophecy had come true. I shivered and sought warmth and consolation in my recent past. Obedient to my call, memories, like flocks of southbound birds, flew by, gradually lulling me to sleep.

I woke up trembling, chilled to the bone. I knew I was ill, but I had little pain. Then, something happened. A stream of fire burned my half-frozen limbs and paralyzed my heart – a stream whose steady flow took the last living warmth out of my body. Helpless, I felt one minute cold, the other hot.

My cell companion slept. I called her, but there was no answer. Hours must have passed. Near dawn, I felt so weak I thought I was dying. I knew I needed nourishment, and with great effort, stretched my arm and took some of the bread and milk that Vala had sent; then I fell back on my bed of wood and lay quietly again, long, long, long, long – half living, half-dead. At dawn, a woman brought bread and water into our cell. She was in and out again before I could ask her a favor. Hours crept by and my discomfort grew. The last drop of life seemed to have left my body – and then there was no pain, no feeling. Nothing.

My eyelids, like two heavy gates, opened. I lived again. I saw a large, bright room and felt straw under my aching body. "Where am I?"

"In the prison hospital," I heard someone say.

I turned my head towards the voice. "But, why? Why am I here? Oh yes – now I remember – I do, I do – I was so sick last night. What happened? I am afraid. Please tell me what happened." The nurse entered and I looked up at her, pleading, "Please, nurse, you were always so kind – tell me what happened."

She looked at me and said, "You lost your almost-three-months baby boy – too bad – but nobody could help it!"

The nurse was very kind. Not only did she work over me for a long time, giving me all the medical assistance she could, she also comforted me mentally – not like a prison nurse, but rather like a close relative – consoling me, trying to explain my condition which, after what the doctor had said, I could neither understand nor believe.

"Impossible, impossible," I kept repeating. But having no strength to speak and explain my doubts, I could only look at her, silently thanking her for her efforts.

"Rest quietly now," she said. "Try not to move at all." Piling the straw up under my knees so that my feet would be set higher, she left.

I did not sleep, but dozed, still wondering. Milk was brought to me a few times and unable to lift my head I drank it through a tube left by the nurse. In the afternoon she returned, sat next to me on a little tabouret and smiled. She was so beautiful and goodness shone through her. The joy of seeing her again gave me strength.

"You look much better, now." she said, sweetly, "How do you feel?"

"Better, I think, thank you."

"Wonderful!" she said cheerfully. " I brought you something that will definitely clear up your doubts."

I lifted myself up a bit, watching her. She removed a piece of white cloth from a large glass jar, and with one hand supporting it from the bottom and the other over it, she held it in front of me.

At first I saw nothing but clear water. "What is it?" "Look carefully and you will see."

I looked. Helplessly floating in the liquid of the jar was something like a little porcelain doll.

"Nurse!"

"Yes, my dear. Now you know that it is true. You needed to be convinced. You can see it is a boy."

Sitting stiff and erect, I looked until tears blurred my sight.

That night, clean and comfortable on the straw, I did not sleep. I thought only of the little being with whom I had shared life for too short a time – a child of ours that circumstances had slain. Open all night, my eyes saw dawn and with the return of the day, I fell asleep.

I heard a loud whisper: "Don't you see her? Here she is!" "Ssh! Do not wake her up – she is sleeping."

"Stop ordering me! I know what to do," came in the same loud whisper. These were familiar voices and in a half slumber I listened to them.

"Oh! You are always ready to quarrel. I'm not ordering you. Listen here. When you speak to her, remember to leave out all your strong words!"

"Ladno, ladno. (OK, OK) But look – look at her," came in a more subdued tone. "She is smiling in her sleep."

Indeed I must have smiled. I knew who they were now. One was Pasha who used to bring me spicy things to eat, the other was Klava. Both were devoted friends of mine from the prison's Criminal Corridor. As soon as I opened my eyes, they came close.

"We could hardly wait to see you!" Pasha said. "We are so glad you are back again and so sorry for all you had to go through. But it's all over now and you'd better forget about it. Just rest and do whatever the nurse tells you to do."

"Yes, we heard all about you," Klava cut in, "and it is all for the best. You wouldn't want to have a son born in prison."

"Oh, Lord! I never thought of that! It would be terrible!" I smiled at the two women, one a thief and the other a murderess, whose faces and attitude spoke of true, sincere interest in me. "Thank you, girls. But enough about me. Tell me how you are."

"I am finishing my three years in exactly two months," said Pasha, "but I shall probably be back soon again. I cannot help stealing. Klava, you know that I love you, but if I meet you on the street, quite against my best interest I'll take everything out of your purse without your even noticing it."

"You will never do it, Pasha! I am sure you are cured now."

"What are you two doing here? Go back to your corridor right away!" The woman who spoke bent over me. "If you need something, ask me. I am the hospital attendant for this week. My name is Maria Semenova."

"Thank you," I said, "I will."

There were only a few very sick women in the large hospital room. The others were recuperating and able to move about. Every one had a kind word for me which made me feel good. There were windows on two sides of the room and I found out that some of them faced the gate.

Soon the nurse came and helped me again. Before leaving my bedside she said gently, "We will not allow them to send you to the Far North this winter. I spoke to the doctor in the men's prison and he's willing to issue a certificate about the inflammation of the tubes. You will remain with us at least until spring." What did she say? What is this about my staying here so long? This cannot happen. I shall be free very soon. I was told – who was it that told me – that I shall be free on the fourth of November, my name day. No, no one told me and yet I remember so distinctly. I heard somebody say that I will be free on that day.

On the second of November, though still very uncomfortable, I managed to go to the nurse's quarters by myself but had to be helped by the nurse and another woman on my way back. My straw bed was right against the wall on one side, and the place on the other side was not occupied. I felt quite private in my secluded corner. Lying there, I participated in the comings and goings in and around the prison hospital. In this way, during the day I had little personal thought except for the sudden recurrence of a sharp grief for my loss. Trying to forget it, I purposely listened to and observed the life around me. Too bad there was nothing cheerful.

I heard the lament of a mother in the cell across from us. She had been arrested the night before and had brought her sick baby along with her. The nurse told us there was no hope for it and, therefore, it was not taken to the hospital but left with the mother. "Sick as it was," the nurse added, "it shouldn't have been taken from its warm bed into the cold winter air."

For a long time there was nothing in my heart nor in my mind but the grief of the poor mother whose sobs reached my ears now and then.

Our nurse was attending to the baby late that night and it was already dark when she once more entered the hospital room. Coming straight to me she handed me some extra medication in the usual little oblong folded paper, saying, "Take this powder after six o'clock – better yet, just before going to sleep. And be careful not to lose it!" Following the nurse's instructions, I carefully opened it very late at night, having a presentiment it was something secret. Indeed, it was not a powder, but a carefully camouflaged copy of a recent letter from Martin. In order to comfort me, Vala had copied Martin's words of devotion in tiny, tiny letters that looked like beads; for precaution's sake as a title for the English text, she had written very clearly in large Russian characters, "POVEST" (a story). Somehow, maybe through Odessky, she had managed to give the note to the nurse.

The only light in the room was dim and it was hard to read the minute letters that Vala, not knowing English, had copied as accurately as possible. "I do not know how to start my letter. You have disarmed me. You have taken away the solid ground on which I so proudly stood. Lisa, darling, I am weeping. I never wept before. Your letter was the lamentation of a soul, not of a mind. It is all so foreign to me. I never possessed that divine inner feeling until now. Teach it to me. Teach me as you will our newborn child. I am also just born. I know so little. I need you as I never did before. There are three of us now. Let it be. If Providence granted it to us, then let us not deny it. I am grateful for your sincerity and affection. Come, come with all your strength and love and faith and make this earth our heaven. Good night, good night, my precious lamb. How many times will I say good night to you without having you beside me?"

He knew nothing of my imprisonment, and nothing about what had happened to me – he still hoped for the baby. What a terrible shock for him! His beautiful letter brought joy and sorrow to me at the same time. I cried and relieved by tears, I fell asleep.

Another day of prayer and expectation and then came the morning of the fourth of November. The friends from the Criminal Corridor had found out about my name day and came early with their gifts. Klava gave me a man's handkerchief, saying that I could use it as a scarf. She must have received it from one of her beaux at the weekly club meetings where the criminal women, together with the men prisoners, heard lectures or watched a movie – privileges that the political prisoners never had. Pasha, the kleptomaniac, must have stolen a little jar of strawberry jam somewhere, because when I asked where she got it, she did not answer.

They told everybody about my name day. Even the Chief, who daily inquired about my health, came to the hospital prison in person to shake hands. While he was there we heard a hysterical cry from the cell opposite. He rushed out, followed by Pasha. She soon returned, announcing in her usual loud whisper, "Her baby died." My eyes were wet and Pasha, noticing my tears, came out with another speech of consolation: "You see now, how much better it was to lose yours before it grew!"

When I was alone again, I remembered that this was the appointed day, the day of my – somehow – from somewhere – promised freedom. A strong electric shock went through me. I must be ready. I must sleep to gain strength, and sleep came at once as though by magic. When I woke up refreshed and hopeful three hours later it was near noon. The call for freedom was usually between eleven and one. "I slept so hard," I said to the nearest woman, "I did not hear a thing."

"You needed that rest," she said. "You slept like a child. I wish you could see your rosy cheeks right now." The woman spoke kindly, but all I wanted to know was whether or not there had been a message for me while I slept. "Nothing special," she said, "except that the nurse told us to send you to her office as soon as you woke up."

Coat over my shoulders, I went. Noon time, I thought, there is not much longer to wait. I tried to steady my steps. The nurse put her hand on my shoulder. "You look so much better today. Congratulations! I heard it was your name day."

"Yes, nurse. And I wish to thank you for your present – the special medicine you gave me last night."

"Did it help?" she asked, whimsically.

"Oh, very much! Thank you."

She looked around the room, then in a low voice continued: "The First Doctor in the men's prison signed the document stating your condition and the Chief of Prison certified it with his signature. In that way you will not be removed from here until spring.

I said, "It's so very good of you to have gone to so much trouble, dear nurse, but I am positive I shall be free today. I am positive!"

The nurse's blue eyes darkened almost to black. She seemed so shocked by my remark that it somehow made me feel guilty. "Dear child!" she said. "I hate to disappoint you, but the Chief signed this document just a few minutes ago and he's the one who should know."

"Still I am sure," I said. "I can't explain why, but I have great faith that I shall be free today."

"I hope so," the kind woman said, "but do you think you are strong enough to go?"

"There will be strength for that," I said.

Pasha was waiting at the door of the nurse's office and arm in arm we walked through the corridor. "There will be some calls for freedom, now. Am I right, Pasha?"

"It's all over," she said. "There was only one called from the Political Corridor."

"There will be some other calls, I'm sure."

Pasha looked at me, sticking her lips far out with a sarcastic "Pooh! 'Other calls', you said? I never heard of such a thing!" Even this did not destroy my hope.

I found my bed all fluffed up and straightened by somebody in my absence. Too tired to ask whose kind hands had done it, but feeling love around me, I sank into the fresh, crisp straw. Rest was all I wanted – rest and hope. There was no chaos in my mind. My mind, in spite of all, was clear while I waited for some strange promise to be fulfilled.

At 3 o'clock, the hospital attendant, Semenova, put a package on my bed. It was from Vala. She had baked a cake for me, the kind that Mother used to make and she had also sent me some fresh clothes and a little bouquet of chrysanthemums.

"Here is your sister," said one of the women standing by the window. "She is waving to us, looking right up here."

I had not seen my sister since the night she and Verochka walked around the north side of the prison through the cemetery. Poor Vala. In no time I was by the window. Looking to the left side of the gate I saw her standing there on tiptoe in the snow, tense, gazing upward, trying to find me among the other heads in the window. She saw me! She bowed low three times. I answered as nearly as possible in the same way, and smiled as broadly as I could. In that very moment I suddenly realized that half the day was gone and I was not yet free. Vala, who probably had expected me home, had come again disappointed. Oh, Lord! I had assured her before leaving that I would be free on the fourth, but would I? For the first time, my faith wavered. I made signs to Vala to go home and dragging my feet, returned to my corner.

Doubt and certitude started a mortal fight. One of them had to win, but torn between the two forces I had no idea how the battle would finish. I felt cold sweat dripping down my forehead while my heart, like a run-away horse, seemed about to leap out of my chest. I do not know whether this conflict lasted one minute or one hour. Finally, a calm voice from somewhere around my galloping heart said, "Wait, wait just a little longer." I knew then that doubt had suffered defeat.

I sat straight up in bed. Evening was approaching but it was not dark yet. The whiteness of the snow seemed to prolong the life of the day. From the little window on the west, the sun rays, like a sheaf of golden wheat, fell into the room and I stretched out my arms toward them. I became conscious of the life around me. I was ready to share Vala's cake with the others when the strident voice of the bereaved mother pierced the air. She cried, "Let me go with him! Let me see where you bury him! Let me! Oh, let me."

I pushed the cake aside, and snatching up my tiny chrysanthemums, begged the hospital attendant to carry them across to the mother for the baby. "She put them right on his little chest," reported Semenova. "The baby looked like a waxen cherub with a halo of golden curls, smiling up from that awkward wooden box – his last carriage." I was amazed at Semenova's vivid, subtle description of the tragic little fellow. Now he was being carried away to the dirge of his mother's inconsolable grief.

I returned to my cake and divided it scrupulously among all. It was a real treat for them.

It was dark now; but even though the activities of the prison's day were about to end, I was waiting – waiting. The usual quiet following the visiting hour seemed even stronger after the cry of the bereft mother. The storm of my own emotion had passed. "Father," I whispered, "Your will, not mine." Peace came to me then and relaxed in mind and body I slept.

THE MIRACLE OF
NOVEMBER 4, 1930

Awakened by the roll call and knowing soon the doors would close for the night, I suddenly realized all the futility of expectation. "My mortal mind took my will for God's will," I told myself, and turning my head to the wall, I grieved. Silence stood all around me. Silence was all I heard and in it I sought help, as one who drowns grasps for air.

"Lisa, Lisa, Lisa!"

What is it, I thought, not turning my head. It was not a whisper this time, but the loud, clear voice of Pasha calling me. What could it be?

"Lisa!" She shook me and pulled my shoulder to make me look at her.

"Lisa – FREEDOM!" The two words hung in the air.

"Pasha, do not joke," I said, trying to control my tears.

"I'm not joking," cried Pasha. "It's true!"

I sat up, bewildered. "It must be the Black Raven. Tell the truth, Pasha, please! At this hour they send only the Black Raven for politicals – and you know what follows. Go, tell them I am sick, that I cannot walk yet, the doctor does not allow me."

"But I was told to call you out for freedom, Lisa!"

I tried to get up from my straw, but fell back again. "Pashenka, go down, make an eye at the soldier, get him to show you the order. Look at it yourself with your own eyes. You told me you read well, Pasha." My forehead was cold, my heart galloping as before, my mind blank.

"By God, it is freedom!" shouted Pasha hoarsely and out of breath. "Get up, now!" But I sank deeper into my straw and did not make a move to rise. The girls, urging me to get up, began to dress me while I was still lying motionless. They chattered around me.

"Freedom at this hour!"

"Whoever heard of such an exception!"

"Never in the history of this prison was anyone called out at this late hour!" someone else confirmed.

"FATHER, IT WAS YOUR WILL!"

Triumphant, I got up.

Only a queen in her boudoir could have as many attendants as I had in that dusky hospital room. Many girls who had been asleep got up to help me and the very sick ones sat up in bed watching the ceremony. I gave myself entirely into their hands. "Get her a chair," one said. "She cannot stand up." "Watch out! You're twisting her arm," another continued. They spoke about me in the third person, going on with their jobs as if I weren't there. It was clear though that one of them took the lead. Her voice was calm and authoritative. I heard someone say. "Shall I put her things together?" Somebody answered, "Good idea." All this scarcely reached my not-too-attentive ear, my essential self still being far away. "Another safety pin, please," the leader said. "Maybe someone has one. She's grown much thinner since her sickness."

This remark brought me back to earth. "I have some safety pins there in my pocketbook," I said. One by one they were used, because my skirt would not hold and my coat had to be overlapped and pinned from top to bottom. Even my felt hat had become too loose and fell down over my ears. I must have been a sight when I was finally ready to leave.

Pasha came in swinging the door wide. "Ready, I suppose," she said.

"Almost," the first lady in waiting answered. I never knew her name. I do not think I had exchanged a word with her before. I do not remember her face, but I remember the spirit with which she helped me and sent me on my new way.

"Walk slowly. Do not exert yourself," she told me, holding my arm and squeezing it for emphasis. Then she said, turning to Pasha, "You take the bundle. Don't let her carry a thing. Leave it in the office until she sends someone for it." I embraced her and looking at the little group of women standing somewhat sadly, their hands hanging useless again, I thanked them for their wonderful assistance.

Now Pasha was leading me out through the corridor and downstairs. "Say!" she exclaimed, stopping abruptly, "Come to think of it – didn't you tell me this morning that you expected to be free today? How did you know? No one else expected you to be free. No one! Even the nurse said she would keep you until spring." She paused for a second, "You are <u>something</u>, Lisa, I swear!" I walked silent, my hand on her shoulder, and she kept on talking. "I shall miss you. I am always better with you around. I wish to straighten out for good, I mean."

"You will, Pasha, I'm sure," I said. "Put that resolution in the very center of your mind and heart."

We were approaching the office. The chief was not there, and an unknown employee checked me out. Pasha and I shook hands and kissed each other. "You were an immense help to me, my dear soul. I shall write and send things to you," I said.

The soldier pointed toward the door. I walked out of the prison into the calm night, stepping on the white carpet of fresh snow. It was the 4th of November, the holy day of God's Mother of Kazan – my name day.

Inside me there was a song, the beautiful melody which led me in some enchantment on and on, as the conductor leads the orchestra to the finale. The baton of the unseen Maestro left me the moment I found myself among the so-called 'free citizens' of Soviet Russia in the crowded streetcar. There was no seat for me. The street car flew through the empty roads of the outskirts. I held onto the back of a wooden bench, hardly able to keep my balance.

Suddenly I felt dreadfully tired, and when the conductor asked for carfare I looked at him. He and the car and the benches all started to turn around and around. Somebody gave me a seat. "Are you sick, Tovarisht?" asked the conductor.

"I do not think so," I said. "Just dizzy, I guess." This ordinary question, not even of concern, maybe – but of plain curiosity, started a reaction in me and for the rest of the trip I couldn't control the flow of tears.

An hour later, the street car stopped in front of the main post office where I had to get off. By that time my pocketbook and part of my coat were drenched with tears and I shook them as one does coming in out of a torrential rain. I felt better, but I walked slowly as I had been told to do, preserving the bit of strength I had. It was dark except for the dim light of the street lanterns. Slowly, cautiously, I walked through the well known streets, wet and shiny from the fast melting snow. I knew every stone, every mark and chip on them, but I thought, would they know me? Would they recognize in this slow, carefully moving figure, the alert light-footed person who never walked, but ran, hardly touching their surface? Would they? I was no longer the one they had known for years. I was a weak sick woman who in most trying circumstances, had had the misfortune of losing what would have been her first born son.

"But we do recognize you," the stones seemed to say. "We have a memory of our own and could even remind you of quite a few things. Here, for instance, your young feet often danced impatiently when your father held you back from crossing the street. And here, countless times we felt your steps glide swiftly on the way to the post office or to your bedridden friend." There was no one on the street and the stones, completely undisturbed, kept talking to me. I listened attentively, looking here at one and there at another. Before starting on my last turn home I stopped at the corner of my street, the street of Peter the Great.

"We remember," the stones continued, "how often you and your mother used to stop here to say a word and give alms to old blind Antony who sat on this corner. Some years later on this very spot you stood tiptoe to give a farewell kiss to a man you never expected to see again."

"Yes, yes. It is true," I said. "But I never thought of it, never put two and two together."

"And if we are not mistaken," the stones went on, "that stranger returned and passed this way again. We recognized his step."

"You are right," I said. "He is my husband, now."

I walked on, lost in reflection. Antony, who a week before he died had told me that his end was nearing, but that he would never cease praying for me – and one night in Yalta, Martin confessed it was that spontaneous farewell that had brought him back. How strange. Antony must have kept his promise. Maybe after all we would be together again; maybe the misfortune of these last months was a test of my trust in God. Maybe after all, we could be happy again. Filled with elation that no earthly fame or glory could give, I whispered, "I love Thee, Lord. I love Thee. No one forces me to say it. I love Thee. From the abundance of my heart these words are uttered. I love Thee."

I sat alone in the familiar room which for fifteen years had served as a background to much joy and sorrow. Memories, leaping out of each corner, assailed me. I thought of my life here first with my parents, then alone with Vala until Martin came. Suddenly he stood before my eyes as on the day he first entered this room, slender and graceful in his light gray suit, a box of candies tucked under his arm. I remember how, in spite of the tension of that moment, spoiled as I was in my youth by exceptional gifts, I had wondered whether or not they were the best brand of candies to be had in America. The profane often introduces itself in grave moments; this was the day we decided upon a civil marriage.

I wondered if Martin knew about the prison and all that had happened. Sister was not at home, and I had to wait to find out. All at once I began to shake with a chill and noticing for the first time that my shoes and stockings were soaking wet, I took them off, curled up on the sofa and fell asleep.

Sister woke me with the touch of a nervous hand on my forehead.

"You are burning, Lisa," she said.

I threw my arms around her and kissed and kissed her. "Maybe I am burning, Vala," I said, "but it does not matter. I am home! And I will be well."

"I remembered what you said the day of your arrest," Sister went on as she set about making me comfortable. "I've been expecting you all day, even after 3 o'clock when I returned from the prison. When night came I lost hope." She told me she had just come back from the Cathedral, in the left wing of which there had been a special service in honor of God's Mother of Kazan. It was there she had prayed, reluctantly giving up hope of seeing me on this appointed day and asking for courage to live through our separation. "I almost cried aloud when I saw you here asleep," Vala said. "Then quietly, I sat on the floor beside you, wondering how and by what miracle you were let out of prison at such an hour." She covered me with a blanket. "I watched you sleep for quite a while, and suddenly I noticed a shiver pass through you. I touched your head and you awoke."

How good it was to be together. How wonderful to read Martin's letters. We spoke of him and sent him a telegram, wording it simply: "LISA IS HOME AGAIN."

I found out that immediately after my arrest Vala, as previously agreed, had informed Martin by cable, "LISA IS SICK AS BEFORE." Martin, disturbed as he was at the time of his departure, must have forgotten our code to be used in case of another imprisonment. He answered immediately, "DO NOT UNDERSTAND. PLEASE EXPLAIN MESSAGE." to which Vala replied, "YOUR WIFE IS THERE WHERE SHE WAS BEFORE YOUR FIRST ARRIVAL."

He understood, my poor Martin, and the letters that followed confirmed his sorrow, his anxiety, his determination to save me. But what could he do from so far away I thought, and yet who knew? Maybe it was because of him that they had set me free at night. The ways of the Lord are mysterious.

Again we spoke of the night of my arrest, when I strangely foresaw the day of my liberation. A daring thought crossed my mind, and I said aloud "It happened, maybe, because at the moment my heart was pure, and it is said that pure hearts can decree a thing and it will be given unto them." I thought of the precious words of Vsevolod S. Soloviev, which I knew by heart (From his book "The Sages", addressed to Zina Kemenea by the parish priest, Nicolai.) "THE LORD, GOD OF ALL POWERS, WILL PROTECT YOU FROM ALL TEMPTATION, ALL EVIL. BELIEVE IN HIS UNSPEAKABLE MERCY, STAND BY HIM, AND FEAR NOTHING. AS LONG AS YOUR HEART IS PURE AND FULL OF LOVE, YOU ARE MORE POWERFUL THAN THE MOST POWERFUL."

The next morning, though feverish, I wrote a letter to Martin. It is in my hands now, written in pencil, its lines uneven. It still amazes me that Martin, always so much against any accumulation of things, saved almost all of my letters.

5 November 1931

Martin, Martin—

I was so far from you these long days and nights. I was not free and had no possibility of communicating with the world. I could not write to you. I could not read your letters. Oh, how terrible for me knowing that you could not understand anything of my silence. I cannot speak about it. But now, my Martin, I can write to you.

Listen, listen to me. Last night, the 4th of November, I got my freedom again. I know nothing clearly; maybe I was taken a second time by mistake. I know nothing. But Martin, how unhappy we were, both of us, Vala and myself.

Yesterday it was my holiday (and the 2nd my birthday), and in the evening I was set free and came home and kissed my sister, my poor Vala. The point I shall not touch for a long time, but over which I wept with her, is the little one, our child, who was not to live. Martin, do you understand me?

I was so weak I could hardly reach my house. Even though I had lost our child in the hospital it now seemed all was ready to be right. Unfortunately I got a severe cold (grippe) and came home with a high temperature. Immediately I cabled you that I am home again.

I hope you have stopped worrying, Martin dear. I shall recover soon. Probably I shall not return to my work. I read your dear letters. I thank you for your love.

Martin, I must send this letter right now. I do not even know what I write today but I hope, I <u>hope</u> we shall see each other once again. Martin, thank you. I wait for your letters. Shall do all I can to speed our reunion. Kiss me. I kiss you.

Lisa

IN LIMBO

Life went on. Refreshed and renewed by a wonderful experience, my spirit was high, but my weakened body had no resistance and I fell sick. My temperature was high, my throat sore, and in delirium Vala said I constantly begged that someone would return my baby.

The first morning after the crisis, everything seemed whiter and newer to me. Outside the sun was shining and the window sills were heaped with snow. Joyfully I realized that I was not in prison, but at home. On the low table by my bed I saw some mail from America but I could not reach it. I called Vala. "How much better you look this morning," she said, coming close. "I hope it's all over now." Yet I had to take it very easy. Even to read one page of Martin's letter took all the strength I had.

Friends began to visit me. Tetia Tonia and Vassinka often brought me something tasty to eat. Zina's chickens laid an egg for me every day. Verochka ran errands while Vala was doctoring me. Marussia S., my former co-worker, inquired about my health but did not come. One afternoon during my convalescence, after a long and healthy nap, the shy, quiet Mme.

R.R. came. Not saying a word, she bent over my bed and kissed my hands. She seemed very excited, and I begged her to sit down and calm herself. She sat at the foot of my bed, small and humble, her white shawl framing her sorrowful face. She remained speechless, shaken by short sobs. She was the wife of a distinguished army general, who retiring from Russia with the White Army, had been unable to take his family along. Unprepared for hardships, she had struggled through life with fortitude. A year ago, she had been informed of the death of her beautiful daughter in Leningrad, and only recently had buried her eighteen year old son who had been unable to fight the germs of tuberculosis. I looked at her, wondering what else that little human being could have lived through, and though she cried there was a radiance about her which I could not understand. After a while she pulled a letter from her pocket. It was from her husband in Paris. She said that he confessed his decision to commit suicide. It was an incredible decision for him, a deeply religious man, and yet it seemed there was no other way: no work, the prospect of being thrown out of his room, and as a climax to all, for two days the restaurant that had been giving him leftovers, had closed the door in his face. She could not talk any more and handing me the letter, pointed out where to read.

"Early in the morning," wrote the general, "I went to the Church of St. Serguey, and for a long time prayed that my weakness be forgiven. Exhausted physically and mentally I returned home, in my mind parting with you, my dear, and also with this beautiful but strange world in which there seemed to be no place for me any longer. In my room I prayed again and again, and having shut tight the door and the window, stretched my hand to turn on the gas. A sudden knock stopped me. Ready as I was to die, I felt that nothing should interfere with my decision and my hand stayed on the gas jet. The penetrating, sickly smell filled my nostrils and lungs, and began to spread all over the room. If only death would come quick, very quick, I prayed. The knock at the door resounded with double strength. It must be the landlady ready to throw me out, I thought. I was sure of it. And the desire to die grew even stronger.

Mr. R. R., Mr. R. R.! Why don't you answer? reached me through my dizziness. Mr. R.R.! A registered letter for you from America! Hurry up and sign for it. I cannot waste my time, shouted the landlady.

So God, through your prayers, my dearest, did not allow me to destroy myself. I shut off the gas, opened the window wide, lingered a second, then excusing myself for having fallen so sound asleep I opened the door. A long American business envelope was handed to me. There was no mistake. My name and address were correct. Only God's mercy over me and your ever sacrificing solicitude could bring this to pass.

The letter, from an unknown American, contained a check big enough for a year's rent, and to let me buy a few bags of oatmeal, my only food. Beloved, the days of miracles have not passed. God bless the generous American."

Through the mist of tears, I saw the radiant face of the little lady. That night I wrote to Martin:

November 9, 1931

My dear,

I received your letter dated October 21, with photos enclosed. Thank you, my dear, but you are so sad in them, and I do not like it. Cheer up now, darling. I hope you are smiling by now.

Did you really think a letter would reach me there? No, Martin dear, during all these days I did not see a line in your handwriting. Yes, it was a heavy experience, but now it is all over and maybe later on I shall understand that these sad days were given to me for my own good. The only thing I can tell you is that though rather surprised and perplexed over that unexpected happening, I went there with a light feeling, knowing well that I had done nothing wrong. And then I hoped that the Lord would not abandon me, and so remained bright and calm in my suffering.

Same day, 4 P.M.

My dear, words fail me to express all, so that sometimes I think I know English very little.

Another joy came to me today. The old man of Clamart, R.R., I wrote to you of, was helped by you at the right moment – Martin, little could I say of my joy and thankfulness to you for having saved his life. I know you will not forget him; you can send him food also. He writes that it came like a miracle – he never expected it. He thanks us, he asks the Lord's blessing upon us, and maybe the prayer of that poor abandoned man reached the Lord. I shall tell you much more about him but now I can say I am happy over his happiness, and it was a very happy Sunday for me. But I wish to be sure you are happy too.

I am still confined to my bed, but hope to finish with it in about 5 to 6 days the doctor said.

I kiss you, Martin. Be well and happy.

Your Lisa

Here is a fragment of Martin's letter answering the above:

...I am sorry that the pictures I took do not please you. As soon as I have a chance I shall take some photos outdoors, with a camera that does not lie. The best picture I have of you is the one you took a few days before I left and it's hanging over my desk.

Lisochka, my love, please come soon or else nothing will be left of your Martin. I walk around in a daze. My mind is not on my work, and the fear of not seeing you soon terrifies me. I live like a man about to be condemned without reason. Lisa, I love you far beyond love's own power of loving, and I suffer much. Good night, darling. Let no ill wind blow your way. I kiss you.

Martin

I had not yet received any reply to my first letter of November 5th, except a cable delivered early one Sunday. It was long and full of entreaties to take constant care of myself. One of his letters mentioned the name of an American newspaper man in Moscow to whom Martin wished me to send a card, thanking him for the interest he had taken in me, which I did. Only years later, did I find out about the strange course of events which took place.

Informed of my new incarceration Martin almost lost his mind. His first impulse was to return to Russia at once but his friends advised him to take action from America. From his two visits to Soviet Russia he knew that he had to rush every possible help or it might be too late. His friend S. G. knew a representative of the American Press in Moscow, and it was to this man that a cablegram of several hundred words was sent explaining the pathetic situation of an American husband whose Russian wife was in prison for the second time, without any guilt whatsoever.

The exact reaction to this telegram and all that followed is related in the book, "ASSIGNMENT TO UTOPIA," written by the same American press correspondent, EUGENE LYONS. In "Chapter X, American Tragedies," he wrote:

One morning I received a yard-long cablegram from a friend in New York invoking my help in the following circumstances. An American furniture manufacturer, while touring the Soviet Union met a personable young lady in Odessa and fell in love with her. His love brought him back to Russia and Odessa for a second visit, and on this occasion he married the girl and applied for an exit visa for her. Local officials stalled him week after week with vague promises and he finally had to return alone. He continued the efforts to get her out for months by long distance without success. Meanwhile, it appeared that he had left his wife in what used to be called 'an interesting condition'. The gentleman was naturally much distressed and begged that I do something.

Upon making certain inquiries in Odessa I discovered that the Russian bride, soon after the American's departure, had been arrested for reasons that I could not ascertain. Reasons are not important in Russia anyhow – the circumstance that she was of bad birth (that is, good birth, old-style) and had associated with a foreigner may have had something to do with it.

I thereupon consulted my typewriter and what emerged was a cable dispatch about love and passports. The gist of it was that the Russian bride of an American businessman, a bride who would soon be a mother, languished in prison while the heartbroken bridegroom and father-to-be fought for her release. This lugubrious tale I laid with a straight face upon the desk of His Highness, the censor. The censor read it and blanched in the two spots on his face not covered by beard. This decidedly was not the sort of story he cared to have spread on record in the American newspapers.

I pretended astonishment at his astonishment. "Why, this is just an innocent little human interest yarn of the sort dear to the American heart. No one denies you have a right to jail Soviet citizens even if they're pregnant and married to Americans."

He looked at me in a way that made further discussion superfluous. "Just leave it with me, Mr. Lyons, and we'll ascertain the fact." Next day I telephoned to inquire whether the facts had been ascertained, ditto the day after that. On the third day the censor's voice had an optimistic lift to it.

"I think I'll have some news for you on that story in a few hours." That afternoon he phoned to say that the story was untrue; the lady had been released from jail. I never had the slightest intention of cabling that story, of course It appears that the order from Moscow was given to liberate me, no matter how late, so that the censor could report to the inquisitive American press man that the story was untrue and that I was not in jail. Thus in some strange way, Martin's action of which I knew nothing at the time, corresponded with the expectation of my faith.

I was up and around now and the first thing I did when finally allowed to go outdoors was to check on my application for the passport to America. A girl in the office politely informed me that it was going through the normal procedure and that I would have to be patient. Often an answer, though negative, given with consideration, does not destroy hope.

I resumed my work in the office but my mind was not in it. Not wishing to be unfair to the good V.V. I thought I ought to resign; but he insisted that I was needed, even though my heart was no longer in my work.

One morning at the end of November just after reaching the office, I suddenly felt sick. I didn't wish to give in, but my general discomfort increased, and V.V. had to take me home in a droshky (cab), My temperature was rising by the minute and some strange dark spots appeared here and there on my body. The district doctor was called but hours seemed to go by and no one came. My condition went from bad to worse. I wondered if some fatal sickness had taken hold of me. I thought of Mother, of her love, of the faith she had in the little star whose mission was to help me through life. Could the little star fade out now when I expected it to shine brighter and brighter?

I had no strength to think any longer, but I felt Mother near me, repeating the prayer:

> Tzar of heaven
> Counsellor, Soul of Truth
> Abiding everywhere,
> Fulfilling everything,
> Come and abide in my child,
> Cleanse her from all evil
> And save, oh Gracious One,
> Her soul.

"She will live," I faintly heard someone say, "Her temperature is coming down."

I had expected Mother to be at my side and, frightened to see a strange woman beside me, I closed my eyes again. "The danger is over," the same voice continued. "When she wakes, let her drink all she can."

"I certainly will," Vala said.

I heard the door open and close. "Who is she, Vala?"

"Our district doctor. She was wonderful to you, God bless her!" The light in the room was very dim.

"Is it night already?" I asked.

"Yes, but do not talk now. Just drink and rest. I shall tell you all tomorrow."

I felt weak, yet relieved of some stupendous physical ill which, in its fury, had been about to consume me. I felt as though something in me had been torn to pieces and it seemed that blood was oozing from my veins, gliding down my legs and arms, dripping from my fingers. In spite of my weakness, I gradually became conscious that new life was being pumped into my body by the greatest Physician and Sustainer of all. The temperature never rose again. Next day I was smiling when the doctor came. She was a tall, energetic woman of about 35 years of age.

"You surely escaped death by a hair," she said, explaining that my sickness developed because the necessary surgical help had not been given me after my miscarriage. As a result of this negligence, blood poisoning had set in a month later, and had it not been for my extraordinary constitution and the purifying strength of my own blood washing out the debris, I would have been dead in the morning. "You lost about two pails of blood, my dear woman," she said. "You must take very good care of yourself from now on, to avoid severe anemia." This was given as a definite order in the tone of a person coldly performing her duty, but the softness of her glance radiated sympathy as she added, "As soon as you can walk, come to the clinic for a thorough examination. I shall expect you."

The hurricane of events had passed, leaving me with more faith in God and more knowledge of myself. I was soon discharged by my doctor who found me in excellent condition except for the anemia. Upon my request, the Exportkleb assigned me to half-day work, mostly for translation of foreign letters.

The middle of December was approaching, each winter day growing shorter as the year drew toward its close. I walked every day, morning and afternoon, to gain strength. Often I walked on Maraslieyskaya Street and across it in Alexandrovsky Park reliving now, when I was free, the awful moments I had so recently lived through.

"On aime revenir aux endroits ou l'on a souffert." ("One likes to return to the places where one has suffered.") says the writer, Henri Bordeaux. What a strange sensation to retrace one's steps on the road where one has trembled with fear and despair. Yet my breathing became deeper and my step more rhythmic as I thought of the strength given me to overcome it all.

Year 1930, year 1930. I could see myself, a schoolgirl, scribbling these figures on a blotter, wondering at them. Yes, it had been fearful, yet wonderful. The ocean of this year had tossed grief and joy on the crest of its waves. Now it was calm again – or was it only a lull? I walked in the healthful, wintry air, remembering, remembering the good and the bad, all mixed in one now – all a total wonder. "So much has happened," I would say, sharing my recollections with the bare trees of the park; and as though in response, the branches creaked with frost. "Now I must wait," I would conclude, "that is all I have to do."

Once I took my long abandoned notebook out of the drawer and wrote:

December 12, 1930

I could hardly find it possible to share a thought with my book this year. I have suffered much, but I have also had other happy experiences, one of which was to meet a man of rare character who from the first glance loved me. He is my husband now. We have been married four months today, but we are still far, far away from each other.

It certainly did not take me long to write my entire love story on the 12th of December, 1930. How characteristic of our prevailing fear is this scantily presented love story where events so dear to me are barely mentioned. These few lines were the only ones written in my notebook since January 31st, the night of my arrest eleven months ago. Days went on, the only pleasure of which consisted in receiving Martin's letters and cables and answering them. On the following pages there are letters which, maybe better than any narrative of mine, will give the picture of my life during those days of anxious waiting.

Odessa, Dec. 15, 1930

My very dear,

Now I am drinking Cocoa in the morning, and trying to eat better; rice is wonderful. We have already received 2 packages which we could take, the duty being something over 12 rubles, and sent one back with the dreadful duty on the soap.

Just imagine, Mrs. Bulgakoff got the notification for the passport parcel, showing the amount of the 136 rublse duty. She was very perplexed, feeling very incorrect to send it back, but I quieted her, saying I told you already that if the duty is great, we send parcels back. Excuse us, darling, but it would be too, how to say – not clever to take it, you understand.

Thank you very much for the parcels. In the future send them in Vala's name and only 5 kilos gr. as I said in my 7th letter.

Oh, please – to the list I wrote you, add one address more for food.

Mrs. E.S.
Pl. Krassnoy Armii
1-44
Dom Popudova
Odessa

Forgive me for all this trouble, but first you offered it yourself, and secondly, sending rice, sugar, farina and other things of this kind is but a trifle in your country's money, and I try to console myself by that and do my best not to blush when adding some more addresses.

I send some old photos of mine which I liked, so as not to forget them later on. Put them aside in a little box and they will wait till I come. You see how strong my hope is.

Your Lisochka

P.S. Darling, I have a request to make. Find out where the Russian church in New York is and on Saturday night or Sunday morning please enter there, buy a candle and light it before an icon for me. I wished to ask you about this since I was so ill and then came home.

Christmas this year was calm, but more prosperous than many previous ones. Through an American tourist, Martin had managed to send a hundred dollar bill to a man in our town, and one evening the equivalent of it in Russian currency was delivered to us with a note, written and signed by Martin confirming the transaction. All of a sudden we were rich. Knowing at what risk for many this money had come to us, we were careful with it.

The extravagance I couldn't help allowing myself was to obtain at any cost something that would look like a Christmas tree, which were not allowed to be sold. To this end, our milk girl was tipped generously and one morning carefully and solemnly, she pulled a rich fir branch from under her apron and with a smile, handed it to me.

On Christmas Eve some of our friends young and old came and together we waited for the first star to appear. Having closed the shutters, we sat around the table with our modest Christmas branch for a centerpiece and broke the fast. We ate baked fish, the traditional "kutia" (wheat grains soaked with nuts and poppy seeds, and "vsvar" (stewed dried fruit). By contrast I remembered the Christmas of my childhood which seemed close to fantastic now.

With a sad note of melancholy Tetia Tonia said this probably was the last Christmas I would spend here under the skies of poor, tyrannized Mother Russia. She was sad. Some of our guests tried to be festive, but most didn't even try. After they left, I reread Martin's last letter and answered it. To write to him made me happier. His faith in our reunion invariably bolstered mine. The last page of this very long letter reads:

"When shall I see you, Martin? Shall I spend next Christmas Eve with you? You see, though you greatly encouraged me, I still wonder and wonder when. I dreamed of you a few days ago. With great difficulty I was going up a staircase, hardly able to take one step more, and there near the top you came and helped me.

My dear, just now, at this very moment, you are almost with me. It is one past midnight here and the evening just begins in your country. Maybe you received my wire. Maybe you are thinking of me as I asked you to in my 12th letter – Martin, sometimes it seems strange to me that we, persons from opposite parts of the world, came together and united our lives, that it was enough for you to look into my eyes, for knowing me, and more than that, loving me. I think this must have been love because only love does not ask questions. You have no idea who I am, what I am, and never asked—

Goodnight, Martin. I shall be with you until sleep takes me away.

Elizabeth

Here is another letter:

Odessa, December 28, 1930

My dear,

I just went out and was enchanted by the wonder of the night – all white and silver. I did not recognize Odessa. I thought for a moment I was transported to Moscow because of the amount of snow. I did not notice any beauty in it this morning, the snowstorm being too strong because of the wild "Northeast" wind, but now it is calm in the moonlit sky. There is no noise in the town either, except the pretty sound of tiny sleigh bells. I love winter; I love Russia, which personifies that snowy season. Though very tired, I couldn't help going out, because of that newly fallen, immaculate snow. Who knows, tomorrow it may already not be the same.

I saw many sleighs driving by and on a large street I saw two of them racing; it was pretty with that brilliant snow dust around them. I thought had you been here we would have chosen the best horse (with a fine net on it and charming bells) and covered warmly, let it go full speed, enjoying the pleasure of that winter drive. But, darling, you are far away, and only your letter received this morning (dated 7th Dec. #19) was with me the whole day – with me during this evening's walk and with me now too, when I am telling you goodnight, kissing, promising to answer it very soon. Sleep well, my Martin.

Elizabeth

Diary

December 31, 1930

It was an exceptionally cold day and toward evening it became even colder; but in our room it is warm and comfortable. Our next door neighbor, Natochka's father, procured some fuel and we built a fire in the huge Holland stove which had been idle for many years. Its glossy white tiles exude a comfortable warmth in our room and theirs. What an unusual New Year's treat! Too bad we cannot keep this fire burning throughout the winter. My desk is not far from the portable stove and today I don't have to bundle up as usual.

Many telegrams with New Year's wishes are spread before me – one from Martin's parents, one from Pauline, another from Gertrude and a very long one from Martin. I think of him and last night I sent my message wishing them health and happiness.

Vala and I decided to stay home tonight and meet the New Year quietly. Is it true that we are going to ring out the old 1930? The premonition of my childhood concerning this year was true. It was an extraordinary one and a happy one because I met Martin. Someday I shall write a book about it.

#20 3rd/4th January 1931

My very dear,

It is 2 hours past midnight. Can you believe it? Tomorrow I shall write to you but tonight I shall only kiss you goodnight and tell you that you gave me immense pleasure by sending the photos together with your letter #20 of December 14th. I also received the touching Christmas card and thank you for all. I like the photos very much and am happy to know where you live.

I am all alone, my darling. Today my dear Vala was sent to a clinic by doctors who are good friends of ours as there is something wrong with her heart. It is still easy to repair if properly treated and there should be no negative results except some fatigue. I think that will diminish with rest. She is going to write to you from there. So darling, I am all alone in this large room, it is night time and the silence is absolute. I just took my bath (in a less comfy bathroom than yours – I could not help making the comparison). Instead of going to bed immediately I am writing to you. No, I should not do it, it is too late. Goodnight, my Martin, come and kiss me. I was so worried these last few days; Vala became very sick so suddenly. Now I am much quieter. Goodnight, my dear. Goodnight, darling. Sleep well.

4th/5th January past midnight

I had an awfully busy day. In the early morning I went to the market and bought 10 eggs (paid 4 rubles) and half a pound of butter (paid 4 rubles 40 kopecks) and a liter of milk (ir.10k). It is very dear, but it is necessary to prepare something to eat.

After work I went to Zina who is not better, poor thing, and about 7 P.M. went to Vala on the opposite side of town. I had one more visit to make and came home about 11 P.M. and only then sat down to eat. Vala is pleased with that place and it makes me happy. I am much happier since I know she will get the necessary treatment. Nikita brought me the wire of Jan. 3rd. I shall answer soon.

It is late but I wish to answer your letters #19 and #20. In the first you speak about Captain Harry Grimston. Yes, he is a very kind man and I am glad you answered him. You must think of all that happened to me when writing letters and sending lists or sheets from the magazines. You seem to have forgotten I must hear nothing but about you. Yes, Captain Harry knew how dear my mother was to me and I shall be glad to have him with us once again.

My darling, since now I am stronger there will be no need for you to come to Europe, better remain at home where you are needed; you must not leave your work at such an important time. Please have someone meet me at the railway station with money because I'm not permitted to have foreign money and it will be embarrassing for me without it.

As to when my passport will be delivered, I know not whether it is going to be delivered or refused. I can address the new petition only in 6 month intervals, so I wait. I often think of Gene Lyons. and of other people who were kind to you. I hope my passport will not be refused. You write that when not busy you feel lonely; Darling, I feel the same.

Thank you for your kind desire to give me some pleasure (which you certainly cannot do) for Christmas. It is so dear of you.

Later you speak of the Crimea but I have already written to you about it and besides I do not want to go there without you.

With all my love,

Lisa

P.S. My dear, please do not forget to thank all your family for the cables I received on New Year's Eve. I hope mine reached you on time.

L.

#24 Odessa, 24 January 1931

My dear Martin,

Tonight I hope to be able to answer all four of your letters. Though I do not have the opportunity to write often, I very often call you to me and talk to you and ask you questions, the same as you do. But there are not many questions to ask before the first (the most important one) is decided. How it will be decided we don't know.

The day before yesterday I was told that a young lady who married a German engineer this autumn and now waits for her passport was refused it. The reason remains unknown.

But let us believe our destiny, dear. The reply must be given about the 4th or 5th of March. I hope that all you did will help our situation.

Your wire tells me that yesterday (the 23rd) you celebrated the opening of the new establishment. Good luck, my dear. I always ask God's blessing upon you. Be well. I leave you till tonight.

Your Elizabeth

I was very busy with the liquidation and other formalities after having finished working (at the Exportkleb, January 15, 1931)

25 1 past midnight, 24/25 January 1931

I know you will be angry with me if I start writing a very long letter after midnight, so I shall not and will go to bed. My #24 is gone this afternoon.

My Martin, how do you feel? Are you not too tired of your work? Do you rest sometimes during the day? Did you get a little stouter? Don't forget to do gymnastics. What are your amusements? Now I must stop. I am leaving you, otherwise I shall talk to you till tomorrow.

Kiss me, Martin. Goodnight.

Odessa, 3rd February, 1931

My dear Martin,

The night of January 31st I felt nervous against my will. It was just a year ago that I had to leave my Vala, leave my house for 3 long months' time; and all that happened that day came back to my mind as if it were yesterday. But Vala having returned that day (January 31st) from the sanatorium was with me, and we felt so happy being not separated as last year. Vala feels much better, kisses you and scolds me for having not yet answered all your old letters, so I am going to do it.

You met your friends at the ball and they asked about me – your "wife". I am not accustomed to that word, it is so new to me. I do feel I am your Lisa, but the word "wife" – it seems to me it is spoken of someone else. So you wear the ring, though it is not a custom in America. It is dear of you. I wrote you that I wear mine too. Yes, Martin, I am right. We received these rings in church the 12th of August, but you wrote 11th instead. It does not matter. But do you remember the man who made them for us from Father's medal? How sincerely he wished us well.

I do remember that night, my dear. I do remember we were walking hand in hand, having the Black Sea wonderfully illuminated by the moon in front of us. It is true we did not speak much, and you never "conveyed all those thoughts that blossomed in your heart." Tetia Tonia and others were with us – In general we have been so little together....

I love and kiss you my Martin. Goodnight.

Elizabeth

February 6, 1931 5 P.M.

Alone in my room, resting on the sofa and admiring the dance of the sunrays on the pictures and walls. Just now a bright sunbeam illuminated wonderfully the gravure of Christ. Fascinated, I looked at the divine face, which seemed alive in the brightness of the sun. And I thought—

In that very moment your letter dated January 13 (sent via S/S Exford - the 14th) was brought to me. Only two hours ago I posted my last one, but I wish to write a few more words to acknowledge the above and thank you for it. I am happy to hear that a very important man is helping us. God bless him. I didn't hear from Gene Lyons since I sent him my New Year's card. But what should he write to me about?

It is growing dark – no more sunshine. I can hardly write. Goodbye, my dear. You say you love my pictures, you love me—Goodbye, my darling. I remain alone in the darkness and think.

Elizabeth

February 9, 1931

Martin darling,

I received your cable and answered about Zina's health at once – she is very ill indeed. We visited her yesterday and found her awfully changed for the worse. Poor Zina, she speaks of death as of something definite, but I still hope. When I visit her I never fail to translate the passages with all your kind and tender words for her.

Food packages are coming regularly, and everyone is so thankful…. you would be perhaps surprised yet pleased to see, had you assisted at our dinner, that all we eat is from your package. For two months now we have had very heavy frosts and a lot of snow, and living grows more difficult than when I wrote last. I wait for the spring; everything will be better then.

To come back to our important subject it appears that if I am refused I can immediately make another application, and will do it. But why should they refuse me, for pity sake! They must not. Don't they understand you are waiting for me, and I wish to be with you so badly?

Since I lost my dear Mother I think of her constantly around this time of the year. I remember how conscious of her condition she was, and how she wanted to make these heavy days easier for us. Poor, dear Mother. She died in the morning of February 21st, 1926. There was nothing but a deep sigh and she was no more with us physically. It will be five years soon, but I never felt her away from me. There is no death for love, it is immortal.

I know you would have loved my mother very much had you known her and she would have certainly loved you, understanding your sincere affection for me.

Be well, my darling, I think of you.

Your Elizabeth

Feb. 16, 1931

My dear,

Thanks so much for the photos – Vala's, mine and those of the details of the new establishment's interior. They all are very good photos and we like them. I am happy your hard work these last months brought fine results and you feel satisfied, and everyone admires the beauty of it. Darling, you say all this effort, all this work was for me. Thank you, dearest, but if it tired you too much, I am sorry. But I feel you like it, that new place, and it is a good enough reward. I am sure I shall like it because I love all that is beauty.

Both Vala and I appreciate the kindness of your youngest brother-in-law, Mr. Hy Selditch, who re-photographed so many pictures of ours. Please give him our best regards together with our excuses for having troubled him so much with our faces, mine especially. Please tell your sisters, Pauline and Gertrude, I am kissing them all heartily and hope to see them soon. Don't forget to give my best to all.

Tonight I dreamed that together with your cable a nice young dog was delivered. Everybody was so surprised, and wondered how that little dog could be sent from America. I laughed all day, remembering the dream. Everyone tried to analyze the dream for me, and it was finally decided that it meant a good, life-long friend. You, of course! Funny thing, these dreams in general.

Goodbye darling

Your Elizabeth

On February 18th, another page of my diary was written. These notes are short and far apart, yet obviously I had a yearning to analyze and review the events of the significant year 1930.

Wednesday 18 Feb. 1931:

I remember how naturally I used to chat with my book, but for a long time now I have kept quiet. One is often silent when one has too much to say. Too frequently this past year, my mind and heart were disturbed by the most unforeseen events, and stunned, I was unable to put my thoughts together. Now it seems I can think more clearly. I tell myself that after a hard test endured without much self-pity, I was led by the hand of God to a new life. My first move was to refuse this happiness, and I rejected the love of a man whom I met by the strangest of coincidences. He left; but two and a half months later he returned. I remember having asked abruptly, "Why did you come?" and he answered, "I could not decide this question by mail."

Ah, those days of torment when I did not know what to do. Though attracted to him, I hesitated to accept his offer of marriage, knowing that many obstacles could come our way, some of which might be too gigantic for us to overcome. I suffered, sensing the suffering of this noble heart who offered me his life, his strength, his love, recognizing in me at first sight, the one he had been looking for all his life. I was greatly moved by the depth and strength of his feeling, yet hesitated to marry him, and asked God to help me to make the right decision. Could one avoid destiny? And what do we know of it, poor humans? This man who came across land and sea to bring me his love was maybe predestined – "Two shall be born, the whole wide world apart, and speak in different tongues, and have no thought each of the other's being, and no heed; and these, o'er unknown lands shall cross, escaping wreck, defying death; and all unconsciously shape every act and bend each wandering step to this one end – that one day out of darkness they shall meet and read life's meaning in each other's eyes."

I still remember these lines by heart from "FATE" by Suzanne Marr Spalding. This was the text of my first lesson in English, written out for me by the handsome British officer of H.M.S. Grafton, Captain Edgar Graves in 1918. I loved and memorized these lines. That evening I was infatuated with the sender of them, whose mission as I see it now was to prophecy my distant future and then fade out of my life forever.

And so I married the man from across the sea, an American not an Englishman, and after a short honeymoon to Yalta he was obliged to leave without me. Then I went through many sad days, but my faith did not abandon me, and the misery of my situation helped me to understand the devotion of my husband. I think God was guiding him all the time. Looking back on the events of last October and November, I realize that if it were not for him and the fact that I was the wife of an American who was desperate for his wife to obtain her passport, I would have perished there.

Now, far away, he waits and hopes I shall soon be with him but the passport has not arrived and it is six months since I last saw him. We write to each other very often. In his last letter he says, "There is nothing important for me, nothing vital, except you."

Feb. 20, 1931 Friday

On the eve of the anniversary of Mother's death, I spoke to her on the pages of my notebook:

Mother, my dear Mother, absent last February, March and April, this year I am here again in the same room where five years ago sick, and oh how weak, you still were among us. You spoke to us, you blessed us. You had the strength and spirit, and presence of mind to uphold us by your unforgettable words. Gradually, you were going away, wholly conscious of it. It was hard for you to leave, yet you never failed to console us. Mother, my dear, dear Mother, I love you as before. I shall never cease loving you. Last year, in all my torment I felt your presence near giving me strength. Not long ago, when I became sick, hardly understanding anything of my ailment, it was you, Mother, who in that sad moment came to comfort me with your prayer.

This February your two daughters are again together. I always pray for you and Papa. I am still here, where we were all together, but where shall I be next year? This, I do not know. What direction will my life take? Of this, I know even less. The only thing I am sure of is that my love for you will remain with me no matter where I am. May the Lord bless your soul, Mother.

20th Feb. 1931

Martin mine,

You are worried, you are sad, you are not in a happy frame of mind so I gather. But please don't, darling. Take all things easier. The most important thing in this world is inner equilibrium. Keep it and you will always have a bright face, and you will smile in all circumstances. A fortune! What is a fortune? Very much, and nothing at the same time. Anyhow, it is much less than health, strength and faith. Martin, I wish you to smile. I wish you to be happy. Don't pay attention to this sudden change.

You are young, you are healthy, and therefore you are rich. Think of all the sufferings I had to endure and I still smile, darling.

Let's smile together.

After reading that sad letter of yours I am so sorry I cannot cheer you up in person, and this letter will reach you only in 2 or 3 weeks.

You think I will come in April – for your birthday! Let us hope, hope and hope –

I kiss you, my dear Martin, and wish you absolute inner peace. It helps so much in life.

Your Elizabeth

Letter from little Natochka:

Feb. 28, 1931

Dear Uncle, Aunt Lisa's husband,*

Thanks for the parcel. I love you and kiss you heartily. I kissed already Aunt Lisochka for the parcel. When Aunt Lisochka leaves, I shall send you something that will seem new to you, to thank you for your kindness.

I kiss you,

Natochka

(*Children in Russia call all adult acquaintances "Aunt" and "Uncle".)

Fragment of Martin's letter of March 27, 1931

.….In the morning I was exceedingly happy on reading your letter #34.

It pleased me that you and your friends had received food and that your health was a bit better, for which I am thankful.

The dear letter from little Natochka was so touching that I kissed it (not forgetting yours).

Fragment from my letter of Feb. 27, 1931:

.….Darling, sometimes, when writing in haste you make some little mistakes and I don't want you making any. You can laugh at me (who makes a hundred times more), daring to point out to you, but my dear, did I not love you I would never pay attention to it, but you see I am afraid you can make the same mistakes when dashing off some business papers. So, note the difference between <u>accept</u> and <u>except</u>: in your letter from Paris last September, for instance, you sent me many kisses and at the same time asked me to <u>except</u> them. You can imagine how vexed I felt after this – so soon after marriage!! Then, you speak about my <u>presence</u> and write <u>presents</u>. It is because you write letters after 2 A.M.!!

Now, if you are angry with me for this, you are not what I expected you to be. But I know you are not angry, dear, dear! Please, if you have time, correct my mistakes. I shall be very thankful to you.

Martin, darling, good night.

I kiss you,

Lisa

Fragment from letter in reply to above:

—I actually laughed out loud for sheer delight. I kiss your dear face a thousand times as a reward for your charm. At that moment you stood before me talking. The little note was your double, it personified your own image. Its tone was as soft as your voice, its contents the all-accumulated wisdom and kindness—

Tomorrow morning I shall send food to all the names you mention, including Aunt B., Nikita and yourself. Please tell me how long it takes for food packages to reach you. Is Zina better? Give her my love. My kindest regards to Vala and all the rest of our dear friends.

Good night, my dearest, kindest, gentlest, and best of women. May health, peace and happiness be yours. I kiss and embrace you with all my heart.

As ever—

Your Martin

March 7, 1931

My dear Martin,

I look at this date, March the 7th, and no information from the passport office – I shall go again and ask about the delay. We had very stormy weather all this month long, with very few sunny days, and no one felt too well. Yes, my dear, it would be wonderful to be with you the 3rd of April, your birthday, but look at the calendar: could it ever be possible if as yet I know nothing of my nearest future? Just think! We did not see each other for half of a year. You can forget how I look! But when shall we see each other. I told you that it will take time and you thought, darling, we shall be together for Christmas.

In your letter #9 you speak of your past-time. Sorry you cannot arrange a regular rest for yourself – you might regret it later. Do take things easier.

You say that since you returned from Russia some ladies have lost interest in you. It only proves how sincere their interest was!! Such ladies certainly do not merit your attention but there are many others, and find an esthetic pleasure admiring them. I earnestly think that not all the women are looking for interest.

As for myself, I cannot say that men have lost any interest in me, though you can well imagine how I care for it, meeting them only mostly when my affairs require it – but as I told you before I always was spoiled by that interest.

And so, my dear, I am still talking to you on this paper, but when shall I hear your voice and you mine? The 7th of March, and I am still here. I hope though that if there is a delay, there will at least be no obstacles.

With much love,

Lisa

293

I was just finishing the above letter when Marussia S. came to see me. "I had almost forgotten how you looked, darling," I said, as we kissed each other. "How nice of you to drop in."

"It is my day off, Lisa, "she said, "and knowing that you had stopped working, I expected to find you home."

"And I am very glad I am home. Has anything good happened to you?"

"Nothing at all. Nothing at all," she said, sitting down without taking off her coat. Impatiently she threw her pretty but much worn purse on the table. "And yet only yesterday Tovarisht M. finally proposed. Right there on the job he stood by my typewriter and poured his heart out to me."

"And you, what did you say?"

"Of course, I refused. Your method, Lisa, still proves to be the best: 'Sorry, I am engaged,' I said. I wish I were, though. But I'm afraid I'll never be married. In these odd times all of the fine men that are left are – or will be in prison, and the others – well, you know."

"It would be terrible for you to be an old maid; you are so beautiful and intelligent."

"Well, such is my sad case," she sighed. "But yours is even more embarrassing, poor thing. Imagine. You married an American last summer and now it is already spring and you are still in Russia, in the same town of Odessa, alone as before. So it does not seem that you are married any more than I am."

"You know very well," I replied, "that they would not let me leave Russia with him. And not becoming automatically an American citizen, I must go through all the Soviet formalities which means waiting and waiting. This I do, trying to be cheerful. I know my husband loves me. He will overcome all difficulties. 'I shall not leave a stone unturned,' were his very words."

"He probably judges by his American stones," she said sarcastically. "But let him try to turn some of the stones of our regime – before he does some smart, clever American girl will manage to make him forget all about you."

"I do not believe it! He never will!"

"Nothing, indeed, can shake your optimism," she laughed.

"I cling to it more than ever," I said.

"What a character, that of yours. Even after a series of imprisonments you aren't crushed. Quite the contrary, you seem more calm and, believe me, even more attractive than before!"

"Do you really think there is no advantage at all in such experiences?" I asked.

"There would be none for me, I assure you. And out of thousands and thousands of political prisoners without guilt, you probably are the only one to have profited by it."

"I think I did," I said.

"But aside from your personal growth, let's see what our general progress has been in the 14 years of Bolshevism....We are still living in

fear, afraid of spies all day, afraid all night, wondering whether the rest of the night will be spent in one's own bed or on the cold floor of some jail. As far as economics are concerned, look at what we eat, what we wear! That bag of mine! My coat – the latest model of 1931 (old already in 1921) – perfect elegance, 'dernier cri' (last word)."

Marussia's laugh was more bitter than amused.

We were sitting on our old, but still beautiful chairs at the round mahogany table, shivering with cold though wearing our coats. We spoke French while having our 5 o'clock tea, hot water and stale pieces of bread. "Too bad you cannot treat me any better, wife of an American!"

"Wait until you visit me in the United States," I told her.

She shrugged, pulling down the corners of her mouth. "I don't think my pessimism will ever lead me there if even you, with your optimism, have only a scanty chance."

"Please speak for yourself. I have had my share of misery. Now I am sure it is my turn for happiness. I do not admit defeat before the battle, and you shouldn't either. Do try to replace your endless 'no' with an occasional 'yes'."

"It's easy to preach, my dear."

"Try, though."

"What's the use, Lisa. I need a strong push even to try. I need some sudden joy, some surprise; but our life is all monotone. Tomorrow I shall trot the same old way to the office where we have so mercilessly wasted our youth, our strength, our life. Sometimes it seems impossible to begin another day."

"Oh, Marussia, cheer up!" I said. "There is actually no choice. Do try to make the best of it."

She left, this beautiful girl – tall, majestic with dark almond shaped eyes and fine aristocratic hands which would type all day tomorrow. Paralyzed with fear, her full lips never smiled, and at the end of the day her body was bent under the weight of discontent and exhaustion. Too bad she never knew the blessing of a sense of humor.

Her pessimism was still floating about my room, and unwillingly I was pulled into the wave of its vibration. "I know Martin so little after all," I thought. "The obstacles may seem too big for him. He might not have enough spirit to overcome them. Marussia thinks I shall never reach America." I turned on my desk lamp, and the pink shade spread a pleasant light. My husband's cable lay open before me: "I THANK YOU MY DEAREST FOR YOUR LOVELY LETTER. KEEP HOPING, AN IMPORTANT MAN IS HELPING US. YOURS FOREVER, MARTIN."

"Yours forever." Is this a common English expression or does he write these words with meaning? What is the matter with me? Why do I doubt? Has Marussia's mood taken away all my common sense? But he loves me. No fast working American girl could possibly take him away from me. Every letter, every cable speaks of his love and devotion to me. Marussia can say whatever she chooses, but I refuse to be influenced by it, even if I have to wait much, much longer. As if relieved of a great weight, I went out to the balcony and admired the blue, starry night. When back at my desk, I glanced through the same cable again: "AN IMPORTANT MAN IS HELPING US." Who could he be? I better tell Martin to be careful.

The floating pessimism tried vainly to affect me. What? Am I doubting again? Certainly not! This "important man" must be a wonderful person. I know he is.

Saturday, Mar. 14, 1931

Darling,

I wired yesterday about the delay of a definite reply as to my permission to leave. You can imagine how I felt when I was told that they still look over all that affair of mine, and that it is good enough that I have not gotten a refusal.

To lose courage is not in my nature, you know, so I still have hope. All you wrote in your last letters only helps me to be patient.

I keep thinking of the "important man" you mentioned in your cable. I am too well trained to ask his name or any details about him, but trust he is earnest in his desire to help us.

They told me in the office that the reply may be given in one or two weeks, in one or two months, but as a rule it does not take more than half or a year's time. Terrible! Of course I shall not see you for your birthday, darling.

Your Elizabeth

PASSPORT TO AMERICA

Diary

March 15, 1931 Sunday

The first splendid day, sparkling under the spring sun. How beautiful it is! How beautiful! My poor Martin suffers far away from me. He waits for me, impatiently. I have more equilibrium, more patience in general than he has because the school of my life was more severe.

Not only did we exchange many letters, but there were weeks when Martin's cablegrams simply bombarded us. April began. I was counting the days and weeks and months since our separation. One afternoon I returned home after a walk and Vala met me at the door holding a telegram. "The second for you today," she said, "but this one isn't from Martin."

She opened it and we read it together, slowly, out loud as in school. Our eyes met. Though expected day after day, month after month, the message still came as a shock: "LEAVE IMMEDIATELY FOR MOSCOW FOREIGN PASSPORT BUREAU."

"Oh, Lord! Why immediately?" Vala said. "Immediately means this minute – not even this hour. How could you leave your home and friends without even saying goodbye?"

I put my hand on her shoulder. "Vala, dear, I cannot take the risk of arguing with the Soviet Passport Bureau, but my 'immediately' will be in two days."

Vala sighed, "I'm glad you didn't say two hours." From the corridor we went into our room, "What shall we do now? What will you take along?" she asked.

Absent-mindedly, I looked around. "There isn't much to take. It could all be done in the last five minutes. Right now I'd better make a list of the friends I must see before leaving, and the first thing tomorrow morning I'll go to the cemetery to say goodby to Mother and Father."

Vala, a little more cheerful, observant as usual, looked at me and said, "Well, don't give in to sadness now, Lisa, it really begins to look as if you're going to join your husband."

"I am not sad, Vala," I said.

But I was – I, who had so eagerly expected this hour. A strange sorrow gripped my heart at the thought that in a short while I would be leaving. I felt guilty about going away to a life of joy and satisfaction, leaving my sister and my friends. I felt guilty about leaving them alone and helpless, and Vala was the only one who, sooner or later, would be with me. It was twilight. Eyes half closed I pictured my father sitting in the arm chair next to me, still healthy, distinguished and good-looking in spite of years of privation. He smiled, his beautiful teeth sparkling, and then it seemed as if Mother came with her light step, and looking at us with loving eyes, asked us to come into the dining room.

"What could you offer us, Olichka? You know we do not like 'bare' tea, and you could not, with all your good will and energy, surprise us with anything else."

"Well, just come and see."

"Vala, where are you?" called Father. "Come on, a surprise!"

It was Father's birthday. I remembered this tea with biscuits and a little jam for which Mother had to trade two hand-embroidered towels – but it was worth it. Our happiness and compliments were far greater than anything she could have expected.

"You act like children," she had said, smiling shyly.

This scene from the past was almost real, and I heard myself say out loud, "Father and Mother, my dears, do you know I am going to America?" Silence answered. I knew that they had heard, that they approved.

Among the numerous letters saved by Martin, there were also many of my cables and this is the one he received, April 10, 1931, "AM ORDERED TO GO TO MOSCOW PASSPORT BUSINESS HOPE AS NEVER BEFORE. LISA."

The time of my departure was set, my ticket bought. Every minute was well used; and two days later all my dear ones stood in a tight circle on the platform of the familiar railway station of Odessa. Suddenly, the small space where they stood was no longer the platform by my train, but the entire, kind and hospitable land of Russia, the country of my birth, the suffering Mother Russia, whose beautiful face had been disfigured by the cruelties and injustice of her sons, whose tired brow was sorrowfully bent before the darkness of the impenetrable future. The group of friends suddenly became my childhood, my adolescence, my youth, all past and present, my life – and this I was about to leave.

Still deep in my thoughts I heard our old nursemaid say to Zina, "Wipe your tears. Don't you understand that she will be happy there? She will never forget you. She will never forget us. You know that."

This helped to change my thoughts. She is right. I will be able to help them much better from America. Not much time was left and shaking off my sadness, I was ready to say a word to each one of them before parting. Tetia Tonia was inconsolable. "Lisa, Lisochka, what shall we do without you? Who will cheer us up in our darkest moments?"

Vassinka stood beside her, his lips trembling. Somehow collecting himself, he said with a pitiful smile, "My joy, my only joy is going away."

To look at him almost tore my heart. It is much easier to bid farewell to the young than to the old. Our nursemaid, forgetting the advice she had just given Zina, was wiping her eyes with her sleeve. She kissed my hands and after I bent to kiss her, she put her arms around me and held me tight, swinging gently from side to side as she used to do when I was a baby.

Mme. E.S., the Romanian lady, came with a present – a small red and gold Venetian vase, a real antique. "This, my dear," she said, "is for your new home. And don't forget to greet your dear husband for us. My mother was very much impressed by him and often speaks of his visit."

Yes, yes, I remembered. They had offered him water with jam in it, which he did not like.

Nikita tried to joke, rather unsuccessfully, and Zina, his wife, who had come along in spite of her advanced ailment, gave me a very neat package of food for my trip. In a faint voice she said, "Goodbye, my angel. God will bless you everywhere. Goodbye," and her eyes added, "forever."

Tears were choking me, but I could not let myself go. I quickly wiped them and lifting my head, saw the dignified figure of our school "Maman" approaching our group, leaning on the arm of her daughter. "Lisa, my dear," she said, "I come to look at you once more, and to ask you to present my regards to your charming husband."

Years of hardship had not succeeded in taking away her poise and grandeur. In her presence I became a schoolgirl once more. "Maman, I shall never forget you," I whispered when she kissed and blessed me.

The young crowd looked and sounded different. "Happy trip!" "Happy meeting with New York." "Greet the skyscrapers for us."

Only Tolia, the promising young actor, looked solemn. "Starting for the New World, Lisa," he said. "And only a few months ago, such hopelessness. Now a new door is open before you. Unbelievable!"

"Quite believable to me," said Verochka, "and Lisa is the one who deserves it."

"Stop flattering me," I said, "You all deserve a better lot. Goodbye, my dear ones."

"Lisa, write! Write to us. Tell us about your trip – your life ..." "I will, I will."

"Oh, here, I almost forgot," Verochka said, passing me a little note. "This is from Marussia. She came this morning and asked me to hand it to you."

They all hugged and kissed me.

Strangers approached too, with problems which would have been impossible for me to solve as the addresses of relatives given were not complete. It was time to board the train. Vala went into the car and I followed. I realized that I was squeezing something tight in my hand. It was the note from Marussia S. Fear, I thought, had kept her from coming. "Lisa, my dear," I read, "So you are going after all! One miracle after the other has happened in your life. Do pray for me."

I had hardly reached my seat when we heard, "Visitors out!" In silence, Vala and I embraced each other. I looked out of the window and in the dusk of the April evening, I saw them all once more. The train was beating its regular rhythm, "Goodbye, farewell." It probably is and always was its business to sing goodbye and farewell, but I had not noticed it before and now could not stop hearing it. Presently, it seemed the wheels were stuck on "farewell" alone – "farewell, farewell, farewell."

It is farewell, I thought, and a real one this time, but it isn't because of these words that I am crying, but because of the expression on the dear faces that aged as I grew, and parting with me looked so unhappy. Terrified by the loss of everything they loved, they clung to me as to their own daughter. I loved them too and was thankful for their love.

The night settled very quickly.

The car I was in was almost entirely occupied by Red Soldiers. As soon as the wooden upper berths were lifted I climbed up on mine and lay down, using my suitcase for a pillow. These berths had no curtains and everyone slept as they were. Below me I heard an animated discussion.

"Certainly you had no right to help that woman."

"But the children didn't stop crying. I had to go in. I thought she was not home, but she was – sick and delirious, and the kids hungry. So I gave her something to drink, fed the little ones and tucked them in. What's wrong in this?"

"The wrong is in the fact that you knew who she was – the wife of one of those who used to call themselves 'blue bloods', and those are the ones who must be exterminated – all of them."

I listened and listened.

"But she was a hard working woman, so patient and loving to her children and so meek."

"They are good actresses. You should have known that."

"After all, I was her neighbor," the accused justified himself, "and I'm glad I helped."

"Tolstovshtina! (Follower of Leo Tolstoy's thinking.) When did you read that stuff, and what will you answer now before Moscow's GPU?"

"Crazy, soft-bodied fool!"

"Imbecile!"

On my upper berth I trembled with disgust. I could not see their faces, but I could guess that the accused was lonely and forlorn among those vandals. My own sadness left me, and for awhile I felt all the misery of this soldier who had had the unhappy idea of helping a noblewoman and who now was on the verge of being charged with counter revolution. All my being protested. The few who want to act decently, I thought, are all accused. What a distorted ideology.

My eyes were closing. The train suddenly began to sing again, "Goodbye, farewell." I didn't hear it long.

The moment I set foot on Moscow ground I found myself burning with the desire for action. I wanted to run to the passport office right away but it was late in the afternoon and the office was closed, so I directed my steps to the house where my friend Katia lived. She had often written me that I would always be welcome. Then I remembered that she would not be home since she usually had dinner with her relatives right after office hours.

I stood in the middle of the station thinking, Moscow, Moscow again. Here, soon after Father's death, I had arrived with Eddy D. and Professor K., full of hope for a good job with the White Star Line. Here, to this railway station, Eddy and I had come many times to inquire about our lost luggage. How happy we were when four months later we were told it had been found! Also about a year later, I met my dear mother who had come from Odessa to visit me. At this moment I relived that meeting, remembering how I saw her from far away in her green wool coat and black fur toque. How I ran to her, kissed her and held her in my arms, rejoicing that for the first time in our lives we were to have some time all to ourselves. Almost ten years had passed since then.

Now I was in Moscow again, or rather going through on my way to America. Subconsciously, I think I had always expected to live in America; but often it is very hard to draw a line between the conscious and the subconscious. I arrived in Moscow in 1922, hopeful of a job, which never materialized. Now, no disappointment could be possible! Had I not been urgently called from Odessa for the sole purpose of obtaining my passport to leave this country? There could be no other reason – but already my uneasy heart fluttered like a bird.

I left the station with Martin's small leather bag in hand and took the bus to Arbat, one of the oldest sections of Moscow. I kept the valise right on my lap. It was almost empty but I was afraid of losing it as it belonged to Martin and I wanted to return it to him. I still was not accustomed to the idea that his things were also mine, and mine his. Martin, having been refused a Russian visa, had promised to meet me in the city nearest Russia, which would probably be Riga. I shall see him in a few days, I thought. I relaxed and in the falling darkness through the window of the bus, I watched the passing silhouettes of old Moscow.

I found Katia lounging on a couch in a pink quilted robe with the earphones of a radio framing her pretty face. Her room reflected her love of elegance and order. Katia, who had lived with her aunt in the United States and finished school there, was fluent in English, enabling her to receive an above average salary. No wonder she sometimes allowed herself luxuries other girls could not even dream of.

"Good to see you, Lisa," she said, stretching her arms out to me. "Look what I have here." She pulled off her earphones and held them in the air.

"Very up to date, aren't you, Katia?" I said, "Even ahead of time. I am sure that few could boast of possessing this modern luxury."

"Very few, indeed," she agreed.

Katia was the only Russian friend with whom I always spoke English. She moved an armchair to her couch and said "Now, sit here close to me, Lisa, and let me hear the news."

"I am here, my darling, to get my foreign passport!"

"Do you really mean it?" she cried, clapping her hands. "You lucky thing! How I envy you!"

I let her read the telegram and she reprimanded me for not having come to Moscow at once. "If I'd received this telegram," she said, "I'd have left the moment I read it."

I shook my head. "Speed was part of your American education, Katia – but it will take me a long time to acquire it."

"Not if New York's going to be your permanent home! Imagine, Lisa, you're almost on your way there…"

"Almost, almost." I said. "I am sure it will not be long now. By the way, would you allow me to stay with you for a night or two and sleep right here on this couch?"

She nodded. "Certainly you may. It's not too comfortable, but I'm sure you won't mind it for a few days."

"Mind it! I couldn't dream of anything better than staying with you. What a relief not having to look for a room in some strange place." I got up and kissed her. "Thank you ever so much, Katia!"

We spoke of her job, of people we both knew, of Martin and his immediate plans, and then went out together to send him a telegram giving my Moscow address. The passport was very much on our minds. Katia thought I was obtaining it unusually quickly. I couldn't agree.

"Waiting eight long months! Do you call that 'quickly'?"

She still thought it was fast since some people she knew had waited over two years.

Back in her room, I set about making my bed, while Katia swiftly made tea and bread with jam. I had not realized until I saw the steaming cups of tea how famished I was. "Katia," I said, "this tea party will surely be written down in the Book of your Life as an especially good deed."

Next morning, seeing me bounce out of bed, Katia calmed me down. "No reason for you to rush; the passport office doesn't open until 10:00 A.M."

I could not believe it. "In Odessa," I told her, "I had to be at my desk at 8 in the morning, sharp."

"Don't forget, Lisa," she said, fixing her hair, "This particular office is not overtaxed with work. Hardly any passports are being issued these days."

"You are right."

I looked at the clock. It was 7:30 AM. Not wishing to be in Katia's way, I sat quietly on my couch while she rushed around, and when she left I took a long time to wash and dress because I wanted to look nice. When I was ready, I still had time. I left the house and strolled through the picturesque streets of Arbat. It was a sunny morning. A few buds could already be seen on the trees. I liked this part of Moscow. Here was the large church of Nikola Yavlenny (Appearance of Saint Nikolas), where Eddy Dailey's car had often waited for me on Saturday nights. Farther to the left was Bolshoy Rjevsky Pereulck (Lane), where we had lived – and there, my window through which I had often looked at that interesting, tiny church, Nikola na Kuryich Nojkach (St. Nikolas on Chickens' Feet). (Now destroyed.) This church was situated not far away from the main street of that section of Moscow, called Povarskaya Uliza (Street of the Cooks), and its little adjoining streets with names like Knife Lane, Table and Tablecloth Lane, etc. Centuries ago all the cooks and servants of the Kremlin used to live on Poverskaya Street. They cooked abundantly for the Tzar and his court, and threw the remainders of the food outside the kitchen on a pile at the very place where Bolshoy Rjevsky Pereulck Lane now stands.

St. Nikolas on Chickens' Feet ... As I pass by this church, I remembered the touching story of the origin of its name:

Long, long ago, there lived a poor but pious man who, after being healed of a severe sickness took an oath to build a church. For years, day after day, he trudged from his humble dwelling to the back of Povarskaya Street, picked up from the pile of leftovers the feet of the fat capons and fowls, went back to the poorer sections of Moscow and sold them to poor folk. At the very end of his life he succeeded in making his dream come true. He built this church, one of the smallest in Moscow, given by his contemporaries the name of St. Nikolas on Chickens' Feet, which it always remained.

Suddenly I realized that I was dreaming. I looked at my watch, 9:15 AM already! I jumped on a crowded street car and hanging outside on the steps reached my destination. I was directed to the second floor. There I sat in an empty room and waited half an hour. Then a clerk with unnaturally measured steps and a face too sweet to please me came to ask my name. He disappeared with no other comment, and for a long time nothing happened. I was not at all impatient. I did not mind waiting longer because my mood was too high to be disturbed. I sat straight, holding the telegram in my hand, not once changing position. For a long time I remained patient. Hours later the same clerk reappeared, noiselessly gliding by like a phantom and I jumped from my seat. "Tovarisht!" I said. "I am the person whom your office called urgently from Odessa to get my passport."

307

Disinterestedly, he looked at me. Then turning the pages of his memorandum, he said, "The order is for you to return to this office in two weeks – two weeks exactly."

"But your telegram says to come <u>immediately</u>" I cried, showing it to him. "Where shall I find a place to live in crowded Moscow?"

Supremely indifferent, holding a pencil by its dull end between his thumb and finger, he rhythmically swung its sharp tip up and down, up and down in my face; for his own amusement or to threaten me I did not know. Standing relaxed on one foot looking far, far away, this degenerate finally asked in a tormenting voice, "Wouldn't any sacrifice, even a year's wait, be worth the <u>hope</u> of maybe getting a passport in the end?"

Now I had the horrible feeling that the issuance of my passport was not as certain as I had thought.

The days were grey. It rained from morning till night. I was so ashamed of being an inconvenience to Katia that I usually left when she did and stayed out until time to go to bed. As a consequence, I caught cold and coughed like a dog. At night it was a torture to not cough while Katia slept. Time passed slowly. My husband's constant cables from Berlin were my only consolation. He was happy and sure I would get my passport. I cabled him, unable to hide my disappointment. His encouragement came back promptly. He did not doubt everything would be all right. My hope revived with each cable.

Not many of my friends had remained in Moscow. I especially longed to find Rica who had moved here last July. I went to the address that I had several times and finally I was told by a person who now lived there and happened to be in, that Rica had married and left for Leningrad.

Of course, the majority of my friends during the period of 1922-1923 when I worked for the American Relief Administration were Americans. Often passing by the mansions they had occupied, which they had called the White House, Blue House, Brown House, Grey

House, etc., I was surprised to find how easily the names of even those whom I had known slightly sprang into my mind: Col. Wm. E. Haskell and his son John, Captain Dalton, the friend of Mr. Harris, John Haynes (transferred from Odessa), Mr. Burland, Mr. Forbes, C. Verdon, Mr. Saycora, Mr. Mangan. I said their names over and over with reverence, adding one to the other like beads of a rosary which I repeated with a certain sense of sanctity. Each of these names represented a kind American who, in one way or another, had lightened and brightened our life in the sad, difficult days right after Father's death. Mr. Holden, Thomas McLaughlin, the Hammer brothers who kept a little bear at the entrance to the Brown House, Mr. James, Mr. Blattner and his wife, Mr. Daley, Mr. Daum, Mr. Queen who replaced Col. Haskell, Mr. Baldwin, Mr. Manley, Dr. Rosen, Dr. Beeuwkes (not forgetting our beloved Dr. Smith who once or twice came to Moscow from Odessa) – all these people whom I might perhaps meet in America if….again and again I repeated the rosary of their names, concentrating on the past in order to forget the uncertainty of the present.

Often as I walked the crowded streets, I studied the faces of the people. They were mostly sad and tense. Sympathetically I smiled at some and once in a while I received something like a fragment of a smile in return – furtive, suppressed and brief. Even the children looked at me like that. Only the babies were cheerful in Moscow. In the spring of 1931 in the squares and boulevards of the city, I saw more babies than I had in my entire life. Like buds, they grew and stretched in the sun, happy and unaware of the sinister reason for their breeding.

Sometimes I took a streetcar and visited remote parts of Moscow. Early one morning I went to the Novo Devichev Monastir cloister built for nuns in 1525 and roaming around reached the gate of a cemetery. Here and there lonely figures bent over the graves, clearing the ground so that the spring flowers could push through. I asked a young woman if she knew where the tomb of Anton Chekhov was. "Right there," she said and pointed. "The monument is pretty tall and shaped like a church steeple."

I thanked her, we walked a few steps together and then parted, smiling at each other. I saw her stop at the gate as two heavy carts were entering. I went to pay my respects to Father's friend, the famous writer. Quietly I sat on a bench by the lofty monument, but unfortunately I had only a short time to concentrate, for suddenly a noise of shattering stones echoed around me. I looked up, unable to believe my eyes. Men and carts were on the central path of the cemetery. One by one, I saw the marble crosses toppled from the monuments. Squads of workmen were performing this act of destruction, some of them knocking down the crosses, others picking up fragments and throwing them into the carts, and as they pulled away others arrived. Memorials, some of them the work of great Italian masters and talented Russian sculptors were being destroyed. I was glad my beloved author, Vsevolod S. Solovieff, was buried in Paris and not here. Nothing past nor present is sacred in the new state I thought and realized that this was one more ignoble act of irreverence to religion. Unable to bear the sight of this vandalism I wanted to run away, but I did not know where to turn. Finally, I made my way through the just ravaged section. I had to carefully step over the fallen crosses and nearly stumbled over the broken wing of a marble angel. On the bases of the monuments I read some of the dates and epitaphs, "Born 1678, died 1733 – Rest beloved until the glorious dawn." On the next flat tombstone, was a philosophical passage. "Passerby, you walk, but you will lie as I do. Sit down and rest upon my stone. Pick up a blade of grass which grows nearby. Reflect. I am home now, but you are still a guest."

On the grave of the Beguitcheffs, I read the famous quatrain of the poet Joukovsky (1783-1852):

"Do not grieve over the dear ones who brightened the world by their presence.

Do not say: 'They are no longer here,' but gratefully exclaim, 'They were.'"

I left this place of ruin to the untouched part of the cemetery leading to the Cathedral, now a museum. Here for a second, I stopped before an ancient urn I had heard about and recognized it. It was white marble, shaped in the form of two outspread wings, symbolic of flying time. Historically, it was attributed to the year 1790, though the plaque with the name and date was missing, and only these few touching words were decipherable: "He was a kind man." It did me good to think that somebody, even long ago, was kind.

Now the way ahead was clear and I ran straight ahead in search of an exit; but suddenly, without apparent reason, I stopped short before a low monument of black marble. The name, covered with hardened mud could not be read, yet an irresistible curiosity got the better of me and I began to clean it off with a little stick and a piece of paper. Letter after letter appeared: V-E-E-V-O-L-O-D, how strange! S-E-R-G-E-I-V-I-T-C-H. Now my eyes were wide open. I fetched some water and nervously, impatiently, began to wash off the last name. S-O-L-O-V-I-E-F-F! Overwhelmed, I dropped my work and sat on the tombstone. How amazing! I could have looked in vain for his place of rest in all the cemeteries in Paris. What unseen force stopped me here? I knelt and prayed at the grave of the man who, through his books, had enriched my life. Then with more water I continued to clean the stone.

"You must be a relative of Solovieff."

"Not by blood, but by gratitude," I said, looking up at the stranger and smiling. "His books 'The Sages' and 'The Great Rosicrusian' have helped me tremendously." I got up and extended my hand to the stranger.

"Sheremetieff." he introduced himself, omitting the title of Count.

"Imagine." I said. "I didn't even know Solovieff rested here. I was told his tomb was in Paris. Some invisible hand brought me —"

The stranger nodded. " ….to show your devotion to our great writer and put me to shame for not having done what you just did. I was his friend – in merriment only, it is true." Then he related some interesting episodes in Solovieff's life. I also learned that the writer's brother, Vladimir, the philosopher, and their father, the priest, were all buried here, one next to the other.

There was refinement in Sheremetieff's speech. He was elderly but his face had a look of youth and his badly patched black cape and weather-beaten felt hat still retained traces of elegance. He told me he was living here and worked on the archives of the cloister, doing some research work for the government. I began to speak to him concerning the outrageous acts of destroying the monuments, but adroitly he changed the subject.

For a long time I was preoccupied concerning all that happened during my visit to the Novo Devichev Cloister.

On the appointed day, in the reception room of the Passport Bureau I sat waiting. I actually prayed that someone else, anyone except the former phantom clerk, would come to speak to me. But no one came. I was called into the office and there a girl with crow-black hair and obvious disdain, asked about my repeated imprisonments in Odessa. This was most distressing. Why stir up the horrible past when I am about to leave this country? Mechanically I answered her questions. Why is she so disagreeable? I thought.

In the same room another girl was speaking on the telephone. Her low voice with kind inflections spread softness all around, and hearing it, I felt exactly as one does when stepping upon a rich oriental rug after having walked on stones for miles.

The black-haired girl, having written down all my answers, lifted her pretty face and began to issue orders in a less disdainful, yet abrupt, staccato manner. "Tomorrow at 2 o'clock – on the Boulevard P ———" It meant that tomorrow at 2 P.M. on Boulevard P., I was to meet a certain Tovarisht X – a tall, slender, middle-aged man, wearing a black coat and hat, his distinguishing mark being a long black beard. Not one word was said about the passport.

What kind of game could this be, I wondered.

"I have never been in that part of Moscow," I said. "I may not find the place. Couldn't Tovarisht X meet me right here in this office, instead?"

"We have told you what to do," the girl said coldly. I walked out, my steps heavy with disappointment. A little later I called Katia on her job, telling her about the new delay. She knew how trying this was for me and reminded me of our hiding place for the key to her room. She insisted that I go there at once and rest. She sounded so very kind and it helped a lot.

Though not over-enthusiastic about my blind date, I nevertheless made a stupendous effort to keep it. I started out early, inquired about the direction, changed streetcars more than once, but just when I thought I was within a block or two of my rendezvous, I found myself in a place diametrically opposite to it. It so happened that people though very willing to help, had directed me wrong all the time, and as a result I missed my appointment. A Muscovite always thinks he knows his city, but he seldom does. Talkative, he often misleads instead of guiding you. I reached Boulevard P. just one hour late, but somehow I did not care. I was fed up with all this postponement and secret procedure, and the whole set up seemed unreasonable to me. The man must have been terribly mad, I thought.

At Katia's there was a message with a telephone number for me to call. Instantly I recognized the deep, soft voice of the girl in the Passport Bureau. She was patient and amiable and never asked why I missed my appointment. She gave me more detailed instructions about the place and the man, emphasizing that I would be expected there tomorrow at 2 P.M. as before. The next day, after a night of unusually sound sleep, I felt well and expected a more fruitful outcome. I found Boulevard P. with no difficulty.

The afternoon was sunny. Light powder-puff clouds were floating over the city of Moscow, remaining round and fluffy in spite of April winds.

From far away I saw the easily recognizable man sitting on a bench in the park. I hurried forward and completely at ease, I greeted him affably, apologizing for yesterday. He got up and politely greeted me by name, not mentioning his. He studied me closely as I studied him. Black coat, black hat, black beard.. To this composition in black, something grim was added by the intensity of two piercing black eyes, accentuated by the morbid pallor of his cheeks. My highly elevated mood had suddenly dropped and I tried to recapture it. "Strange," he said, "you appear to be much younger than the age shown in your papers."

I felt on an equal basis with this man who for the second day had waited for me in the park and laughingly remarked, "Nothing escapes your eye. There is, indeed, a slight error in my document, but I was told it would take too long to correct it."

We both sat down, half facing each other. It was a rather secluded place with few people around. In my heart I thought the whole set up seemed more like an appointment in response to a matrimonial advertisement than a questioning by the secret police. Adjusting his coat and passing his long fingers over his beard, he continued, "It would take too long to correct it you said? You are very much in a hurry, aren't you? But who could possibly persuade us that it is true love that makes you want to hurry out of the Soviets?"

"What do you mean, Tovarisht?"

"I mean that we know only too well that your marriage is a marriage of convenience, not a marriage of love."

God All Powerful, I thought. What is it now? My heart began to beat faster and I could feel my temples throbbing. I closed my eyes and saw darkness through which stripes of black and white flew like arrows. My nerves, awakened to danger, were on edge. I was furious and frightened at the same time; yet I controlled my emotions and calmly said, "You are mistaken, Tovarisht."

He shrugged. "I doubt it, and if I were you, I wouldn't begin with any justification."

"All right, I will not. What is it all about?"

Then taking the glove off his left hand he inserted it slowly in his right inner pocket.

Disheartened, I watched.

"I have here a letter," he said, pulling an envelope out of his pocket, "from the American Senator, William Borah, the only one whose request we might consider." (Senator William E. Borah of Idaho was at that time chairman of the U.S. Senate's Committee on Foreign Relations, and was in favor of trade with the Soviet Union.) He opened the letter and holding it so that I could not see it, continued, "We understand that you plan to rejoin this so-called 'husband', who appears to be very adroit at attempting to help you get out of this country."

"I do not like you to—" I began, but raising the large pale palm of his hand he stopped me and went on.

"It might surprise you to learn that we already know that soon after your arrival you will be left alone and possibly very unhappy in this big foreign metropolis. Foreseeing this, we offer you some work for our cause in America."

A chill ran through my bones. "Tovarisht," I said indignantly, unable to retain my outward calm any longer, "I go to my husband whom I love and who loves me, and I will be loyal to him and to his country."

"An illusion," he said. "These prearranged marriages seldom last." He looked at me harshly. "You'd better come down to earth and for your own good consent right now to do what we ask of you."

"But what is it – specifically? Please come to the point."

"Nothing much – just to receive our mail in America, deliver it to the address given by us, and carefully follow our instructions."

I stiffened. "This will not do – I will not! Within the four walls of the prison, no one was able to force me to do secret or spy work. And now when I am free, surrounded by the fragrance of early spring, do you really think I will change my mind?"

He drew himself up. "Nobody speaks of spying, but of working for the interest of your country."

"My work will be to raise a family."

"But before you begin to raise it, you must get a passport," A demonic smile crossed his lips.

I got up. I had to feel the ground under my feet. "I see now," I said. "This is what you have been leading to. Well, if this is the cost of my passport, I must refuse it!"

"There certainly isn't much patriotism in you, Tovarisht Kraevsky," he said without moving.

My voice kept rising as my emotion grew, and almost hysterically I answered, "After all, aren't we taught to replace it with internationalism?"

Brusquely I turned away from him and had started to walk off, when his voice reached me. "Our conversation is not finished, Tovarisht Kraevsky."

"I have nothing else to say." I moved quickly, quickly – conscious only of the necessity of a physical distance from that place. I stopped only when I stumbled over something and I looked around. The day was gone and in the darkness I did not recognize the street. I felt lonely, extremely lonely. Why? I wondered. Suddenly the entire scene in the park unrolled before me: the man, his sardonic smile, his doubt of Martin's love for me, the frightful white palm of his hand stopping me from saying what I wanted. What was it I wanted to say? I did not want him to speak of Martin as my "so-called husband." How pitiful! I was not allowed to say one word to defend Martin's love for me. He wickedly suggested that Martin would leave me and I would be alone, all alone – in the "big, foreign metropolis." Alone, alone – we both are going to be alone now and the fault is not Martin's, but mine. He would never leave me. It is I who would leave him. This man's dishonorable conditions would force me to do it.

Was it today I saw the powder-puff clouds in the sky? Was it today that I was happy? It seemed impossible. I felt cold as I looked at the people slowly walking by seeming very comfortable. I understood that the cold came from my heart, frozen at the thought of the immense grief my decision would cause Martin.

Noiselessly, I pushed open the door of Katia's room and on tip-toe passed her bed on the way to my corner. It must have been nearly eleven for Katia was already asleep. That was fortunate, as it would have been impossible for me to speak to her or anyone, stunned as I was. I sat down on the couch, my feet burning painfully. The night of despair was before me. Again, as in prison, they had dug into my soul with their dirty hands! Again, why this infamous bargaining and why was that meeting arranged in the park? Were they afraid of me or what? Were they afraid of Senator Borah, the only man whose request they "might consider"? Senator Borah must be the 'big' man Martin mentioned a few times in his letters. What of it now? I have refused the passport. In the stillness of the night I shook with sobs.

I almost had it, I thought, but lost it forever. To bargain with this man? No, I could not. I could not even talk to him any longer. How could I ruin all of Martin's hopes? How could I? What should I write to him? "My dear Martin – I shall never come." No. This would be impossible. I was not that cruel. I could not write those words – but I would have to. I had to face it and he had to face it too. Senator Borah must be a very important man! How I wished to hope! Yet, I knew what I had done. I had told the strange man I did not want the passport. How could I have told him anything else?

"Oh, Lord," I prayed, "Do not abandon me. Teach me how to write to Martin so as not to hurt him too much." On a piece of paper, by the faint light coming through the window, I wrote.

"My very dear,

It was so wonderful first to dream, then to believe that soon we would be together, that your Lisa would come to America, smiling and triumphant – with a light heart and joyful after all the suffering. Only in such an elated state of mind and heart could your wife join you in

317

your beautiful and free country. Not otherwise. Only when true to myself can I breathe and live and be happy.

Today the best of me was challenged. And as a result, <u>I refused the passport.</u> I cannot explain it to you now. Forgive me, beloved.

Your Lisa.

The light of the day was breaking through the night. I could easily read my letter now. Like a child, I thanked God for having helped me to write it. My tension was gone. "Abide in me, guide me," I prayed, feeling that the light of God, as the light of the day, had broken through the density of my grief. "Abide in me, guide me," I repeated, as gently, but firmly, sleep took me away into the realm of peace and forgetfulness.

The next morning I was awakened by an official telephone call. I ran to answer it. "Are you Elizaveta Antonova Kaevesky?" I heard.

"Yes, I am."

"You can come anytime to get your foreign passport."

LEAVING RUSSIA FOREVER

I was on the train for Riga, Latvia. We were approaching the border. Here on the Soviet side one had to undergo a personal search and the custom house inspection of our luggage. I was nervous. I hope they will let me through! I do hope! I do hope! I kept saying faster and faster as the speed of my heart increased. "Nothing but wrist watches and marriage rings to be taken across," was announced as we got off the train. I had never parted with my cross and chain – never, even in prison. Would I do it now? Could I? Some past experience flashed through my mind, and with a strange inflow of spiritual strength my nervousness disappeared. Calmly I entered the inspection room.

A tall, blond woman with no words to spare began the search by examining my mouth and ears and undoing my hair. Next, her hand followed the links of my long gold chain, Mother's gift, and her fingers touched the outline of my cross. Her face remained expressionless and no comment was made. She didn't inspect the rest of my garments. She only glanced through my pocketbook; then lifting her head she smiled at me and motioned toward the exit.

Greatly relieved, I walked into the adjoining room where some employees were admiring Martin's valise. I gave them the key. They looked at me in disbelief as though there could be no possible connection between me in my modest attire and this rich piece of luggage. However, they seemed reassured when upon opening it, they found nothing but a pillow on one side to give it a fuller appearance, and mostly notebooks on the other.

"What kind of writing is this?" one asked. How desperately I wished to protect my diaries. To this day I do not know how and where the answer came from.

"These are my University notes, Tovarisht." I said an innocent lie for his and my convenience; because had they begun to translate the endless pages of my diaries, written in French, I probably would have been frozen on the Latvian border for years. It was a unique experience watching the man turn the precious pages, holding the copy book upside down.

Satisfied with his inspection, he closed the valise and patting its soft leather, said, "Send it to me when you get another one." I would gladly have sent him even a better one had I time left to write down his name.

The inspection was finished.

Passing my right hand over my dress to feel my cross, with my left hand firmly holding the valise, I rushed to the train. Once inside the car, I closed my eyes and prayed. Still trembling I waited for the wheels to turn on Latvian soil. Hesitantly at first, then with more assurance, more rhythm, the train moved ahead. We were leaving our country now, all three of us, my cross and my diaries and I for a brighter and better future. My little star did not fail me, Mother dear.

We had left Moscow the day before, Tuesday, May 12th at 7:35 in the evening, and now it was Wednesday noon. The weather was bright. As I looked out of the window I saw nothing but an emerald sea of grass. Up a little farther, a grove of birch trees appeared. From far away they looked like slender maidens dressed in white and green.

The peasant houses and the little farms seemed more and more prosperous as we pushed ahead, away from the Soviets. I was leaving my unfortunate land, known before as Russia. I was saying goodbye to the country of my birth which I so deliriously loved. I was saying goodbye to my past which in spite of trials, privation, suffering, irreparable losses, was such that today, lighthearted and serene I could smile to the entire world. Goodbye, poor Mother Russia. Goodbye to you, long-suffering Russian people. Let your only possession, your faith in God, save you too.

"Riga in ten minutes!" I heard the conductor call. My breath failed me.

I felt dizzy.

Freedom in ten minutes!

Happiness in ten minutes!

Dear Lord, help me to live through these ten minutes.

On the platform I saw Martin. He looked tense as he stood there, eyes fixed on the moving train. I couldn't wait. I jumped off before the train stopped. I ran to him and hiding my face on his chest begged him, "Martin, my Martin. Hold me tight. Hold me. I am afraid!"

His arms were around me. "No reason to ever be afraid again, my love."

Elegant hotel rooms, vases of long-stemmed roses, an atmosphere of long forgotten luxury, love and freedom all at once were mine! I could not believe it anymore than I could believe that in the dazzling white tiled bathroom there was all the hot and cold water my heart and body desired. I must have spent a full hour in the bathtub experimenting and assuring myself of this fact until my wondering and, I presume, a little impatient husband knocked on the door, tactfully asking me if everything was all right.

We had a late dinner in a fine restaurant where waiters in full dress were noiselessly gliding between the tables sparkling with crystal and Louis XV pink satin chairs. Champagne, violins – more than once I closed my eyes for the joy of opening them again and finding that the dream was not dispelled.

Riga, the threshold of my happiness! In my diary, I find just these few written lines:

Dear Lord, where am I? Is it true that I am free, free to say, free to write what I choose? Is it true that after all the seeming impossibilities, I am free and abroad with my husband who came for the third time from America and met me here at the station in Riga? Yes, it is true, but how soon will I wholeheartedly believe it? I am still afraid when Martin is not with me. To fear has become a habit.

My sister, my poor sister, if only she were not in danger back in Russia!

Indeed, the contrast between yesterday and today was tremendous, and to relax completely was still impossible. I imagined that some Soviet agents were still after me, and though I tried hard to persuade myself to the contrary I continued to be very tense. I would avoid speaking on the streets, and only when alone and safe with my husband would I become happy and talkative again and chat and laugh to my heart's content.

We had our solemn moments speaking of our endangered and almost lost happiness. Now Martin knew the whole story of why I had decided to refuse the passport.

"Stop, stop," he would say at times. "This is too much!"

As for myself, I wanted to hear more of the important, kind man who helped us. I learned about the career of Senator Borah as a statesman, about his being so different and powerful in his opinions. I learned that a woman lawyer whom Martin met while trying to save me, presented his petition to Senator Borah, and that it was on his own accord and moved by his own heart that the Senator, though extremely busy, found time for me. How thankful I was to him for having taken an interest in my life! I felt I must write and thank him right away, but Martin said it would be better to wait until I came to America.

The formalities at the office of the American Consul being finished, we left Riga on the 19th of May for Berlin and stayed in the very same hotel on Friedrichstrasse, where many years ago Mother met us on our way from France to Russia. Hans Arndt was with her – our friend the linguist, whose death so deeply saddened me. Memories! The person who remembered it all seemed well known to me, and yet she seemed to have lived and died some kind of death for awhile, and only now began to live again.

We took the day express train from Berlin to Paris. Here, people sat opposite each other and toward the end of the trip they became acquainted. Almost immediately Martin engaged in conversation with a red-haired Englishman, and I was satisfied to be left alone with my thoughts and impressions, trying to file them the best I could in my mind. Last May and this May, I thought. Is it true?

It was good to relax on the train, knowing that we were no longer separated. Looking at Martin to make sure he was there I sat quietly in deep meditation. It was a wonderful hour or two. With my eyes closed, I saw a great light. Gratitude, like a surging fountain, was beating out of my heart to the highest of my consciousness. Absolute certitude came to me through faith, and because of clinging to the best in me, problems were overcome and peace and love replaced them.

More people moved into our compartment. Martin was still discussing some political questions with the Englishman and I returned to my peace, when I heard someone say in perfect Russian, "Beyond any doubt, Madame, you are a Russian."

"Indeed, I am," I answered to the smiling man. Some minutes passed.

"You are very beautiful," the voice continued.

"Sorry," I said, "My mind is intensely busy now. I would prefer not to converse."

He excused himself politely but soon after lunch succeeded in introducing himself to my husband who in turn, introduced him to me, saying that his wife would enjoy speaking Russian to him, whereas he does not know a word of it. Martin should have known what this Russian was up to. The stranger began with a long dissertation about the differences in Russian and American characters, which sounded very scientific at first, but finished with a sudden, yet intent persuasion for me to leave my American husband and run away with him. I could have slapped him in the face had not the situation appeared too ridiculous, too funny, for anger. Once more our happiness was in danger!

I succeeded, though not without difficulty, to save the piquant story of my new conquest until the moment we were alone in our lovely penthouse of the Hotel Rond Point des Champs Ellyses.

"Just another case of love at first sight," said Martin very casually.

I laughed. "To me," I said, "it seems the height of nerve and stupidity," and here I almost choked with sudden fear, "what if he were a GPU agent testing my love for you?"

Yes, fear was leaving me too slowly. Fortunately, Paris was farther away from Soviet Russia than were Riga and Berlin. Paris was so beautiful that spring! Every evening at sunset we drove through the Bois de Bologne and ate delicious French food in restaurants of renown. "I never could imagine that such delicacies existed!" I would say, which only made Martin spoil me more and more.

It was high time for me to think of a new wardrobe, but our days were so full that involuntarily, I postponed my shopping from day to day. Besides, the need of it was not too urgent as Pauline and Gertrude, my sisters-in-law, sent me some casual things with Martin, some of which fit rather well. However, Martin mentioned right from the start that in Paris I would have to dress from head to foot. One morning he simply insisted that I do nothing else but shop.

The amount of money I was given frightened me. "You don't expect me to buy the entire Galleries Lafayette?"

"No, but buy all you want." he said. "It will be simple and pleasant for you to shop, knowing the language."

I wished Martin could go with me, but I knew that he had to change our steamship tickets as we were leaving Paris a little earlier than expected. I could not remember ever having shopped alone. In our childhood most of our clothes were made at home or to order. When it came to shopping it was always with Mother, our governess or Vala.

During the last fourteen years there was nothing to shop for in Soviet Russia. We simply refreshed our old dresses by turning them from one side to the other an endless number of times.

In spite of it, I was sure I would succeed. Martin wished me to be well dressed and I intended to please him. Alas, I failed in spite of the money, the language, and the obvious interest the salesgirls took in me. It seems ridiculous to me now, and probably incredible to many, that a young woman with a certain background would be absolutely incapable of selecting things and determining what would be right for her to wear. Yet, I could not blame myself completely. After years of total privation, a certain re-evaluation of values is bound to develop, and a sudden leap from an empty closet to the abundance and opulence of the Grandes Maisons de Paris leaves one puzzled to say the least. The dresses which I now would consider to be rather on the conservative side then seemed to be fit for an actress on the stage or for an eccentric demimondaine.

To this day I am sorry for not having purchased one particular gown. "Cela vous va a merveille!" (It suits you to perfection!) the salesgirl exclaimed. I looked at myself and could not help agreeing. My severe hairdo, sleek at the temples with a Grecian knot, suited the dress with its low square neckline, trimmed with a dawn of yellow ostrich feathers. It was followed by a wave of exquisite powder-blue material, tight at the bodice, flowing gracefully down to the floor, forming a train which was slightly lifted from the ground by the same light yellow feathers which trimmed the neckline. The eyes that looked at me from the mirror – my eyes – were bluer than ever and my complexion fairer. This surely does something for me, I thought – but the square décolleté and the train?

"Vous avez l'air d'une reine," (You have the air of a queen.) said one of the girls in sincere admiration; and it was exactly this remark that confirmed my doubt. The dress is not for me, I thought; it is for the stage. "Vous allez la regretter, Madame," (You are going to regret it.) said the girl – and I did.

Surely, this must have been a unique case in the history of human relations; that a wife being given a large sum of money for her own use, after a day of shopping returns it all, gently putting it in the lap of her bewildered husband! (Any husband reading this must envy Martin!)

"You will need a new evening gown for at least three nights of our four day's crossing," exclaimed Martin. But it was too late to obtain them. By previous arrangement the next day we took a trip to Versailles with our friends, followed by dinner in Paris. The following day our sojourn in the French capital was over.

We were in the harbor of Cherbourg. Far away, the silhouette of the liner which was to take us across the ocean reminded me of another steamer. "It looks exactly like the boat we took from Odessa to Yalta last year, doesn't it, Martin?"

"You mean the 'SS Krim'? Let me see! Let me see!" he repeated, examining the far-off liner very carefully. While looking at him, I could not help seeing some irresistible humor in his eyes. "Wait until it comes a little closer," he added very earnestly, "I shall be able to judge better."

The joke, of course, was on me and for a long time my comparing the massive liner Europa with the SS Krim became Martin's favorite story. I tolerated it very graciously in spite of the exaggerations, although I was not totally wrong. The two steamers were built in the same boatyard and by the same company in Holland and, therefore, with some allowance, Krim could be taken for the miniature of her big sister ship Europa. This is the same as saying the Opera House of Odessa is a miniature replica of the Grande Opera de Paris.

The lack of evening clothes was not too painful for me. The sea was high most of the time and I remained in our cabin, resting and eating very lightly while Martin the good sailor, felt perfectly well and ate for both of us. We had only one splendid day and I spent it almost entirely on deck dreaming, slumbering, intoxicated by the ocean air, completely relaxed; I was somewhat more secure in the middle of the Atlantic than ever before.

We met a surprising number of people. Among them, Alice Hughes, the successful journalist and a woman of rare heart who became my lifetime friend, and her husband the late Leonard Hall. That evening I watched all the first class passengers dance, but not without a tinge of regret for not having bought the powder-blue gown which, after all, was rather modest compared to some.

At dawn – AMERICA! The skyscrapers – my first steps on free soil – my beating heart, my tears.

BORN IN RUSSIA –
REBORN IN AMERICA

June 2, 1931

I am still here among you and at this moment, I feel as emotional as the day I came. My book is finished. Something very powerful compelled me to write it. My gratitude for all is not only constant, but ever growing. Soon after my arrival I wrote a letter of thanks to Senator William E. Borah, and a reply came by return mail!

Dear Madame:

Your grateful letter is compensation enough, and more than enough for any service I may have been able to render you. I am happy to know that you are safe and free under the Stars and Stripes.

With very best wishes for your continuous happiness, I am

Sincerely,

(Signed) William E. Borah

I received quite a few letters from the Senator, my American father, and one day I went to Washington to meet him personally. Approaching the Senate I felt so much in tune with all that is beautiful and loving that I forgot to be nervous. In his large office Senator Borah greeted me warmly. I bent and kissed the hand which heartily shook mine – the hand that had reached across the ocean to save me. This was my unique chance to tell the Senator about the immensity of his help, and of the depth of my appreciation. I did not search for words. They came by themselves – warm, sincere and true; they were words that do not write well on paper, because with too much feeling they belong to the realm of the intangible. Tears filled the Senator's eyes. Tears were in mine – unforgettable moments!

The Senator wanted to know if there were any worries he could relieve me of.

"You have already done so much for me, Senator," I said. He insisted that I open my heart.

"I really have only one worry," I finally said. "It is my sister, Vala, all alone and possibly in danger in Soviet Russia."

"Let us take your only burden upon our shoulders," he said. He did. My sister came to America in 1933. Oh, how generously he gave me this new happiness! "I wish you all the good in the world, Child. You deserve it," he said.

I was drinking in each word. "Goodbye, dear Senator Borah. God bless you!"

Now, though no longer among us, he lives in our hearts and in the hearts of our children. With his good wishes my happiness and my gratitude are ever growing. Once, during our Thanksgiving dinner, I made a spontaneous toast.

> "I am thankful for so many good things I possess,
> Our fearless home, our children, and for my new green dress.
> But most of all, I thank Thee God, for having well foreseen
> My need, and given me a man who is neither dull nor mean."

Of course, during all these years we have had our "ups and downs," but with love, mutual respect, and a little common sense, we have transformed our problems into worthwhile challenges. My husband still possesses an endless amount of enthusiasm, energy and initiative. In brief, we are happy and I feel younger than on the day I stood at the railway station in Riga, afraid of my own happiness. At times, I must be alone to meditate, to write, and Martin respects my solitude.

I do not think, however, that at this point I should attempt to tell much more about my life with Martin. I cannot help saying that we still ascend the ladder of happiness and that on our way we have been given three lovely daughters, Olga, Tania and Natasha. We live by the calm waters of Indian Creek in Miami Beach, Florida, in a spacious and original house full of young laughter, understanding, love and peace. We often hear from people that our house reflects happiness. Thanksgiving never leaves my lips!

> New land, I owe my gratitude to you
> and a love I am unable to restrain
> since one clear day when I first felt the dew
> on youthful soil and joined your free domain.
> America, to you I owe my best
> that was not killed in me the final year
> of trial, year that strengthened me through test,
> when God protected me from human fear.
> I consecrate my heart to you, my pen,
> and faith that dawns in a triumphal day.
> Great country! Hope of freedom-hungry men.
> Heal sick humanity, show it the way
> until the boughs of brotherhood will bear
> the fruit of understanding everywhere.

This sonnet, as well as my book, are tokens of my gratitude to America for the warm and permanent welcome, for the blessings of freedom we all enjoy; and they are at the same time a warning to preserve this freedom by greater inner and outer vigilance.

EPILOGUE

As a child growing up you are not aware of the effect your parents have on the world around you. Both of our parents did in very different ways. Our father, who was influenced by the European styles introduced at the Worlds Fair in Paris in 1926, later founded Modernage Furniture in New York City and was recognized as starting the Modern Furniture Movement in America. In the 1930's when high society and movie stars were eager to have the newest styles, Modernage had the designers and factory to supply the demand. We moved to Florida in 1939 and he established the Modernage Corporation in Miami Beach. The first store was opened later that year at Lincoln and Alton Road. It was a beautiful modern showroom which Army Intelligence occupied during World War II. After the war a chain of nine showrooms were build in other Florida locations. Modernage was sold in 1971 and remained in business until the year 2002.

How strange it must have seemed to Momma, arriving in America and sailing past the Statue of Liberty, to be met by total strangers who were to become her instant family. After all the years of expectation she was welcomed with great warmth by Father's two sisters and their husbands. With time she left unforgettable impressions on all of them.

Our beautiful Mother never met a stranger; all she had to do was say hello to you and you felt loved. Momma spoke Russian to us, which we spoke before we learned to speak English, and we had fun speaking with her in Russian when we didn't want Daddy to understand what we were saying. In addition to rearing her family Momma was lecturing and writing in English, French and Russian. She was a member of the Poetry Society of America and was published in a number of magazines and publications.

During our teens we traveled to Europe in the summer and for six weeks attended school in Switzerland while Momma and Daddy traveled. When traveling together Momma was our interpreter as she spoke six languages. In Civitivica, Italy we met a talented young artist, Bruno Barbarini, at an art exhibit. Daddy bought several of his paintings and invited him to come to America, stay with us for two years, and paint here. He became our adopted brother. We traveled in our own automobile which was aboard ship with us. It was always thrilling to see the 1949 Kelly Green Cadillac swing through the air from the ship to the dock when we landed. The car always got a lot of attention winding through the narrow streets of Europe as the people had never seen one like it before. They were wonderful years with Momma and Daddy – what an education they gave us!

In 1961 the family took a trip to Russia; Daddy wanted to see family and Momma wanted to visit her parents' graves. The trip was very difficult during the communist period; every step we took was watched as we were required to always have an Intourist guide with us. In Moscow only relatives who were over 80 years old dared to visit us; the young were afraid of losing their job or going to jail. For many years Momma had sent money to a friend in Odessa to take care of the graves but when we arrived we found them unkempt and overgrown with weeds. Her friend had died. In Kiev Daddy had an angry encounter with the Intourist Russian Customs Official; consequently we had to leave Russia ahead of time and fly to Vienna. When we returned home Momma was so happy to be in America she kissed the ground and said she never wanted to see Russia again.

334

At the 90th birthday party we gave for her she was overwhelmed by the touching stories of all the guests about how she had inspired them and how much they loved her. She passed away at home in 1986 at the age of 92. She had told us she would always be with us – and she is.

Daddy also lived to be 92 and passed away at home in 1992 with us at his side.

Surviving family members are Olga and David Melin and granddaughter Gina Melin of Florida; Tania Sudduth, grandson David Sudduth of Colorado, and granddaughter Tammy Rae Sudduth Scott of California; Natasha Kimmel, granddaughters Lisa and Tatianna Kimmell and grandson John Kimmell of California.

Milton Keynes UK
Ingram Content Group UK Ltd.
UKHW040714200324
439767UK00006B/287